Chile's Free-Market Miracle:
A Second Look

Chile's Free-Market Miracle: A Second Look

Joseph Collins

AND

John Lear

A FOOD FIRST BOOK
The Institute for Food and Development Policy
Oakland, California

Library of Congress Cataloging-in-Publication Data

Collins, Joseph.   1945 –
    Chile's free market miracle : a second look / Joseph Collins & John Lear ; with a foreword by Walden Bello and epilogue by Stephanie Rosenfeld.
        p.   cm.
    Includes bibliographical references and index.
    ISBN 0-935028-63-3 : $15.95
    1. Chile — Economic policy.   2. Free enterprise — Chile.
3. Chile-Economic conditions — 1973–1988.   4. Chile-Economic conditions — 1988-   5. Chile — Social conditions
— 1970-   I. Lear, John. 1959-   .   II. Title.
    HC192.C575   1994
    338.983 — dc20   94-30596
                                                              CIP

Printed in the United States of America
10 9 8 7 6 5 4 3 2 1

To order additional copies of this book please contact our distributor:

Subterranean Company
Box 160
265 South Fifth Street
Monroe, OR 97456
(800) 274-7826

Please add 15% for postage and handling ($2.50 minimum)
California residents add sales tax. Bulk discounts available.

Design and typesetting: Harvest Graphics
Cover design: Lory Poulson
Cover photo: © Alvaro Hoppe Guiñez

Table of Contents

ARICA

IQUIQUE

CALAMA
ANTOFAGASTA

Sa.- OVERA

COPIANÓ

LA SERENA
COQUIMBO
OVALLE

VIÑA DEL MAR
QUILPUE
VALPARAÍSO
SANTIAGO

RANCAGUA

TALCA
TALCAHUANO   CHILLAN
CONCEPCION

TEMUCO

VALDIVIA
OSORNO
PTO. MONTT

CUCAO

PALENA
PARQ. NAC.-
-IS. GUALTECAS
RIO CISNES
PUERTO CISNES

IS. GUAYANECO

Duque de York

Almagro

PUNTA
ARENAS

c h i l e

Foreword

Walden Bello

It is fashionable these days to refer to the "Chilean Miracle." This is an ideologically loaded term, one which subtly renders acceptable the social and environmental costs of the 17-year economic experiment presided over by Gen. Augusto Pinochet. Better than any other work, *Chile's Free Market Miracle* by Joe Collins and John Lear captures the different dimensions of the economic and social disaster that befell the majority of the Chilean people as a vengeful ideological elite dragged the country through two major depressions in *one* decade and produced by the end of the Pinochet period an economic outcome that consigned 40 percent of Chileans, or 5.2 million of a population of 13 million, to life below the poverty line.

Indeed, Collins and Lear question whether, even by the narrow standards of economic growth, a miracle took place at all. And they are right: the growth in gross domestic product during the Pinochet years (1974-89) averaged only 2.6 percent a year, or below the rates registered in the decades of state interventionism, 4 percent in 1950-61 and 4.6 percent in 1961-71.

This book helps fill a disturbing vacuum in progressive analysis. For it appears at a time that most intellectual and political elites in Latin America and the Caribbean have been incorporated in varying degrees into the neo-liberal or structural adjustment consensus. After being elected on anti-adjustment platforms, populist leaders like Michael Manley of Jamaica, Carlos Menem of Argentina, and Alberto Fujimori of Peru turned 180 degrees and imposed Draconian neoliberal programs on their economies. And to a great extent, they were encouraged in this betrayal by the lack of solid advice on alternative policies from progressive intellectuals,

many of whom had become convinced that there was no alternative to neo-liberal adjustment. For both politicians and intellectuals,
the Chilean experience has been central in their tragic pilgrimage
from militant radicalism to hesitant conservatism.

Since the Chilean Miracle, like the "East Asian Miracle," has
been disseminated internationally as a model for the whole Third
World by enthusiasts like the World Bank and the International
Monetary Fund, this book has something very important to say
not only to Latin Americans but also to people of Africa, Asia, the
Middle East, and even in the former Soviet Union, where some
economists have boldly contended that Pinochet-style free-market
economies cum authoritarian controls would be a step forward
from the post-socialist crisis.

In periods of great economic difficulty such as today, Southern
leaders and intellectuals are very vulnerable to panaceas, especially those that are packaged as "bitter but essential" elixirs to regain
economic dynamism. The Chilean neo-liberal model is one of
those panaceas, and as Joe Collins and John Lear so effectively
argue, this is one medicine that is likely to be much worse than
what it purports to cure.

Acknowledgments

Over the four years we were researching and writing this book we incurred untold debts. Ideally we could acknowledge by name each of the many individuals and institutions who generously helped us. Some individuals, however, explicitly asked us not to use their names. Many others are acknowledged by name in the Notes. In case, however, we failed to keep proper track of the names of all who helped us, mentioning some here would run the risk of unintentionally slighting others. We have chosen, therefore, to make general acknowledgements; they may be less personal, but they are more complete.

Chile is a country known for its numerous institutions researching and publishing on economic and social issues; their achievements and collegiality made from the outset our ambitious project feasible. We interviewed and held discussions with economists, sociologists, educators, government officials, health professionals, social workers, engineers, legal experts, politicians from various parties, labor union and community organizers, writers, journalists, poets, priests, and human-rights workers. We are grateful to them for sharing with us their insights. We also wish to thank our colleagues in Chile and the United States who generously made the time in their busy schedules to comment on our drafts.

We also learned immeasurably from the Chileans we met on the streets, in buses, in health clinic waiting rooms, in sweatshops, in vineyards, in schools, in restaurants and snack bars, in fishing villages, in shantytowns and country clubs. Many invited us into their homes and spoke freely about their lives. Their personal stories above all made vividly concrete for us the impact of free-market policies.

Finally we wish to thank all our many friends, old and new, who helped us in so many ways along the road.

PART ONE:

CHILE AND NEO-LIBERALISM

1

Why This Book

Chile has moved farther, faster than any other nation in South America toward real free-market reform. The payoff is evident to all: seven straight years of economic growth. . . You deserve your reputation as an economic model for other countries in the region and in the world. Your commitment to market-based solutions inspires the hemisphere.

President George Bush in Chile
December 6, 1990[1]

I challenge you to find another country in the world that has such nice stats. It's almost too good to be true, and people wonder where the downside is.

Curtis W. Kamman
U.S. Ambassador to Chile
May 10, 1992[2]

Free-market or "neo-liberal"[3] economic and social doctrines have taken the world by storm. By millennium's close, free-market ideology is likely to have radically altered the lives of far more people and nations than any other ideology in history. The best government is the least government, we are told. Government planning, government regulation, government corporations and government social programs are all losers. Let private enterprise, market forces, and free trade reign!

Especially since the collapse of the government-planned economies in Eastern Europe and the Soviet Union, free-market policies are widely touted as the obviously correct course to pursue. Democratization in the former Soviet world is often now

3

defined as synonymous with free-market "reforms." Assistance from the U.S. government and the World Bank and the International Monetary Fund to these nations as well as to the debt-strapped nations of the Third World is now conditioned on their embracing free-market policies — privatizing government-owned companies, lifting price controls, giving free rein to private enterprise, slashing government budgets especially for consumer subsidies and social services, and pulling down barriers to foreign trade and corporate investment.

While nations everywhere to one degree or another are now rushing — or being thrust — headlong into the realm of "the market forces," one nation has already been long and thoroughly subjected to free-market policies. Starting in 1975, Chile was turned into a laboratory for free-marketeers. And their experiments in Chile have been more thorough than elsewhere because their patron was General Augusto Pinochet whose long and ruthless dictatorship (1973-1990) ruled out effective opposition. Chile therefore affords us an exceptional opportunity to document and weigh the economic and social implications — positive and negative — of the ideas today powerfully promoted and adopted around the globe.

The impact of free-market ideas on the Chilean economy and society deserves close scrutiny not only because Chile over a long period has been a free-market laboratory; but, more importantly, because free-market advocates have pronounced the results a shining success. Since the mid-1980s, top officials of the World Bank, the International Monetary Fund, and the U.S. government, the most influential U.S. media (in particular the *New York Times*), multinational corporation executives, and prominent neo-liberal economists such as Milton Friedman have celebrated Chile's free-market experiment. They hold up Chile as a development model for nations around the world, from Russia to India, from Ghana to Bolivia. Chile has even been catapulted into the ranks of perhaps the only other nations widely acclaimed today as models — the Asian economic "tigers" such as South Korea and Taiwan.[4]

Leaders of countries across Latin America, Eastern Europe and the former Soviet Union make pilgrimages to Chile to seek the recipe for moving from a government-planned economy to a market-driven economy. Many of the Pinochet government's economic counselors are now well-paid consultants, dispensing advice to governments elsewhere.[5]

By 1990, when the first elected president in seventeen years took office, impressive macroeconomic indicators gave credence to the notion of an economic "miracle." That is, if one doesn't probe back before the mid-'80s. For since that time at least Chile has experienced strong economic growth, a boom in exports, a positive trade balance, a comparatively low inflation rate, stepped up foreign investment — and it has continued to make timely payments on its sizable debts to foreign banks.

Chile's macroeconomic indicators look especially impressive when compared to the deep development crisis in most of the Third World. Most third world nations in the early 1980s fell into a deep and prolonged recession. The United Nations in 1990 estimated that in many third world countries the percentage of the citizens deprived of jobs, adequate food, housing, health and education was higher than even during the worldwide depression in the 1930s. In Latin America the 1980s came to be called the "lost decade."

The Third World has been undergoing not only a crisis in development but also a crisis in development models. Earlier prevailing models for achieving development, both "capitalist" (protected markets, industrialization through import substitution, government strategic investments and subsidies, stages of growth, etc.) and "socialist" (central planning, redistributive reforms, collectivization, public ownership and government subsidies) have been widely discredited or discarded. In this context of appalling economic and social conditions compounded by unprecedented disorientation, free-market proponents have advocated — and in many countries advanced — radical reversals and restructuring. Their prescriptions include selling off government-owned companies, allowing prices even of necessities to be determined entirely by supply and demand, privatizing many services that for generations were viewed as the part of the proper role for government (health care, schooling, old-age security, utilities, recreational parks, prisons, etc.), sweeping deregulation of private industry, removal of protective tariffs along with other impediments to free trade and multinational investment, stringent limits on labor unions as well as on professional and trade associations (all said to "interfere with market forces"), and reduced taxation on corporate profits and individual wealth-making.

Free-market advocates themselves regularly refer to their prescriptions as "shock treatment." Anyone protesting the resulting tremendous dislocations in people's lives — depression-era joblessness, widespread bankruptcies, slashed subsidies and social services — is admonished that those countries that stay the free-market course will, albeit perhaps after years of "bitter medicine," become "another Chile."

But what is Chile *really* like? Champions of free-market policies do not provide (or do not have) a complete picture of Chile. While neo-liberal Chile is held up in many influential circles as a model to emulate, few outside the country have solid information about the economic and social realities there after more than a decade and a half of free-market transformations. What were the consequences in terms of growth, equity, employment, sustainability, quality of life, the environment, and natural resources? What has been the impact of free-market policies on the key sectors of the economy: agriculture (especially fruit cultivation), fishing, mining, forestry, manufacturing, finance and services? What have been the results of neo-liberal reforms — privatization and "choice" — in education, health care, housing, social security, and the development of human resources? And how much have factors other than free-market policies been at work in the declared "successes"?

Determined to obtain a much fuller and realistic picture of neo-liberal Chile, we started our fieldwork in December 1989. It proved to be an especially appropriate time. The day before our arrival, Pinochet's hand-picked candidate in the first presidential election since 1970, a neo-liberal economist and one of the principal architects of the regime's free-market policies, was soundly defeated. The imminent end of authoritarian rule (the formal end came with the inauguration of Patricio Aylwin in March 1990) mitigated Chile's "culture of fear."[6] For the first time in over sixteen years many Chileans in all walks of life would dare to speak their minds — although still often in hushed tones.

We set 1973 to 1990 as the scope of our assessment, the period during which free-market policies were implemented under the Pinochet dictatorship. Such a period seems sufficiently long to document fairly the consequences, positive and negative, of the neo-liberal package of free-market policies. We carried out our research in Chile during three separate two-month stays between December 1989 and January 1992. Where appropriate and feasible, we have updated data. Stephanie Rosenfeld, who has carried out the Chile component of an Institute for Food and Development Policy study of nations going from long military dictatorships to elected democratic governments, has added to our book an Epilogue on the post-Pinochet period through early 1994.

When we began to dig deeper into the Chilean reality, we discovered many things at odds with the rhetoric and claims of the free marketeers. For example,

- The celebrated economic growth of the late 1980s must be viewed in the light of the two catastrophic recessions (in 1975 and 1982). Only by 1989 — 14 years into the free-market policies — did per capita output climb back up to the level of 1970. Indeed the "miracles" refer to recoveries from depression-like collapses that can be attributed in large part to the free-market model.
- Poverty widened dramatically: from 20 percent of Chileans in 1970 to 41 percent in 1990; among the impoverished, the percentage forced to live in extreme poverty doubled.[7]
- The rich got richer. They did so mainly at the expense of many middle-class Chileans: between 1978 and 1988 the richest 10 percent increased their share of national income from 37 to 47 percent, while the next 30 percent saw their share shrink from 23 to 18 percent.
- Thanks in large part to free-market policies, Chile's foreign debt shot up from $5 billion to $21 billion, one of the highest per capita debts in the world. In the laissez-faire climate of sweeping deregulation (and with shades of the U.S. taxpayers' bail-out of the scandal-ridden savings and loan companies), much of Chile's sizable debt was recklessly contracted by private operators; when they went bankrupt the public got stuck with the tab, keeping the foreign creditors happy.
- Pressured to step up exports in order to meet payments on the debt and with the laissez-faire attitudes toward private business, Chile has plundered its rich forestry and fishery resources. Diversified native forests were leveled — often cheap grist for

Japan's computer paper mills. While the free marketeers decried subsidies for needy Chileans, the government handed out lucrative subsidies to lumber companies for planting monocultures of non-native pine and eucalyptus. Similarly, unregulated access to the seas has pushed three major commercial species of fish to the brink of depletion.

- The percentage of Chileans without adequate housing increased from 27 percent in 1972 to 40 percent in 1988, even though according to neo-liberal social dogma the private construction industry combined with supplemental vouchers for low-income households would solve the housing problem.
- A pioneering and much-praised national health care system was gutted. Government expenditures on health were slashed from $28 per person in 1973 to only $11 per person in 1989. Seventy percent of Chileans cannot afford the private for-profit HMOs; they have no choice but to remain "stuck" in the severely run-down public system.
- Profit-oriented private enterprise has no interest in public health. With government health budget cutbacks and free-market mentality, outbreaks of typhoid fever and hepatitis A soared to epidemic levels after decades of steady decline.
- Workers' rights to organize and bargain collectively have been greatly curtailed. Employers' total "flexibility" has been the hallmark of neo-liberal labor policy: many Chileans have been involuntarily reduced to short-term contract work. Despite the rhetoric of "modernization" working conditions are often so exhausting and hazardous that they are reminiscent of 19th century capitalism.
- Free-market principles applied to Santiago's urban transport led to clogged streets, bus fares that are the highest in Latin America and beyond the reach of many of those most dependent on public transport, half-empty buses, and some of the worst urban air pollution in the world.
- Sell-offs, generally under value, of government-owned companies now mean several hundred million dollars in reduced revenues for the public purse since many of Chile's public sector companies had been respectably profitable.
- Per-pupil school vouchers, the encouragement of for-profit schools and the municipalization of the national public educa-

tion system — all decreed in the name of "choice" — have greatly magnified the differences in educational opportunities and results.

- In the fruit export industry, one that has "boomed" and "modernized," 80 percent of the workforce can obtain only temporary work with no benefits and is legally prohibited from organizing or striking for a fair share of the profits.
- The armed forces have not been included in the the neo-liberals' much-touted "shrinking" of the government. Chile's military budget is guaranteed in real terms at 1989 levels as a minimum, and military salaries are indexed to the cost of living unlike those of other government employees. The military budget in 1989 outstripped by $432 million the housing, health and education budgets *combined*.

As we completed our research and have spoken formally and informally in the United States about what we learned of the realities of Chile's free-market world, the most frequent response has been, "That's just what's happening here!" Indeed another good reason for a focus on Chile is that long before the imposition of the free-market policies Chile developed into a society with a large middle class[8] and several other social indicators and democratic institutions roughly comparable to those in our own country. A second look at free-market Chile, therefore, can help us peer down the road on which our own society is already traveling — and hopefully debate whether that is where we want to go.

2

Chile Before Chicago

Chile became a pioneer in Latin America soon after it first gained its independence from Spain early in the 19th century. While most of the continent's fledgling nations underwent recurrent rebellions and multiple constitutions, Chilean elites quickly established a stable conservative order under the strong arm of Diego Portales. The Constitution of 1833 lasted almost a century, and with few exceptions, power passed smoothly from one elected president to another.[1]

Despite its limited economic role in the Spanish empire, independent Chile quickly inserted itself into international markets. During the decade that followed California's '49er Gold Rush, Chile was an important supplier of wheat to that region until California became self-sufficient from its own agriculture. The predominant free-market ideology of the nineteenth century, preached particularly by British merchants, diplomats and industrialists, called upon the new nations of Latin America to open their economies to foreign trade and investment. Chile was an early convert. The port city of Valparaiso took on a decidedly English flavor in the 19th century as British merchants married into elite society and initiated Chileans into such peculiarly English habits as high tea (known in Chile as *las once*). Foreign companies, mostly British, exploited Chile's "comparative advantage" by exporting raw materials from Chile to industrial countries and importing manufactured goods. From the 1880s through the 1920s, the primary engine of the Chilean economy was nitrate exports, to fertilize the agricultural fields and supply the armaments industries of Britain, Germany and the United States. The invention of synthetic explosives and fertilizer after World War I brought Chile's nitrate industry into decline; but during the 1920s, with redoubled U.S. investment in Chile's rich copper mines, mining again became key to the development of the economy.

The mines of Chile were the classic enclave economy of Latin America: they operated amid the great deserts and mountains of the north far from the populous central valleys, and they were controlled by foreign investors. Export activities were partially linked to other areas, through railroads linking up mines, cities, ports and agricultural areas and through the flow of large numbers of workers back and forth between rural areas, mines and cities according to the economic ups and downs of mining. Foreign mining operations benefited the national economy to the extent that the government succeeded in taxing profits in order to provide services, economic infrastructure, and jobs to a growing middle class.

A brief civil war in 1891 pitted President José Manuel Balmaceda against Congress. Two issues at stake would reappear periodically over the next century: first, Balmaceda attempted to push Chilean development by increasing government intervention in the economy against the interests of the traditional alliance of Chilean landed elites and foreign mining companies; and second, Balmaceda sought to strengthen the presidency vis-à-vis Congress. Balmaceda was defeated, and wealthy landlords continued to dominate Congress. Even so, in the congressional model of government lay avenues for broader political participation. At century's end Chile's embryonic democracy far surpassed the "enlightened dictatorships" that ruled from Mexico to Peru.

What is striking about Chile when compared to most other Latin American nations is the early presence of middle and lower classes in national politics, resembling in many ways the political systems of more developed European countries. In 1920, the flamboyant candidate Arturo Alessandri ushered in mass politics by winning the presidency with the support of broad urban constituencies against the traditional dominance of rural estate owners. Five years later, a group of young officers led by Carlos Ibáñez pushed Alessandri to suspend Congress and submit a new constitution to the public by plebiscite. The resulting Constitution of 1925 strengthened the presidency and introduced election of the president by direct popular vote.

Prior to the 1973 military overthrow of the elected president
Salvador Allende and the long authoritarian rule of General
Augusto Pinochet, Chileans took enormous pride in their democratic traditions. As just recounted, only two times after the establishment of the Constitution of 1833 was the legal handing over of
political power violated: first in the brief 1891 civil war and again
in 1925 when strongman Colonel Carlos Ibáñez assumed the
presidency through threats of military force. All told, from 1830 to
1973, Chile was under direct military rule for only thirteen
months.[2] Between the resignation of Ibáñez in 1933 and the 1973
coup, Chile was the only country in Latin America in which the
presidency passed continuously and peacefully from one political
party or coalition to another.

The Great Depression dramatically undermined the free-
market economic philosophy and the pattern of economic and
political development that had predominated in Chile until then.
First, the country's excessive dependence on mineral exports and
on foreign investment and financing became painfully obvious as
mining exports fell disastrously and Chile suffered through the
worldwide depression in far worse shape than countries less exter-
nally dependent. Second, vocal sectors of the middle and working
classes increasingly protested the persistent inequalities in Chilean
society.

From the economic crisis and social and political ferment of the
1920s and 1930s, Chile again emerged as a pioneer in Latin
America, this time as a "developmentalist" nation. The idea was to
foster greater and more diversified economic development, lessen
the country's vulnerability to swings in the world economy, and
reduce inequalities at home. At bottom was the rejection of an
unfettered market and the belief — similar to that underlying
Keynesian and social welfare policies that had taken hold in developed countries — that government could play a fundamental role
in promoting economic development and social equity.

Starting in the late 1930s, the Chilean government aggressively
guided economic development. U.S.-owned copper mines
remained the main sources of exports and government resources,
but governmental organizations such as the development agency
CORFO (Corporación de Fomento), founded in 1939, invested in
infrastructure and in private and public enterprises considered

strategic to economic development and diversification. With the assistance of international public financial institutions, CORFO helped to set up a national steel industry, electrical plants and distribution networks, and transportation and communication systems. Government credit policies and protective tariffs made possible the formation of a diverse industrial base in textiles and light manufacturing, producing goods for a rapidly expanding domestic market. From the depths of depression, the Chilean economy responded to the new policies by diversifying and growing rapidly.

The Chilean government also pioneered policies to provide social services to Chileans unable to satisfy vital needs on the open marketplace. Government spending on education, health, housing and social security increased significantly during the 1920s, slowed only slightly during the 1930s depression and grew substantially after World War II. The implementation of new social laws and institutions, however, was piecemeal: laws covered one group (for instance, salaried workers) before new laws expanded the benefits to another (waged workers). This led to complex and inefficient social programs, in which the bulk of benefits didn't always go to the poorest Chileans for whom the programs supposedly had been created.[3] Social services also became an ever greater fiscal burden on a government reluctant to tax personal incomes to the degree necessary to finance them.

From the 1930s through the 1973 military coup, the Chilean political system was characterized by widespread participation and conflict. A variety of political parties competed for expanding constituencies, which gradually moved beyond elite circles to include the growing middle classes, urban workers, women (1949), farm workers and finally those unable to read and write (1970). Coalitions of parties of the left and the right competed for the allegiance of middle-class voters who might otherwise vote for the middle-of-the-road Radical Party or later the Christian Democrat Party. From 1938 and through the 1940s, elected governments were part of a "Popular Front" alliance led by the Radical Party with the participation of the Socialist and Communist parties. This alliance fell apart in the Cold War chill fostered in Chile by the United States. The Chilean Congress banned the Communist Party in 1948 — a year after it had won 18 percent of the vote in

municipal elections — and extended the vote to women the following year. The ban and the initial conservative electoral leanings
of most women voters put an end to the Popular Front and paved
the way for a center-right coalition to return to power in the
1950s, under the governments of the aging Carlos Ibáñez, followed by Jorge Alessandri (son of the 1920s president and scion of
one of Chile's largest family-owned conglomerates).

By the 1960s, the political system was increasingly divided into
left, center and right-wing coalitions. No president, therefore,
could count on the firm support of more than a third of the electorate, or more importantly on the cooperation of Congress, which
controlled the budget and confirmed all cabinet appointments. In
the short term, this factionalism forced political compromise; in
the longer term, however, the ever greater politicization of the population (intensified by the Cold War, the example of Cuba, and
competing visions of reform) escalated conflicts between the right
and the left, and between Congress and the president.

Frei and the Revolution in Liberty (1964-1970)

By the 1960s, Chile faced a development crisis. Following two
decades of rapid expansion, economic growth slowed to 4 percent
a year. The impressive expansion of domestic industry and the
broadened coverage of government social services had been largely financed by budget deficits that fueled spiraling inflation. Public
payrolls — key to Chile's sizable middle classes — were bloated.
Chile's economy was still overly dependent on copper (80 percent
of exports by value) which moreover remained in the hands of the
U.S. companies Kennecott and Anaconda. Agriculture stagnated
under the domination of large (and for the most part notoriously
underproductive) landholders. Meanwhile, a revolution led by
Fidel Castro in Cuba had put radical reform on the agenda
throughout Latin America, and the Kennedy administration's
"Alliance for Progress" championed more limited reforms with
the hope that they, together with increased military aid, would
stave off radical reforms.

In this context, Chile's presidential election in 1964 took on
special internal significance. It pitted the reformist Christian
Democrat Eduardo Frei against the Socialist Dr. Salvador

Allende. The traditional parties of the right decided to back Frei rather than run a candidate of their own for fear of throwing the elections to the left, since Allende had lost the previous race to Jorge Alessandri by only 3 percentage points. Allende was again backed by a coalition of left parties, called the Popular Unity, that included his own Socialist Party and the now legalized Communist Party. President Kennedy's "Alliance for Progress" held up Frei and the Christian Democrat platform as models for reformist policies in Latin America that could undercut revolutionary nationalist insurgencies. The CIA and multinational corporations funneled millions of dollars into Frei's campaign — double the amount per voter that the Johnson and Goldwater campaigns together spent per voter in the United States that same year.[4] Waging a virulently anti-Communist campaign, Frei won the elections by a wide margin with 56 percent of the vote.

From 1964 to 1970, President Frei and his Christian Democrat Party tried to implement a reform program. The stated goal was a "revolution in liberty" that would "re-make capitalism with a human face" through limited government interventions in the marketplace, including modest curbs on foreign influence, an agrarian reform, and an expansion of social services such as housing and education.

One of Frei's most important interventions in the economy was the "Chileanization" of the copper industry, by which the government bought 51 percent of the stock of copper and nitrate operations from U.S. companies. But the substantial tax breaks Frei gave the U.S. mining companies allowed them to continue to take out enormous profits.[5] Their unwillingness in these years to comply with agreements to expand investments in copper production further provoked the left parties and Chilean nationalists in general, who advocated expropriation. The Frei administration, however, accepted aid and loans from the United States on terms that made it impossible to reduce the foreign influence in the economy.

The other significant government intervention was in the rural economy. In 1964 huge estates comprising a mere 7 percent of Chilean farms controlled over 80 percent of agricultural land, a pattern prevailing since colonial times. In that year rural workers won the legal right to form labor unions, engage in collective bargaining, and conduct strikes, which dramatically shifted the balance of power in a countryside long dominated by a handful of large estate owners. The acceleration of rural organizing, backed by political parties looking to enlarge their constituencies, soon forced the question of agrarian reform. Frei's 1967 agrarian reform law put limits (albeit high) on the size of agricultural holdings and attempted to establish worker cooperatives on expropriated and redistributed estate lands. But by the close of Frei's term in 1970, implementation of even this guarded agrarian reform fell short of his announced goals and far short of the heightened expectations of the impoverished rural majority.

In his reform efforts, Frei faced bitter resistance in Congress from the parties of the right, which opposed all reforms, and from the parties of the left, which criticized Frei for not fulfilling his reform pledges and urged more radical measures. At the same time, poor Chileans who had mobilized to claim vacant urban land for housing needs or rural land for cultivation were increasingly frustrated by the government's slowness and inability to respond to their demands. Internationally, the Frei reforms, however modest, and his earlier close ties to Kennedy were enough to guarantee Frei the hostility of Richard Nixon, who was elected to the U.S. presidency in 1968.

In Chile's 1970 presidential election, the new Popular Unity coalition of left-wing parties again ran Salvador Allende of the Socialist Party. The Christian Democrats chose Radomiro Tomic, whose platform of radical reform was closer to Allende's than to Frei's. Outraged by even the moderate reforms of Frei, the right-wing parties put up a candidate of their own, the ever popular Jorge Alessandri, who had defeated Allende in the 1958 presidential election and who after a term out of office was again eligible to run. Alessandri was the preferred candidate of foreign corporations and of President Nixon, who viewed the Christian Democrats and Tomic, in particular, as too radical. This time, Allende edged out Alessandri to win with 36 percent of the vote, while Tomic trailed a distant third. Allende thus came to the presidency with the combined hostility of much of the electorate, the majority of the members of Congress, the conservative and Cold War-indoctrinated armed forces, foreign corporations, and the U.S. government.

Allende and the Democratic Road to Socialism (1970-73)

President Allende moved beyond the limited economic interventions of President Frei to propose a "peaceful and democratic road to socialism." Allende and his advisers planned to expand the government-owned sector to take control of "the strategic heights" of the economy in order to overcome patterns of uneven development that they viewed as rooted in exploitation by foreign companies, feudalistic structures in the countryside, and a backward, near-monopolized industrial sector. By breaking with previous structures, they sought to improve Chile's earnings from its exports as well as to diversify exports, redistribute income (a 1968 study showed that the top fifth of the Chilean population captured over half of national income, while the bottom fifth wound up with less than 5 percent[6]), increase production and national consumption, and raise living standards.

The Popular Unity government was continually split between its goals of structurally transforming the economy and of gaining the support of the poorer classes while fending off trenchant opposition from at home and abroad. Almost immediately after taking office in November 1970, Allende used his executive powers to grant large wage hikes and freeze prices, which jump-started the economy and boosted his popularity. During 1971, the economy grew a substantial 9 percent, and unemployment dropped by more than half, to 4 percent. The economic surge helped increase the support of the Popular Unity coalition, whose share of the vote rose to 50 percent in the crucial municipal elections of 1971.

In the longer run, such policies were not sustainable economically or politically. By 1972 many manufacturers were refusing to produce at the fixed prices and either stopped producing or sold their products on the black market. Scarcities and long lines in stores became notoriously common. The government continued to resort to deficit spending and printing money to fund social programs. This recourse resulted in part from the opposition of the majority in Congress to a tax reform and because administration officials seemed more concerned with delivering on populist promises than with how things were to be paid for. The annual inflation rate climbed to 150 percent by mid-1973 and to even higher levels in the months leading up to the September coup.

Ironically, the Popular Unity government's need to expand its political base to support its attempts to transform Chile's economic and social structures pushed it to indulge in irresponsible fiscal practices that undermined the viability of its program of transformation.

One important structural reform the Allende administration did carry out was the complete nationalization of the copper industry in July 1971. The law creating the publicly owned copper company, CODELCO, passed the Chilean Congress unanimously, and fulfilled a long-standing aspiration of many Chileans. The Popular Unity government also broke the private monopoly control of the financial sector, buying all but three of the country's largest banks as well as many industries controlled by family conglomerates. Most of these nationalizations, however, were carried out by administrative decree over the opposition from the center and right-wing parties in Congress, utilizing a 1932 law that allowed industries to be temporarily requisitioned in the public interest. The last key structural change of the Allende presidency was to greatly accelerate the agrarian reform. By the September 1973 coup, over half of the country's irrigated land had been affected.

Right and center parties, Chile's propertied classes, multinational corporations, the CIA and other agencies of the U.S. government, and right-wing vigilante groups such as *Patria y Libertad*, all bitterly opposed the government's policies at every turn through demonstrations, economic sabotage, "destabilization," and violence. At the other extreme, radical elements within the Popular Unity coalition (and the workers, urban squatters, and landless peasants whom they helped to organize) pushed the scope and speed of change toward socialism. Although continually torn between the moderates and radicals within his coalition, and between his program of strategic and legal transformation and the vociferous pressures from below to go beyond it, President Allende often reluctantly supported popular confiscations of factories and land holdings that were not considered strategic or large enough to warrant expropriation.[7]

"Spontaneous" expropriations alienated many medium-sized (and even smaller) business and land owners who either lost their properties or feared losing them. As political polarization grew in what would turn out to be the final year of the Allende administration, these middle sectors — convinced more and more by the right-wing predictions of an impending Cuban-style regime — increasingly opposed Allende. Business people stopped producing and investing. Enormous sums of money illegally converted into dollars were spirited out of the country. Merchants hid away stores of scarce goods or sold them at high prices on the black market. Middle-class consumers banged on cooking pots in front of the presidential palace to protest shortages. In October 1972 and again in July 1973, truck owners' strikes were backed by strikes and closures by many shopkeepers, bank clerks, doctors and lawyers, pushing the country further into economic and social chaos.

The climate of pervasive uncertainty could be even more debilitating than inflation or actual shortages. As Gonzalo Martner, Allende's Minister of Planning comments, "Many people repeatedly refer to the economic chaos of the last year of the Popular Unity. Yet the drop in production in 1973 was 6 percent, while under Pinochet both in 1975 and 1982, it was as bad as 15 percent." The problem was not simply one of economic production "but the manipulation of information and fear."[8]

Nationalization of the U.S.-owned copper companies and government interventions in many of the holdings in Chile of other multinational companies such as ITT further aggravated tensions between the U.S. and Chilean governments. The Nixon administration[9] cut off all aid and credit programs to Chile (except military aid) as well as access to loans from international agencies controlled by the U.S. such as the World Bank and the Inter-American Development Bank, which in the past had helped to fund many of the Chilean government's development projects. During the six-year Frei government, U.S.-economic aid had totaled $1.2 billion; during the three years of the Popular Unity government, the total dropped to $68 million, of which $33 million was military aid.[10]

As the right-wing media played upon fears of Cuban-style rationing and government economic control and fanned unfounded rumors of armed peasants and workers plotting a coup, political polarization deepened. Nevertheless, in the mid-term Congressional elections of March 1973, the Popular Unity coalition increased its representation in Congress, winning 43 percent of the vote. This was a considerable increase over its vote in the 1970 presidential elections, but a decline from the 50 percent the Popular Unity coalition had won in the municipal elections of 1971. At any rate, it was not enough to wrest control of Congress from the increasingly united opposition of the center and right-wing parties. During the following months, the leader of the Christian Democrats, Patricio Aylwin, continually rejected Allende's calls to negotiate with the Popular Unity coalition. Confident that they would inevitably inherit power from any ousting of Allende, the strategy of the Christian Democrats played into the hands of those from the political right and the military who plotted a coup.

In the early morning of September 11, 1973, the Army surrounded the presidential palace as Air Force jets bombed from above. The siege ended hours later as President Allende died defending the constitutional government. While many Chileans without doubt were relieved that the uncertainties of the Allende government were over, few anticipated the brutality of the repression that was to follow and the many years it would continue. The brutality of the coup was unprecedented, with thousands of Chileans killed, tortured or forced into exile. Over the next months, military wrath fell on those with ties to parties of the left, unions, intellectuals, and organizations of peasants and urban working-class neighborhoods, as the military junta fabricated the pretext of a civil war to justify the ferocity of their reprisals. Repression extended to all levels of Chilean society: the Constitution remained suspended, universities and even high schools were put under the direct charge of generals and admirals, the Congress was shut down, the media were subject to censorship, and political parties were eventually either banned or severely restricted in their activities.

President Allende and his Popular Unity coalition still evoke strong emotions from most Chileans. Many of the workers, shantytown dwellers, students and others who actively supported Allende and the Popular Unity coalition today speak of a time of extraordinary hope, solidarity, and democratic participation that was sabotaged by industrialists, the military, and the imperialists and interventionists of the United States. Others, in particular those confessed supporters of the armed forces or at least of the new economic and social order they brought about, express their visceral hatred of the "communist" government that brought Chile to the "verge of economic ruin and totalitarian dictatorship." Many Chileans alive then, even as they came to despise the military regime that replaced Allende, still have vivid agonizing memories of the shortages of many goods, the long lines and the pervasive anxiety and social clashes that reigned in the last months before the military coup. These memories were systematically manipulated and exaggerated by the armed forces for the next seventeen years, as they insisted that they were the only alternative to the "communist horrors" of the Popular Unity.

3

Dictatorship and the Free Market, 1973-1990: An Overview

The Pinochet-led military junta, advised by a group of Chilean economists mostly trained at the University of Chicago, imposed a radical program of free-market policies. The junta did so by decree, without the constitutional rule and democratic institutions that had once been the pride of Chile. Nonetheless, the actual course of implementation of free-market policies was shaped by the changing political context of international and domestic pressures, trends in the global economy, and the roller coaster of booms and busts in the Chilean economy. Looking back, it is useful to distinguish five periods in the economic history of the seventeen-year military rule.

- 1973-1975: repression and economic retrenchment

- 1975-1979: "shock treatment" and the initial implementation of free-market reforms

- 1979-1981: the "Chilean miracle" based on monetary manipulations and massive foreign borrowing; major reforms in social programs

- 1982-1984: the financial crash and deep economic recession

- 1985-1990: economic recovery and consolidation of the model

First, a little background. In June 1955 four professors from the University of Chicago, Theodore Schultz, Arnold Harberger, Simon Rottenberg and Earl Hamilton, arrived in Santiago. They all came from the university's Economics department. Their "Chicago school of economics" was known for its strident anti-Keynesian, free-market economics. The professors came to Chile in order to help launch an extensive program of technical cooperation between the University of Chicago and Chile's Catholic University. The U.S. government[1] liberally funded the program through 1961, and thereafter support came from Chilean businessmen and others.[2]

The program consisted of creating within the Catholic University a center for economic research, professors from the University of Chicago teaching in Chile, and sending Chilean economists to Chicago for postgraduate studies. Between 1956 and 1961, some 150 promising Chileans received full graduate fellowships at the University of Chicago.

These "Chicago Boys" were sons of the Chilean right. "Middle- and upper-class students at the Catholic University in the 1950s and 1960s, [they] shared a conservative religious background, a visceral rejection of socialism, and a contempt for Chile's free-wheeling, mass democracy."[3] As students at the University of Chicago they would have all these sentiments only reinforced. Under the rigorous tutelage of the Chicago economists — most notably, Professor Harberger and the charismatic Professor Milton Friedman — they would become immersed in unadulterated free-market doctrines.[4] The precepts in which these Chileans were schooled in Chicago ran directly counter to Christian Democrat as well as Marxist prescriptions to cure Chile's underdevelopment that captured the minds of most of their peers.

Many of these Chicago Boys took on the theoretical certitude of their mentors and returned crusader-like to Chile. They rapidly gained footholds in academia (primarily the Catholic University), conservative think tanks, influential media organizations such as El Mercurio, and prominent corporations. At least fifteen Chicago Boys would occupy top policy-making positions in the Pinochet military government.[5] By the mid-1970s "Chicago Boy" had become a household name, even among the poor. The U.S. government and the other sponsors of the University of Chicago's "Chile Project" certainly got their money's worth.

I. September 1973 to April 1975: Political Repression and Economic Retrenchment

On September 11, 1973, for the Chicago Boys, shut out from the corridors of government power during the many years of the Christian Democrat and Popular Unity administrations, it seemed their time had finally come. That night, while jet fighter planes still buzzed terrifyingly low over Santiago, the lights were burning at the Lord Cochrane publishing house. Inside the photocopy machines were whirling non-stop, cranking out copies of a thick document known to the Chicago Boys and their sympathizers as "the brick."[6]

"The brick" was a 500-odd-page plan for reversing the economic policies of Chile implemented over the previous half century. No ordinary time and no ordinary publication, the plan's authors wanted copies to be placed before noon on the next day on the desk of every general in the new military regime. Eight Chicago Boy economists and two other like-minded economists had formed the core of the task force that put together the voluminous draft document. They had been diligently meeting and drafting for months, called into action by a group of high-ranking Navy officers and certain business leaders. They were galvanized by their sense that it would not be much longer before the military would overthrow President Allende. Their efforts were financed by SOFOFA, Chile's main private industry lobby, which in turn received funding from foreign companies as part of a "war plan" to destabilize the Popular Unity government and outline a plan of action for a "replacement government."[7]

The Chicago Boys' preparations to insert themselves into positions of power in the military regime would largely meet with success, but their rise to power was neither immediate nor smooth. For one thing, the junta in a manner characteristic of the military, placed in decision-making positions only those on whom they could fully rely; proven loyalty was the first criterion and aptitude only second for the position. Thus, while several key Chicago Boys were called to serve within the military government, at first they were only advisers to uniformed ministers and directors of purely technical departments.

More prominent among the junta's first economic policy advisers was a mix of civilians from the Christian Democrat and Nationalist parties — largely the old guard from previous administrations. While agreeing with the Chicago Boys' goal of loosening government controls on the economy and giving incentives to foreign investment, they nevertheless believed in a strong economic role for government. They desired only to eliminate Allende's "excesses" and thought that whatever changes were to be made should be carried out gradually in order to minimize traumatic social costs.

There is no evidence in the decree laws of the first months of a coherent economic ideology. At first, Pinochet and his uniformed colleagues moved with caution. They summoned before them advisers with conflicting views and heard out their often heated debates.

The Chicago Boys and their foreign mentors seized every opportunity to undermine the prestigious old-line economic tacticians on whom the military initially most relied in their efforts to turn around Chile's disastrous economic decline. They threw themselves into working to win over General Pinochet and the other ranking military to their free-market precepts.

Many military officers worried about the political repercussions of the first two concessions to the free-market proponents — a drastic currency devaluation along with the "liberation" of the prices of most goods and services. Both moves automatically hiked the price of imported goods on which Chile was very dependent and only further fueled inflation throughout the economy. The admiral who was then finance minister who had taken the decision was sharply rebuked by junta member Admiral Merino: "We've all been deceived. When we took the decision to devaluate no one told us that the price of wheat [much of which was imported] was going to go up and up and therefore also the price of bread and many other things was going to increase. It's intolerable and it creates problems for us. The military junta cannot be increasing prices. We will be accused of killing the people with hunger."[8]

Additional influential opposition to the free-marketeers was mounted by major interests in industry and agriculture as well as right-wing politicians. They had battled both the Popular Unity and the Christian Democrat governments but were nonetheless threatened by any ideas of cutting government subsidies, lowering protective tariffs, and ending joint ventures with the private sector. Strong opposition to the Chicago Boys' notion of "shrinking the government" also came from within the armed forces. Many in the armed forces (not least of whom were ranking officers appointed by the junta to manage many of the large public sector companies) believed "national security" required the government to control the nation's major economic institutions.[9]

Decrees during this period reveal the junta pursuing a gradualist approach to economic reform. In addition to lifting price controls, the junta gave back most industries confiscated by the Popular Unity government to their owners, shifted many of the smaller farms resulting from years of agrarian reform out of the hands of farm workers towards investors, reduced taxes on foreign companies, lowered tariffs, and trimmed government spending. Nevertheless, Chile seemed mired in merciless stagflation: consumer prices continued to skyrocket at an annual rate of 375 percent while joblessness reached unprecedented levels and wage hikes fell far behind increases in the cost of living. The budget deficit, despite spending cuts, ran at about 32 percent.

On the political front, it soon became clear to civilian politicians who had supported the coup that the junta was by no means ready to hand power over to them. In 1974 the junta proclaimed in its "Declaration of Principles of the Government of Chile," that "the Government does not intend to be a mere caretaker." Instead it would "take upon itself the historic mission of giving Chile new governmental institutions that [would] embody the profound changes occurring in modern times." The declaration ominously signaled the junta's intention of "reorganizing the economy, destroyed to its very roots by Marxism" and of "imposing authority and discipline in production and labor relations."[10]

By mid-1974, the continued repression of the military regime was more than the Christian Democrat Party could stomach and the leadership asked its members in government posts to choose between the party and the junta. Only a few stayed on in government, leaving the path to power that much less obstructed for the Chicago Boys.

II. April 1975 to 1979: The "Shock Treatment"

The more the gradualist reforms seemed to fail, the more the Chicago Boys lobbied for more radical measures. They pulled out all the stops in March 1975 with a visit to Chile by Professor Milton Friedman, the best known of the Chicago economists (and soon to be awarded the Nobel Prize), accompanied by his colleague Arnold Harberger. In numerous public appearances and television interviews during the whirlwind visit, Friedman's theme was unmistakable: economic reforms by the military government to date were mere palliatives and unless "the diseased parts of the economy were amputated the final costs would be higher." Acknowledging that there would be a surge in unemployment resulting from his "medicine," he predicted that the unemployed would rapidly find work. ("You'd be surprised how fast people would be absorbed by a growing private-sector economy," he told his audience.[11]) Continuing to deploy medical metaphors, Friedman in a speech at the University of Chile called for "shock treatment." Friedman also "trooped over to Pinochet's office to give the general a one-hour course," according to *Fortune* magazine.[12] Friedman counseled the dictator to ignore his extremely bad press abroad and to cure once and for all the "disease" that is "suffocating statism," specifically, government playing the leading role in the economy.[13] The immediate prescriptions from Chicago included slashing government spending by a further 20 to 25 percent and removing constraints on — but also subsidies to — private businesses. *Fortune* commented that, "The Chicago Boys realized that the Friedman-Harberger road show was good public relations for the drastic steps they were about to take."[14]

The Chicago Boys were rapidly advancing in power, gaining on their opponents. Shortly after the Friedman-Harberger visit, Pinochet appointed Sergio de Castro, a leading Chicago Boy and Harberger's close associate, as the Minister of the Economy, replacing Fernando Leniz, a business type who was one of the two greatest obstacles within the government to the radical free-market advocates.[15] General Pinochet then decreed the centralization of all economic policy under the Minister of Finance. This "super-minister" was the newly appointed Jorge Cauas, who, though an alumnus of Columbia University as well as an alumnus of the

Christian Democrat Party, had become an ardent convert to the University of Chicago doctrines.

The Chicago Boys (in particular de Castro and Cauas) wasted no time drawing up a plan to implement free-market policies. They worked on the detailed plan inside and outside the government without the knowledge of the Minister of Economic Coordination, Raul Sáez, the other influential opponent of the free-market prescriptions inside the government. Sáez, who in the 1940s and '50s had helped promote Chile's industrialization through publicly owned companies, was willing to see market forces being given freer rein in the economy but adamantly stood for government playing the leading role in marshaling and directing resources for economic development.[16]

In April 1975 there was one final debate before the junta.[17] At a weekend meeting at the presidential retreat in coastal Viña del Mar, Cauas presented the plan. Sáez objected strenuously. Joined by several uniformed advisors, he warned that the drastic measures would greatly worsen the recession. Sáez objected to such aspects as the removal of all controls on interest rates banks could charge. Most of all, he opposed the fundamental change in Chile's economic system whereby the government's economic role would be greatly reduced, indeed coming into play only when the private sector could not rise to the occasion. The debate lasted for several hours. At about 9 p.m. the session ended when General Pinochet pronounced his approval of the Chicago Boys' plan.

The plan quickly became known throughout Chile as "*el tratamiento de shock*," the shock treatment. As *Business Week* commented, "An already severe anti-inflationary policy was turned into one of Draconian harshness." Milton Friedman's comment was that his "only concern" with the plan was "whether it would be pushed long enough and hard enough."[18]

The plan slashed government spending and contracted the money supply. As predicted, these moves worsened an already bad recession. By the end of the year (1975), economic output shrank by a depression-like 13 percent, the purchasing power of wages plummeted 40 percent from the level of 1970, and unemployment climbed to 20 percent.[19] But at least inflation did start to drop. The Chicago Boys pressed on, determined that the economy would be managed on technical rather than social criteria.

At the same time the junta and their civilian advisors began to devise economic and political institutions to replace "rule by force and fury." The generals envisioned a new political order that would not simply cut out the "Marxist cancer" of leftist parties from national politics but eliminate politics itself. They blamed politics, in particular the inevitably demagogic promises of politicians and the irresponsible demands of their constituents, for the national crisis under the Allende presidency. Their political prescription had two principal ingredients: a tight security apparatus to insure social order, and a technocratic bent to an authoritarian government that would *de-politicize* national decisions. Both components were to be presided over by a strong and independent executive; by 1975 General Pinochet, eclipsing his colleagues in the junta, had a firm grip on this role.

As the economy finally started to recuperate in 1977, de Castro and his team began to push through their broader free-market agenda. The regime sold off the principal government-owned banks as well as a multitude of small publicly owned companies. The financial sector and the transportation and the fishing industries were substantially deregulated, and limits on foreign borrowing by the private sector were abolished. High tariffs on imports were further reduced — by 1979, down to a uniform 10 percent. The government opened wide the door to foreign investment, allowing, for instance, for the almost unrestricted remittance of profits abroad. Finally, through a less-than-free-market manipulation of the peso's exchange rate with the dollar, inflation was brought down at last to a tolerable annual 30 percent. Chile was poised for its long-promised "miracle."

III. 1979 to 1982: The Chilean "Miracle" and Major Reforms in Social Programs

Vigorous growth from 1977 to 1981 barely got the economy back to the production levels of 1970, but it did afford Pinochet and the Chicago Boys a margin of maneuverability to impose sweeping changes in social programs. Human rights pressures from Europe and the Carter administration in the U.S. also pushed the junta to move from rule by emergency decree to a more institutionalized order, a move which culminated in 1980 with a new constitution.

Major free-market reforms of social services were begun in 1979. Among the most important were the creation of a voucher system that gave subsidies to private schools, the replacement of the public social security system with one run by private investment companies, and the dismantling of a national public system of health care in favor of private health insurance companies. In addition, the regime decreed a new Labor Code that severely curtailed the organizational and collective bargaining rights of workers. The Chicago Boys liked to refer to these and related changes as the "Seven Modernizations."

The results of the so-called economic "miracle" of this period were mixed and rested on the shakiest of foundations, as in due course would be clear to all. Exports did show signs of diversifying and growing, notably in fresh fruit, fish and forestry. By contrast, most traditional industries, especially manufacturing and agriculture for the domestic market — which the Chicago Boys exposed to "the winds of international competition" — did not fare well as the lowered tariffs afforded little protection from goods on the world market. Unable to compete, numerous firms and farms were forced into bankruptcy, helping to keep official unemployment above 15 percent.

Contrary to what one might expect from free-marketeers, government policy makers in 1979 pegged the peso at 39 to the dollar and artificially held it there until the end of 1981. The resulting overvalued peso on top of the lowered tariffs made Santiago reputedly one of the least expensive places in the world to buy goods from Asia, the U.S., and Europe. This overvalued peso and the eagerness of foreign banks awash in "petro-dollars" to make loans put up the greater part of a steeply mortgaged "miracle."

Nevertheless, for more than three years even many low-income Chileans enjoyed an "easy money" bonanza, for instance, buying foreign-made electronics goods for the first time in their lives. Speculative investments and conspicuous consumption, largely financed by heavy borrowing, were the hallmark of the miracle. Real estate prices soared; wealthy Chileans found they could buy homes in Miami for less than in Santiago. The number of cars, mostly imported, tripled between 1975 and 1982, mirroring a tripling in the foreign debt to $16 billion, one of the highest per-capita levels in Latin America.[20]

In the midst of this shopping spree and a pumped-up economy, Pinochet's freshly crafted constitution won 67 percent approval in a carefully controlled plebiscite on September 11, 1980, the seventh anniversary of the "Day of National Salvation." Drawing on the theoretical framework of University of Chicago philosopher Friedrich von Hayek, the Chicago Boys had drawn up a charter for the strong authoritarian rule they saw as necessary to enforce the rules of economic freedom.

The new constitution consolidated into a juridical framework the free-market economic and social reforms of the "Seven Modernizations" while bequeathing a "protected democracy" on future generations of Chileans. Presidential powers were strengthened, and Pinochet's own presidential term guaranteed through 1989, with the possibility of an additional eight-year term to be decided in a plebiscite. Along with the eventual election in 1989 of a new Congress, the constitution created an autonomous National Security Council and a bloc of junta-designated senators sufficient to veto major legislation and guarantee the military a continued executive and legislative grip. To further preserve the rightist order under what was proclaimed as the "Constitution of Freedom," leftist parties were to be permanently outlawed, along with "all groups contrary to morality, public order or security of the State."[21]

IV. 1982 to 1984: The Crash

Pinochet and the Chicago Boys rode into 1981 with the all the confidence they had consolidated in the previous year with the constitutional plebiscite and an almost 8 percent growth in the economy. Virtually all of the key free-market reforms were in place, and in the national and international media, the deep recession of 1975 was but a distant memory. By the end of 1981, however, the strength of the economy and the legitimacy of the government, or at least of the Chicago Boys, stood in serious doubt. The recession in the United States, brought on in part by President Reagan's monetarist policies (also inspired by the Chicago school of economics), proved just how vulnerable an open economy could be to shifts abroad. The global tightening of credit and higher interest rates burst the bubble of prosperity in Chile.

Starting in November 1981, a series of banks and businesses began to fail, including several of the principal conglomerates that had benefited most from privatizations of government-owned companies and sweeping financial and business deregulation. The result was a drastic contraction of the economy that rivaled the worst years of the Great Depression. The gross domestic product (GDP) dropped by 14 percent in 1982, and official unemployment rose to over a third of the labor force (and in reality even higher). Suddenly the Chilean "miracle" had little to show for itself except a heavily indebted and failing private sector and an economic base incapable of supporting such high levels of debt.

The military government responded by distancing itself from free-market policies, at least long enough to bail out the private sector. The government intervened massively in the financial sector. Over the next two years, the government absorbed the debts of many large businesses, restoring them to soundness before selling them off to private interests. Other companies were sustained through preferential exchange rates with which they could pay their dollar debts. The government wound up taking on as public debt some $16 billion in foreign loans, most of which had been originally incurred and often recklessly spent by private Chilean conglomerates.

By contrast, middle-class families watched with disbelief and anger as the balances on their home mortgages, indexed to the dollar value of the peso, soared; but the government offered them no relief. Even though these and other debts for millions of Chileans rose with every peso devaluation, in 1982 the government ended all indexing of wages and salaries for inflation, and the Labor Code decreed in 1979 severely restricted protests and collective bargaining. In Chile's worst economic crisis since the global depression of the 1930s, one out of eight Chilean workers wound up in government emergency work programs, typically jobs planting trees or sweeping streets and subways at less than the miserably low minimum wage. It's little wonder that 1983 witnessed an unprecedented wave of anti-government protests among unions, shantytown dwellers, and even some middle-class and professional groups that had supported the coup a decade earlier.

V. 1985 to 1990: Recovery, Consolidation, and Electoral Defeat

For all the severity of the crisis, Pinochet and his economic advisers refused to back away significantly from free-market policies. In 1985, overall economic policy passed into the hands of wunderkind Hernan Büchi (a Chicago Boy in fact graduated from Columbia University) who in previous years had quietly participated in the design of many of the free-market changes in health care and other social services. With some pragmatic adjustments and concessions, Büchi regained the support of Chile's dominant classes for the free-market model. Concessions included selective debt relief to businesses, an undervalued peso that encouraged Chilean exports, slightly raising certain protective tariffs and a system of agricultural "price bands" for crops grown for domestic consumption.

The Chilean foreign debt peaked in 1985 at around $21 billion, equaling the total value of the country's entire economic output (GDP) in that year and forcing Chile to drastically cut imports and to prioritize exports in order to meet its loan payments.[22] The Pinochet's government dutiful payments to the foreign banks and its persistence in free-market reforms (by this point strongly championed by Reagan in the U.S. and Thatcher in Britain) won Chile the favor of the IMF and World Bank, which funneled short-term credits to help pay interest on the debt and supervised the financial restructuring. A drop in the world price of oil, a rise in the price of copper, and decreased shipping costs for Chilean exports all favored recovery after 1985.

When the government completed the sale of companies that had failed in the crash, the Chicago Boys launched a second wave of privatizations that included Chile's largest traditional public companies, such as electric utilities and communications monopolies. The companies were sold off at bargain prices to domestic and foreign investors. Further neo-liberal reforms in social programs were stepped up in the months before the 1988 plebiscite on Pinochet's continued rule, since his future and that of the Chicago Boys hung in doubt.

Strong growth in the economy after 1985 — especially impressive compared to the stagnation or worse in the rest of Latin

America — led supporters of free-market policies in and outside the country to again speak of a "Chilean miracle." Once again the miracle was not all it was made out to be. Only in 1989 would per capita economic output get back up to the level of 1981 or, for that matter, that of 1971. Wages fell sharply with the crash of 1982 and remained stagnant throughout most of the decade, even as GDP recovered and surpassed previous levels. Unlike the first Chilean boom, much of the growth in the late 1980s was based on an expansion of exports, particularly such non-traditional exports as fresh fruits, seafood, and forestry products. But recovery and expansion after 1985 depended on two ingredients that are unsustainable over the long term and in a democratic society. The first ingredient was the unregulated exploitation of nonrenewable natural resources such as native forests and fishing areas, which amounted to a one-time subsidy to domestic conglomerates and multinationals. The second was an intensified exploitation of the labor force.

In the 1988 plebiscite, voters rejected an additional presidential term for General Pinochet. In December 1989, voters chose the Christian Democrat Patricio Aylwin, candidate of a center-left coalition, as the first civilian president to succeed Pinochet. The candidate of the right was Büchi, Pinochet's economic czar and architect of many of the free-market reforms of the previous decade; he received only 29 percent of the vote. But whatever the interpretation of the vote, Pinochet remained as head of the armed forces, and with the support of the appointed hand-picked senators, held in effect a likely veto over fundamental change. The economic program of the Chicago Boys was firmly in place and watched over by the structures of "protected democracy."

4

The Worldview of the Chicago Boys

The bulk of this book examines the concrete consequences of free-market economic and social policies implemented under authoritarian rule in Chile. First, however, a brief overview of the theoretical underpinnings of those policies can help orient us.[1]

The philosophy to which free-market economists adhere is often referred to by both its champions and its critics as "neo-liberal."[2] As with Adam Smith (1723-1790), the Scottish political economist and founding father of "liberal" thinking, the focus is on liberty. For Smith as well as the latter-day neo-liberals, the focal point is the individual: only if individuals are free to pursue their individual gain will the best interests of society be promoted. The transmission belt by which individuals pursuing their own interests winds up to be in the interests of the society at large is the market. The marketplace is society's locus of salutary competition among individuals.

The classical liberal as well as the contemporary neo-liberal worldview goes far beyond what today is generally (and quite narrowly) understood as the scope of economics. It is an all-encompassing ideology. And, as Juan Gabriel Valdes notes, "Neo-liberal economists are priests and preachers; they are social and moral philosophers; they are educators and propagandists."[3]

An emphasis on freedom or liberty is the distinctive element of the neo-liberal worldview, on which everything else turns. Freedom is defined in terms of *individual* autonomy. Key to that autonomy is that the individual not be hemmed in or coerced by society. Freedom is defined negatively, that is, in terms of the absence of outside intervention.

Quintessential freedom is economic freedom, the right of each individual to carry out economic initiatives in the marketplace without being hindered by the government. Without fully realized economic freedom, political freedom is meaningless. In other words, economic freedom is the right to make choices as a producer or a consumer without government interference. Centralizing economic activity in government or governmental efforts to regulate the market not only leads to the negation of individual liberty, but also thwarts the development of a prosperous economy by undercutting the creative capacity of individual entrepreneurs and enthroning bungling bureaucrats.

To function properly, the market requires private property, private management of economic enterprises, and unfettered competition between enterprises. The freedom of the individual results from the free functioning of the market. The market organization of economic activity, according to Milton Friedman in his book *Capitalism and Freedom*, prevents one person from interfering with another in respect to most of his activities. The consumer is protected from coercion by the seller because of the presence of other sellers with whom he can deal. The seller is protected from coercion by the consumer because of other consumers to whom he can sell. The employee is protected from coercion by the employer because of other employers for whom he can work, and so on. And the market does this impersonally and without centralized authority.[4]

At the foundation of the neo-liberal vision of the market is the concept of the individual as a rational optimizer of self-interest. Operating on the market involves the constant calculation of advantages presented by the ever-changing conditions of the marketplace.

In a market free from interference (from government, price-fixing, "interest groups," etc.), prices for products or services will find their "natural level" determined by the "law" of supply and demand. According to the neo-liberals, this market mechanism, ever objective, maximizes efficiency and benefits all individuals who participate.

From the neo-liberal understanding of freedom it follows that government is the foe of individual freedom. The role of government should be highly circumscribed and, as a consequence, its size reduced. "The least government is the best government" was a favorite refrain of the neo-liberals long before Ronald Reagan. Neo-liberals also oppose any other institution or organization that in any way limits the full range of options for each individual. For them, intermediary organizations such as professional associations, guilds, cooperatives and labor unions interfere with and distort free, competitive market behavior; therefore such obstacles to individual freedom should be discouraged or severely circumscribed.[5]

For neo-liberal theorists, individuals — social animals that we are — do create social institutions but only to pursue specific ends. These social institutions, beginning with the family, culminate in the state. Here enters the neo-liberal "principle of subsidiarity:"[6] No higher-level social institution should undertake activities which could be performed by a lower-level institution. Thus the area of competence of the national government begins where the possibilities of effective action by the individual or the family or, say, the municipal government have been exceeded. In the economic arena, the government ought not to play any role, carry out any type of activity, that could be done by private individuals or companies. National defense is one of the few appropriate roles of government because it is beyond the capacity of lower-level institutions. Delivering the mail is not. From this principle flows the neo-liberals' doctrine that publicly owned companies should be privatized except perhaps for the few considered "strategic for national security."

Proper to the government's restricted role is the defense of private property and, if necessary, the enforcement of the rules of the free market — for example, rules against "market-distorting" monopolies or cartels.

Banishing government from much of the economic arena, neo-liberals reject any notion that the government should play a role — let alone be a leading actor in economic development (as the Chilean government had been for a half century). The proper engine of the economy is individual profit-seeking. If given free rein, private initiatives will best promote development; ultimately, everyone benefits.

Neo-liberals thus would do away with governmental goals such as promoting industrialization, stimulating a depressed economy, encouraging investment in areas considered priorities for the society, and assisting certain groups with credit, tax incentives, or subsidies (for example, small businesses). Such interventions by government in the marketplace invariably generate inefficiencies in the allocation and utilization of resources. Any measure which discriminates in favor of certain groups will introduce market disequilibriums. Only freely working market mechanisms can assure that economic policies have neutral distributional effects, that is to say, that they don't discriminate in favor of some to the exclusion of others. The neo-liberal economic prescription is always the same: swiftly privatize the economy, liberate markets of government regulations and other obstacles, and open up the national economy to international trade and foreign investment.[7]

On this last point of the prescription, neo-liberals staunchly advocate that underdeveloped economies open themselves to "the winds of international competition," particularly by lifting protective tariffs and restrictions on foreign investment. Such barriers to free trade coddle inefficient national industries usually at high costs to local consumers and often to taxpayers as well. Local enterprises and industries that survive international competition will do so by becoming more efficient. Those that identify and build on local "comparative advantages" will be rewarded in the global marketplace.

Neo-liberals also reject the social amelioration role of government. In accordance with their principle that the government do only what the private sector is incapable of, and their goal of reducing the cost of government, they would stop government from providing a whole array of social services that most governments have tended to assume responsibility for since the French Revolution (education, health care, public health, housing, social security, recreation, etc.); private enterprises freely competing on the marketplace will be more responsive and more efficient in cost-benefit terms. Moreover, government economic and social interventions tend to rack up budget deficits, bringing on inflation, and inflation is unfair to the majority and most heavily penalizes the poor.

The government should assist, neo-liberals admit, those citizens so poor that they cannot on their own satisfy their basic needs (such as for adequate food, health care, housing, and education) through the market. Neo-liberals view such "extreme poverty" as the product of previous governmental meddlings in economic markets that, whatever the fine intentions, generate bouts of inflation and unemployment. Truly indigent people will not be in a position to take advantage of the economic opportunities offered by the marketplace to get out of the vicious circle of poverty — they are too poor to get and hold a job. The government, in fulfillment of its subsidiary role, should step in and enable such persons to take advantage of market opportunities. Even then it should use market mechanisms: for example, rather than grant food the government should give food vouchers that enable the recipients to shop on the open market; or, rather than build and operate public housing the government should supplement the buying power of the homeless poor so that the private housing industry can profitably respond to their needs.

Neo-liberals would cut government social spending by focusing resources only on the "truly poor." Without careful "targeting," they argue, social spending does not benefit mostly the poor but winds up benefiting middle-class and even rich citizens. Whenever government in the name of promoting equality and social justice grants exemptions, subsidies, and other privileges to certain groups, invariably those who capture the lion's share of the benefits are those who organize into pressure groups — not the poor. The end result of government interventions aimed at a more equal distribution of benefits is a more unequal distribution.

The ethical goal therefore should not be social equality understood as equality of results — no matter how different the individual effort expended. (Moreover, the neo-liberals claim, history has abundantly demonstrated that the pursuit of such equality leads to repression and to totalitarian dictatorships of the left.[8]) The equality and justice to which neo-liberals avow they are committed is equality of opportunity — equality in the marketplace. They define equality of opportunity as the absence of discrimination against any individual actor. That in turn is conceived of in opposition to government interventions: equality of opportunity will be achieved only when the free market — which submits all decisions to impersonal and uniform rules and not the arbitrary power of public bureaucracies — regulates the supply and consumption of goods and services. The (free) marketplace, according to neo-liberals, is the only arena in which everyone is formally equal and there is no discrimination based on personal attributes and access to power. Opportunities are distributed equally — "impersonally" — that is, without regard to person. When the market operates free from government social engineering, no inequalities will be generated that are not either "from God or the result of merit." In sum, as long as the government limits itself to seeing that all have access to essential goods and services, the only inequalities in a society will be attributable to individual efforts, to varying propensities to save or splurge or to varying God-given endowments.[9]

The free-market system is the path, according to the neo-liberals, away from a weak society of mediocrity to a strong society, one that stimulates individual creative capacity and rewards hard work. In the neo-liberal version of social Darwinism, the most capable and most hardworking are the ones who triumph. The free-market system, concludes Chilean sociologist Pilar Vergara in her insightful study of neo-liberal ideology, mercilessly punishes "those who make mistakes, who are ignorant, who are incapable and who fail to live up to the rules."[10]

The neo-liberal stance that all but the indigent be "free" to satisfy their needs as they see fit in a marketplace of competing providers (in contrast to universal and mandatory government programs) should, they point out, not only shrink the size of most governments but reduce payroll costs to employers, thereby helping to make local industries more competitive on the global marketplace.

Neo-liberals like to identify their programs as "modernizations." Shifting the provision of basic social goods and services from government to private enterprise (and letting the rules of the market regulate access to them) is often referred to by proponents as "social modernization."

Free-marketeers, consistent with their principles, also oppose public ownership of facilities such as parks. In their view, such services in the hands of government tend to result in a tax burden on virtually everyone whereas private enterprise could charge only those who make use of them. (True free-marketeers, in advocating all-out privatization, view government ownership with user fees sufficient to recoup operating costs as a half-way measure.)

Monetarism is a basic component of the philosophical framework of the neo-liberals and particularly of Chicago school economists such as Friedman. Inflation, not unemployment, is viewed as the primary economic problem[11] — "a disease of the social body that only responds to strong and prolonged treatments."[12] Furthermore, in Friedman's own words, "Inflation is always and everywhere a monetary phenomenon, produced in the first instances by an unduly rapid growth in the quantity of money."[13] Keynesian-inspired government interventions, such as combating unemployment by job creation, do more harm than good by expanding the economy too rapidly, not to mention the likelihood of government budget deficits. The resulting inflation inevitably requires a tightening of the money supply in order to slow down economic growth and thereby hold down prices — in other words, a recession and widespread unemployment. Monetarists argue that the economy — and therefore everybody — would be better off with a constant non-inflationary rate of growth in the money supply.

Since governments often deal with their budgetary deficits by printing more money, for monetarist neo-liberals it is crucial to keep a tight lid on the size and cost of government. Thus monetarism fits well with the overall neo-liberal view of the proper, i.e., highly circumscribed, role of government. Reducing government means taxes can be reduced, one of the key ways neo-liberals aim to help private enterprises become more profitable and thereby, they believe, generate higher levels of investment, economic growth and employment. Indeed the best social program, from the neo-liberal worldview, is a limited, deficit-free government.

****

As for *political* freedom, Chile's neo-liberals (and perhaps also their collaborators in Chicago[14]) seemed unperturbed by the glaring contradiction of employing a decidedly interventionist — indeed authoritarian and repressive — government to enforce "economic freedom." A taunt repeatedly hurled at the Chicago Boys over the many years of iron-fisted rule was, "If consumers have the freedom to choose what to buy or not to buy, why can't they have the same freedom with respect to political alternatives?"[15] For them, however, it was all only a paradox, not a true contradiction. "We are making a policy in order to lose power, so how can we be concentrating it?" a seemingly bewildered leading Chicago Boy exclaimed when he and his colleagues were accused of being anti-democratic.[16] The Chicago Boys would have the world think of them as "apolitical" technicians, unappreciated though they might be at the time, laboring to lay the foundations of economic freedom that eventually would be the pillar of political freedom. They argued that a long "period of transition" was needed in order to transform individual and social values and habits.[17]

Constable and Valenzuela, in their study of the "culture of fear" in Chile under Pinochet, perhaps come closer to the heart of the matter: "To these men [the Chicago Boys], the only kind of freedom that mattered was individual economic freedom, which [Chicago Boy] de Castro argued was best guaranteed by an 'authoritarian government' with its 'impersonal' method of exercising power." Yet, note Constable and Valenzuela, "their definition of economic freedom was highly selective: businessmen were 'free' to move capital and raise prices, but workers were not 'free' to present collective demands or strike for better working conditions."[18]

Pinochet's authoritarian rule offered the Chicago Boys — indeed the entire Chicago school of economics — what they had always wanted: guaranteed protection from political, institutional and even social pressures while they had a real country on which to prove their theories. "Public opinion was very much against [us], so we needed a strong personality to maintain the policy," de Castro recalled in 1979. "It was our good fortune that President Pinochet understood and had the character to withstand criticism."[19]

And what did the General see in the Chicago Boys? Part of their appeal was that, like military commanders, they called for swift, get-tough measures. There was also an appealing simplicity about how to implement the model. The Chicago Boys laid out their ideas clearly, making them all the more persuasive, regularly trouncing their opponents in their debates before the military.

Another factor is that the Chicago Boys were not affiliated with a political party, for the men who carried out the coup d'etat intensely despised political parties and politicians. The Chicago Boys appeared self-sacrificing. They presented themselves as dedicated to the salvation of the nation and impervious to political pressure, exactly as the men in uniform perceived themselves.

Pinochet also was drawn to the radicalness of the Chicago Boys' aims to transform the economy and break with the orthodoxies of the past. He believed that to deal once and for all with "the Marxist threat" it was necessary to thoroughly overhaul Chilean society. He scorned those who in the final analysis wanted only to restore things to how they were before the Popular Unity. "The General yearned to be identified with a historic act of national renewal, and he decided these bold technocrats held the key to a new, prosperous future that would forever distinguish his rule,"[20] write Constable and Valenzuela. Pinochet in a 1982 interview said that he "thanked destiny for the opportunity it gave me to understand with greater clarity the free or liberal economy."[21]

Then there was the long period the Chicago Boys said was required to implement the free-market agenda in Chile. This fit well with the aspiration of Pinochet and his colleagues to remain long at the helm. The neo-liberal project of society-wide transformation seemed a ready-made rationale for a long authoritarian rule.

Last, but not least, Pinochet hoped that the Chicago Boys, with their sophisticated U.S. credentials and connections, would help win badly needed financial support from the multilateral banks and foreign private banks at a time when many governments were shunning the dictatorship because of its internationally publicized human rights violations. This tactic paid off: Chile's free-market economic team at once became the darlings of the international financial institutions. Over the ten years after the U.S. Congress blocked U.S. bilateral aid to the Pinochet regime the World Bank and the Inter-American Development Bank made 46 loans to Chile totaling over $3.1 billion.[22] By 1979, loans by U.S. private banks to Chile since the coup were thought to total over $2 billion.[23]

****

One final comment on the neo-liberals and their worldview: Even more than other social theorists, neo-liberals in their public discourse are notably dogmatic and technocratic. The Chicago Boys routinely put forward their economic program as the "true," "modern" economic science, the only rational option,[24] the only one backed by "absolute knowledge" of a "scientific" character.

Their program alone is "value-neutral"; all other economic policies are driven by "ideologies." Criticisms of their program are labeled as nothing more than the product of ignorance or the defense of special interests.[25] According to neo-liberals, key decisions about the economy should be made by economic technicians rather than politicians, and these technicians should be sheltered from political pressure. They are the "experts," the only depositories of scientific knowledge.[26]

The chapters that follow document how the free-market theories of the Chicago Boys played themselves out in the real-life world.

PART TWO:

NEO-LIBERALISM AND THE ECONOMY

5

Privatizing the Common Wealth

In Washington and other international circles of policy makers, *privatization* has been a buzzword since the early 1980s. Publicly owned companies and other government-run institutions have been portrayed as the bane of economic progress. The message is unequivocal: Be it in the Third World, the former Soviet Union, or the United States, private is good, government is bad. Private equals enterprising, efficient; government equals bungling bureaucracy, corruption, and chronic budget deficits. Reagan liked to sing the praises of privatization, as in this speech excerpted by the U.S. foreign aid agency: "We already know what works: private ownership, the freedom to innovate, healthy competition, reliance on market forces, and faith in the strength and inventiveness of the individual citizen. Privatization is premised on all these principles and offers us the surest road to economic renewal for families and nations."[1]

Between 1975 and 1989, Pinochet's Chicago Boys sold off government ownership in 160 corporations, 16 banks, and over 3,600 agroindustrial plants, mines and real estate holdings, in addition to returning property expropriated by the Allende government.[2]

Publicly held companies have had a long history in Chile. As in most of the rest of Latin America, a series of foreign trade crises, notably the 1930s depression and the two world wars, stimulated the development of local industries that supplied many previously imported goods. The public sector played a crucial role in building infrastructure, supplying the credit, and erecting tariff walls to protect local fledgling industries.

In 1939, a populist coalition government created CORFO, the

Corporation to Foment Production, a government agency that would provide credit, conduct research and development, and foster numerous public enterprises and mixed private-public companies over the next three decades. CORFO encouraged joint ventures by the public sector with local investors and industrialists, and international investors and lenders including the World Bank. The agency selected projects for strategic reasons of national security or economic development, and which the private sector was unwilling (due to insufficient projected profits) or unable (due to the requirements of capital and technology) to take on.

CAP (Pacific Steel Company), for example, was formed by CORFO in 1946 as a joint venture and became a leading steel producer in Latin America, generating useful linkages to mining and manufacturing industries. LANCHILE, the national airline, was formed in 1941 by CORFO in collaboration with the military. The national electric company, ENDESA, and several other regional electric companies were set up by CORFO to supply electricity to provincial areas where private companies were unwilling to invest.

Many Chileans who became government employees during the CORFO heyday still speak proudly of the tradition of efficient and non-partisan administration of public holdings. This tradition, they emphasize, is relatively unique in Latin America.

The Popular Unity coalition (1970-1973) in its initial program contemplated a limited number of expropriations of private companies thought essential to its goal of placing the government in control of "the strategic heights" of the economy. The hope was that the government could redirect the economy to break patterns of uneven development widely believed to be due to exploitation by foreign companies, feudalistic structures in the countryside, and a backward oligopolistic industrial sector. One of President Allende's first pieces of legislation, unanimously enacted by Congress, was to nationalize the foreign-owned copper companies, turning them into the giant public company CODELCO.

Political pressures, production sabotage by Chilean and foreign owners antagonistic to the government, and factory takeovers by workers and political activists, forced the Allende administration to use emergency powers to take control of many more enterprises than it had originally envisioned — certainly beyond what made economic and management sense. By the September 1973 military coup, the public sector formally included the country's 19 banks, 185 other companies, and, de facto, an additional 350 "intervened" firms.

The First Wave

Once the Chicago Boys came to power, the rapid return of properties expropriated during the Allende government was high on their agenda. The process was completed by 1975. It nevertheless left the traditional public sector and CODELCO intact.

In addition, the Chicago Boys put Chile's traditional public sector through two later waves of privatization, the first lasting from 1975 to 1981 and the second from 1985 until Pinochet surrendered political power in 1990. The first wave focused on the banks traditionally belonging in the public sector. Usually an entire bank was sold to a single buyer. These privatizations further concentrated wealth among the handful of families that had dominated Chile's finance and manufacturing industry during the previous half century. Yet, by the end of this first wave, six of the ten largest corporations in Chile were still in the hands of the government.

The Chicago Road to Socialism?

The financial collapse and recession beginning at the end of 1981 constituted a major stumbling block for free-market ideologues. Much of what they had wrought up until then was virtually undone. Huge losses by the most important Chilean banks (and the companies owned or indebted to them) meant the government had either to come to their rescue or simply let them fail, as prescribed by free-market doctrine. The government (at the urging of the IMF and World Bank as well as Chile's other major international creditors) opted to take over the failed banks and businesses, in the process making the government and the Chilean public responsible for $4.7 billion in foreign loans contracted by private Chilean banks and other companies. Of the 19 banks that the government had privatized in the 1970s, all but five failed and fell back into government hands, along with 90 other bankrupt firms. The government-controlled portion of the economy in 1983 rivaled that of the final year of the Allende administration. The irony was not lost on free-market critics who mockingly referred to this phenomenon as the "Chicago road to socialism." The regime engaged in an unacknowledged doublespeak. So rigid was the regime's ideology that, although the public purse had bailed out the privatized banks and other companies, the government refused to classify the companies as public. Instead the government created a bureaucratic category called the "rare area," which these companies occupied while their debts were assumed by the public, and then they with their assets were sold to private interests.

The one bank that had not been privatized and the other publicly owned companies survived the crisis in relatively good shape. Chilean public companies had a tradition of conservative investments that stood in stark contrast to the recent (and historic) proclivity of the private sector towards speculation and short-term profit-taking.

Virtually every major publicly owned enterprise was turning a profit, generating for the government in profits and taxes 25 percent of its total revenues. In 1985, the profits from and taxes paid by public companies accounted for 25 percent of government revenues.[3] Thus the public companies that had escaped the Chicago Boys' privatizations (especially the copper company CODELCO) enabled a financially strapped government to resuscitate the failed privatized banks and companies.

The balance sheets of the public companies were improved by a process of "rationalizations" within the public sector. Workers were dismissed in the name of efficiency (though often on the basis of their political beliefs), wages frozen, prices of products and services increased, and further investment and development discouraged. Between 1981 and 1985, electric rates rose 45 percent faster than inflation, and telephone rates 64 percent. In retrospect, this process can be seen as preparation for a second sweeping wave of privatizations.[4]

Privatizations Redux

The second wave of privatizations began in late 1985 when the government announced plans to privatize most of the remaining large public companies. Repression and the complete absence of democratic institutions afforded the regime considerable leeway to thereby pursue its ideological program and respond to the pressures of international creditors. It therefore redoubled efforts to complete its agenda to transfer assets and financial authority from the public to the private sector.

Right up to the defeat of Pinochet's candidate in the December 1989 presidential election, the Chicago Boys continued to privatize companies, including the national airline, LANCHILE, and the long-distance telephone company, both once thought sacred. Even in the weeks before the inauguration of an elected president, the military junta transferred properties out of the hands of the government and issued decrees that tightly limited the activities of the remaining public holdings. By August of 1989, 24 of the largest remaining public companies had been turned over to the private sector, and nine more had been partially privatized.

In the case, however, of CODELCO, the publicly owned copper company, the military government pursued self-interest over ideology. Pinochet's Constitution provides that 10 percent of CODELCO's gross revenues go to the armed forces as a no-questions-asked supplement to the armed forces budget; CODELCO remained in public hands.[5]

The Price is Right?

Public holdings were sold off at minimal prices, often in government-financed deals in which buyers put down as little as 5 percent of the purchase price and covered the rest with a long-term, low-interest credit from CORFO.[6] Buyers were sometimes allowed — despite the supposed neo-liberal antagonism to government subsidization — to use the company to be purchased as collateral.[7]

One of the companies privatized in the first wave was INCESA, the national cement company. It was sold in 1978 to Bio Bio Cementos for just under $3 million. This sum, according to a government internal audit at the time, amounted to 10 cents on the dollar for the value of INCESA's assets on the books. At the time of the sale INCESA's working capital alone exceeded the sale price by more than $1 million. The combination of low prices and easy credit terms for the sale of publicly owned companies generated considerable public criticism.

The announcement in 1985 of the second wave of privatizations gave the impression that new procedures would put an end to the virtual giveaway of publicly owned assets to financial elites. Before long, however, it became clear that the post-1985 privatizations would continue to substantially undervalue the companies being privatized by setting prices according to a fledgling and depressed stock market rather than the value of assets or level of earnings.

One of the most notorious abuses occurred with the sale of CAP, at the time Chile's most important manufacturing corporation and third largest public company. CAP's value was estimated at $700 million in late 1985 when an initial package of company stock went on the market at rock-bottom prices in the wake of the recession. In 1987 CAP negotiated with CORFO to buy back and retire almost half of the stock that remained in the public sector in exchange for $72 million in CAP's working capital. This operation was of dubious legitimacy; after all, CORFO, as holder of 83 percent of CAP's stock, was accepting, to that extent, its own money for the sale of much of the stock it held. The sale was a windfall for the private stockholders, whose combined share in the company automatically tripled to 49 percent. One happy shareholder was the CAP director (and later president) Roberto Andraca, who bought up shares for himself and family members during the month while negotiations with CORFO were underway. (Andraca later argued he was merely demonstrating confidence in the corporation he ran.) The company's profits in the next two years, all paid out in dividends rather than plowed back in investments, earned back all of the investors' entire outlay of $18 million.

All told, the privatizations were bargain sell-offs of public assets. Mario Marcel, an economist for the Chilean think tank CIEPLAN, calculated that the twelve companies privatized during 1986 and 1987 were sold with what amounted to a subsidy from the national treasury to the buyers of 27 to 69 percent, depending on which of various recognized ways the value was determined. Economists Marin and Rozas estimate the loss to the national treasury from the selling off in the late 1980s of three of the largest companies (CAP, Chilectra, and Soquimich) at $1.4 billion.[8]

Audits of CORFO privatizations done by a government accounting office are damning. IANSA, a sugar refining company, with a conservative book value of $81 million was sold for $34 million. IANSA profits for the first years after privatization (1986 to 1988) totaled $52 million, far exceeding the purchase price. Soquimich, the nitrate and fertilizer company, was sold off for $120 million, an amount which, given the dividend levels of 1988, would have been recuperated in under three years. In the case of ENDESA, the electric company whose privatization was completed after the 1988 plebiscite, internal auditors of CORFO put the total loss at almost $1 billion. One CORFO official conservatively estimated that losses to the national treasury from privatizations during the years 1985 to 1989 surpassed $2 billion, the combined result of undervalued sales and earnings forfeited — this in an economy whose GDP in 1987 was less than $20 billion.[9]

Throughout the privatization process, with no free press, no public discussion of policies, and frequent changes in whatever goals and procedures the government did reveal, it was easy for insiders to maneuver in their own interests as well as those of relatives and friends. Commonly the administrator of the privatization of a public holding moved to the top post in the newly privatized company. Julio Ponce Lerou, Pinochet's son-in-law, was director of Soquimich (the nitrate and fertilizer company) from 1980 to 1983 when it was public, then emerged as president of the privatized Soquimich in 1987. Several other Pinochet relatives were installed on the board or became major stockholders. Pinochet labor minister Jose Piñera became the vice-president of ENDESA, the privatized national electric company.

When Pinochet surrendered the presidential sash in March of 1990, many key figures from his long dictatorship were firmly (and comfortably) ensconced in the privatized banks, manufacturing and service companies.

A Quick Fix

Revenues from sales of public corporations provided one-time boosts to government finances, allowing Pinochet the luxury of balancing the budget from 1986 through 1988, pleasing the IMF, making timely payments to foreign creditor banks, and even cutting taxes. Since most of the companies sold had produced revenues for the government rather than deficits, such gains were brief and illusory — accountants' sleights of hand that papered over government budget deficits. (It is unorthodox to add the one-time proceeds from such sales into yearly income totals; in reality, income-generating assets were lost forever.) Estimates for lost revenues range from $125 to $200 million annually for the years 1990 to 1996. The higher estimate equals the total new social spending the transitional civilian government hoped to marshal for 1991.[10]

Popular Capitalism?

Proponents proclaimed Chile's second wave of privatization the road to "popular capitalism," because employees in many of the companies undergoing privatization could opt to acquire shares by drawing from their workers' compensation funds, or in lieu of increases in wages and other benefits. For many, the opportunity was irresistible, and indeed those who held on to their shares have done well (so far).

In 1989, the total number of employees holding shares in privatized companies was 30,000, well under 1 percent of the labor force.[11] Where employees do have stock holdings, those holdings are a distinct minority of a company's total shares. Chile's relative handful of "worker capitalists" receive dividends but not much else. Only in a single case have workers managed to gain a seat on the board of directors. Management-level employees and professionals are more able to take advantage of stock offers. (In fact, many blue-collar workers quickly sold their stock, no doubt out of a need for cash. In Chilmetro, a regional electric company, workers purchased 7 percent of the stock, but within a few months had sold all but 3 percent.)[12]

There was significant opposition to the second wave of privatization. Union leaders from public companies organized the Commando for the Defense of Public Enterprises, which conducted an energetic campaign against further privatizations. Opposition politicians, intellectuals and some former government officials formed a parallel organization, the Committee for the Defense of the National Patrimony. In the face of brutal government repression, however, these mobilizations rarely moved beyond the unions and those immediate allies, and they proved largely unsuccessful.

When the privatization wave rolled on after the 1988 plebiscite, presidential candidate Aylwin threatened to undo the last-minute privatizations of the outgoing regime. By 1992, however, his administration had not reversed or called into question a single sale.

With the Pinochet privatization agenda largely completed, strong vested interests have emerged to defend its "accomplishments." In the case of one public firm, ENDESA, stock was made available for purchase to government employees outside the company on similar terms as to ENDESA employees. By far, the largest percentage of stock (about 21 percent) went to members of the armed forces, who now form a rear guard of property owners which staunchly opposes any efforts to bring such companies back into the public domain or even review the process of privatization itself.

Privatization and Foreign Ownership

Multinational corporations have gained a stronghold over the Chilean economy through privatizations and through their control of financial companies that control employees funds (see also chapters on debt and social security). Competing private pension fund companies (AFPs) were set up in 1980 as a mandatory replacement for the government social security system. After the crash of 1981-1983, several of the most important AFPs failed and passed over into the government's "rare area." When they were re-sold in the following years, foreign financial consortia purchased controlling shares in many. For example, a Bankers' Trust holding group (which includes three other international banks that hold Chilean debt) bought a controlling interest in the largest AFP. Aetna bought 51 percent of the next largest AFP, and the American International Group another. The three companies together by 1989 controlled 55 percent of Chile's privately held retirement funds.

By 1989, the retirement funds had been used to acquire an average of 32 percent of the stock of the privatized companies.[13] But Chileans who pay into their retirement accounts do not actually own stock in the AFPs and therefore have no say in how their funds are invested. Bankers' Trust and other financial groups have that power and can use it to look out for their own interests. So much for the claim that "popular capitalism" has made some 3 million Chileans part-owners of the privatized corporations through their pension funds.

The same multinationals also made direct investments in a number of privatized companies. Bankers' Trust now has investments in 13 companies, including the steel company CAP, the nitrate and fertilizer company Soquimich, and several regional electric companies, all privatized by the Chicago Boys. Aetna has important investments in six privatized companies.[14]

Privatizations and debt swaps have become prime mechanisms for increasing the weight of multinational companies in the Chilean economy. Debt swaps, in which an international loan is bought at a discount (around 30 percent below face value in the case of Chile in the mid-1980s) and spent at near-full face value in local currency within the debtor country, became an irresistible way for international banks to cut their losses on loans that might never be paid back and for the purchasers to acquire some of the most attractive assets within debtor countries at big discounts. Using debt swap leverage to acquire a company being privatized at an undervalued price gave a double subsidy to foreign capital. By mid-1988, 13 completely privatized companies were controlled directly or indirectly by foreign multinational corporations.[15]

The engineer Raul Saéz, a former CORFO official and short-lived Minister of Economic Coordination in the Pinochet government, who then headed up the Committee for the Defense of the National Patrimony, questions whether "the new owners, national and foreign, [will] be willing to forgo dividends in order to build new steel factories or new electrical power plants?"[16] Because of private sector unwillingness, this has been the historic role of the public sector in Chile.

An official who has observed three decades of changing public and private sector roles from within CORFO complains that the free-market government simply handed over natural monopolies like electricity and telephones to the private sector and foreign capital without establishing any regulating power or any other significant counterweight that might substitute for the absence of market competition. "These new financial groups are as powerful as the drug lords in Colombia, powerful enough to bring down any government" which might attempt to regulate them, he says.[17]

Privatization has made foreign companies more powerful in Chile today than they have ever been before.

To declare all privatizations necessarily bad would be a mistake. But the balance sheet for Chile's privatization experience is very different from what its proponents boast. They argue that privatizations eliminated an inefficient and politicized public sector, reduced government fiscal problems and helped to disperse ownership. In fact, most of the largest companies privatized in the second wave of privatizations were producing significant profits, not deficits, for the government. Control of the common wealth of the entire nation passed to a handful of national and foreign interests that captured most of the subsidy implicit in the rock bottom prices. Political maneuvers, insider information and outright corruption created industrial barons almost overnight. Sergio Bitar calls the privatization process in Chile "the greatest diversion of public funds that has occurred in our history, without the consultation of public opinion or accountability to a congress."[18]

Revenues from sales of public companies provided a one-time financing of the budget deficit at the cost of a medium-term future of severe fiscal constraints. The government has been stripped of most of its potential to shape a truly competitive economy which serves the interests of the majority of Chileans. This is the legacy left by General Pinochet and his Chicago Boys.

6

In Debt to the Free Market

The year 1982 is known throughout Latin America as the year of the debt crisis — the year the "easy money" stopped and the bills started to come due. It marked the end of a decade of a torrent of international credit, itself the product of banks awash in petrodollars, that flowed indiscriminately towards Latin America. For much of the eighties, first and third worlds bickered over how much of the borrowed hundreds of billions were to be repaid and when.[1]

The endless stop-gap negotiations over debt issues have been dominated by a united group of creditor nations led by the World Bank and the International Monetary Fund. Debt renegotiations have afforded them the perfect leverage to impose a whole gamut of free-market reforms on Latin American governments. In this context, Chile's performance is paradoxical: free-market orthodoxy got it mired in foreign debt in the first place; and the remedy applied by the Chicago Boys, while following the dictates of the World Bank and the Fund, violated a key free-market principle often cited by the Chicago Boys.

An Original Debt

Chile's debt crisis stands out from those of other major Latin American debtor countries in two ways. Most striking is that the borrowing abroad was done mostly by the private sector. When the Chicago Boys began to implement new fiscal and monetary policies in 1975, 85 percent of Chile's foreign debt — a modest $ 5.5 billion — was owed by the government. By 1981, over 64 percent was owed by the private sector, a far higher share than that in any other country in Latin America. The second difference is the degree of debt. Chile's debt in 1982 was $16 billion, seemingly modest compared to that of such super-debtors as Brazil and Mexico, yet with a population of under 13 million, per capita debt far exceeded that of Mexico and Brazil and more than doubled the regional average.[2] How did this happen?

We have already reviewed the series of drastic measures by which Chile became an open economy in the mid-1970s — banks were privatized and deregulated, and tariffs were virtually eliminated. In addition, we saw that starting in 1979 the government (following an extreme version of neo-liberal monetary policy) fixed the currency exchange rate at 39 pesos to the dollar. This "dollar standard" was supposed to provide an automatic mechanism by which imports would increase only in balance with increases in national production and thereby stabilize inflation levels. In theory this device had all the elegance of the nineteenth century gold standard. But at a time of abundant international credit and high international interest rates, the Chilean peso quickly became over-valued.

Dollars in effect became very cheap relative to the fixed peso, and therefore it took fewer pesos to buy imported goods. This came on top of the free marketeers having cut import duties down to an average of only 10 percent — Chile became something of a big duty-free store. Chilean consumers found they could, for example, purchase an imported tractor in early 1981 for 30 percent fewer pesos (even adjusted for inflation) than in 1976. According to the monetarist theory, the dollars for increasing imports should have come into Chile through earnings from an expansion of its exports. Instead foreign loans provided the dollars to pay for an ever-rising flood of imports. And exports rose only moderately, in part because the overvalued peso made Chilean products expensive abroad.

Dollars borrowed abroad by private Chilean banks were recycled, often at very high interest rates, to private borrowers. Government officials insisted that mushrooming private foreign debt was a private affair, and thus the government could not be held accountable for its repayment. Far from regulating or even monitoring the level of national debt, the free-marketeers encouraged Chileans to borrow money freely, indeed almost considering it a patriotic duty. The operative neo-liberal theory, roundly endorsed by international lenders, was that in a free-market economy, the private sector would invest borrowed dollars where they could best increase the productive capacity of the economy. As the Chilean economist Ricardo Ffrench-Davis notes, "In the country's official circles. . .the belief prevailed that a foreign exchange crisis was impossible because the debt was mainly private and thus would be efficiently used."[3]

In reality, the Chilean elite more likely used borrowed dollars to buy Mercedes Benzes than to invest in machinery or other productive inputs. From the late 1970s through the 1982 crisis, Chileans went on a shopping spree, using privately borrowed billions. Over half of the mounting foreign debt went to import consumption goods, mostly consumer durables like cars and appliances, rather than machinery and parts that might have increased Chilean economic output. Easy money also went into real estate speculation and debt-financed takeovers by the financial conglomerates of one enterprise after another.

For a few years the benefits of easy credit extended even into Chile's poorer neighborhoods. Chileans with anything close to a steady job were for the first time offered what seemed like easy terms on imported electronic goods such as radios, cassette tape players, and televisions.

Abundant foreign loans gave the Chile of these years an illusion of growth. In 1980 the economy reached GDP and wage levels that had not been seen in a decade. Inflation came down dramatically for the first time in decades. But Chileans were not saving and investing in their economy's development.

The flood of cheap imports wiped out much of Chile's traditional manufacturing sector, which had produced goods for the local market. Some firms survived by turning themselves from production to importing and retailing of foreign-made goods. Free marketeers argued that manufacturers were obviously inefficient if they could not compete in an open economy, and that investment would instead flow into more competitive sectors. But the rate of investment in productive capacity from 1978 to 1981 dropped below the average during the 1960s.[4] By comparison, during the same period in Brazil most of the foreign debt was taken on by the government. The government was then able to direct credit to specific industries seen as strategic, and to investments in national infrastructure. As a result, at least the productive capacity in these industries was boosted during the decade of easy foreign credit.

At that time the Pinochet government started to talk about the "Chilean miracle," and without doubt considerable numbers of Chileans in 1980 felt a certain euphoria. On the eve of the referendum on a new authoritarian constitution, which would guarantee Pinochet at least another decade of rule, he declared that Chileans could rest assured that the peso would stand at 39 pesos to the dollar for the indefinite future.

The Crash

In 1981, the rise in international interest rates and a downturn in the global economy brought an end to the flow of cheap dollars and therefore to the illusory well-being of the Chilean economy. A moratorium on debt payments declared by Mexico in August 1982 cut off new international lending throughout Latin America. In any case, it had become increasingly obvious that debt levels in Chile were not sustainable without any commensurate increase in production and foreign earnings. With an open economy, the peso-dollar exchange rate fixed, a heavily indebted private sector and little government economic intervention to absorb the massive external shock, Chile's GDP dropped a drastic 14 percent in 1982. Chile's debt crisis drop was far worse than that of any other Latin American country.

Although various countries wielded the threat of a temporary moratorium on debt to improve their negotiating position vis-à-vis the creditor banks and multilateral agencies, Latin American countries failed to unite in a region-wide negotiation that might have brought an overall solution to the overwhelming debts. Each country thought it could negotiate a special deal, and the united lenders divided and conquered.

Chile proved to be the most compliant debtor nation in Latin America. The government first carried out a series of devaluations of the peso. Since individual consumer debts had been indexed to the dollar value of the peso this automatically increased the indebtedness of many consumers (by 70 percent in peso terms), a devastating blow to many Chileans given the depression-like collapse of employment and wages.[5]

Although free-market ideology called for government letting businesses sink or swim according to their efficiency, the Pinochet government decided to bail out the indebted private banks. For the most part, it simply took over the operation of virtually all of the key private institutions. This was tantamount to the "nationalization" of the banking sector, undoing a decade of privatizations and deregulation. In the process, the private debt of the financial sector became public debt. The percentage of government-guaranteed debt shifted from 36 percent of total national debt in 1981, to 85 percent of national debt in 1986. Not surprisingly, the international lenders led by the International Monetary Fund and the World Bank, which had encouraged private sector debt in the first place, successfully pressured the Chilean government to take over this debt. A variety of governmental guarantees and additional borrowing undertaken by the government's Central Bank drained over $8 billion from the public coffers in the process of assuming the private liabilities.

As we saw earlier, the government-intervened banks, once "sanitized" of their debts, were handed back over to private hands. The influential conservative newspaper *El Mercurio* was allowed to continue operating despite its heavy $100 million debt to the intervened banks, thus insuring the government unconditional media support during the crisis from that influential newspaper.[6]

Life after Debt?

For the foreign bankers, Chile has been a model in its harmonious relations with creditors and multilateral institutions. Its unwavering pursuit of the prescribed adjustment policies since 1982 has earned it the joke of being "more orthodox than the International Monetary Fund itself."

From 1981 to the mid-'80s its debt increased steadily as Chile renegotiated with its creditors, essentially borrowing more in order to make interest payments. National foreign debt peaked at around $21 billion in 1985, equaling the total annual value of the GDP.[7] Since then debt has remained relatively constant — in 1991 it stood at $18 billion dollars — partly as a result of debt swaps.[8]

As previously explained, debt swaps are government-sponsored transactions in which international debt can be bought outside of the country at a discount (in the case of Chile, for around 30 percent below face value during the years of the swaps) and spent in the country at near full face value converted into local currency. This arrangement amounted to giving foreign investors a hefty discount on Chilean assets.

Nowhere in Latin America were debt swaps undertaken as extensively as in Chile. Chile swapped over $6 billion of its foreign debt by 1990. As already mentioned, foreign companies used the debt swap mechanism to acquire privatized companies, as well as valuable natural resources such as forest lands and mining rights. This type of purchasing was done without bringing any significant fresh investment into Chile, and in fact may have displaced fresh foreign capital that might otherwise have occurred.[9]

The huge debt Chile took on under the Chicago Boys' watch became the instrument by which many important national assets passed into the hands of foreign companies. While in the short run the net flow of capital out of Chile to make payments on the debt was reduced, foreign companies that acquired Chilean assets through debt swaps could begin remitting their profits abroad after only four years. The total remittances of this capital abroad could well far exceed the interest that was not paid on swapped debt.

Chilean foreign debt was incurred privately, primarily by a small group of financial groups and a wealthy minority who indulged in a consumption binge. When the bottom fell out, the professedly free-market government moved in to bail out the banks with the public treasury, meanwhile leaving most Chileans saddled with unpayable debts. The fiscal crisis that resulted from the government's assumption of the foreign debt of the private financial institutions also gave a rationale for, and an urgency to, other elements in the neo-liberal program such as further cuts in social spending.

Chile shares the debt problem of all of Latin America, but much of its foreign debt was due to free-market policies. The remedies, as with so much of the free-market agenda of the Chicago Boys, privatized benefits and socialized costs.

7

Working on the Free Market

Industrial and labor relations in Chile have been "modernized," according to José Piñera, Pinochet's Minister of Labor (1978-1981) and the chief architect of the Labor Code of 1979. Piñera and other free-market technocrats claim that "politicized" labor leaders and their "privileged fiefdoms" have been eliminated, that workers no longer hold "monopolies" on job positions, and that the government no longer intervenes in labor disputes. Instead, negotiation within individual firms is now left up to "individual responsibility and the discipline of the market."[1]

Piñera's "labor revolution" has been central to the free-market project. Beginning in the mid-seventies, a series of government interventions changed the structure of the manufacturing sector, and wages began to drop drastically as a result of high unemployment levels. In 1979 new labor legislation divided workers and limited their efforts to organize lest they demand that the costs and benefits of the free-market revolution be shared more fairly.

With high levels of unemployment and little job stability, workers in Chile have had to resign themselves to being just another commodity to be bought as cheaply as possible and only when needed. Employers unilaterally set the terms of employment, while workers float from one demanding job experience to another, often with periods of unemployment in between.

The free market's effects on workers are observable throughout Chile. Typical is workers lining up every Monday at construction projects in order to underbid each other for the week's work.[2] In the Santiago *población* of La Pintana, women board fruit company buses at 4 a.m. in order to pick fruit two hours away, one of the

67

rare employment opportunities available to them a few months of the year. Driving in southern Chile a couple days after Christmas (1989), we stopped for three men hitchhiking the 20 miles from Puerto Varas to Puerto Montt. They were on their way back, they explained, from attempting to land jobs on a road construction crew. Maybe next week, they had been told. We asked if the pay was good. "Yes, 60 pesos an hour (20 U.S. cents)." Later another hitchhiker, not yet fifteen, had just finished working five weeks in a fish packing plant and was headed back to Santiago, hoping to find work as a houseboy. He told us he was "too exhausted" from the work in the plant. When we looked at the incredibly long hours and yet low wages on the pay stub which he showed us we understood why.

Could such realities simply be attributed to the transitional poverty of a developing country — as the Chicago Boys argue — or were they at the heart of the free-market model?

Before the Coup

Chilean workers have a history of struggle and social achievement dating back to the organizations of nineteenth century mine workers. At the turn of the century, a series of strikes for better wages, working conditions and participation in workplace decisions resulted in violent, government repression. To this day, these massacres symbolize for the Chilean labor movement a legacy of resistance.

In the 1930s, organized labor became solidly incorporated into Chile's political system. Worldwide depression and social protests undermined the economic and political status quo in Chile. Continuing pressure for reform from workers and the rapid growth of an urban and industrial work force had led to a new political order in which basic labor rights were guaranteed. In this new order the government mediated between workers and employers.

With the Labor Code of 1931, the government guaranteed the enforcement of certain minimal work conditions and the right of most workers to organize. When conflicts in the collective bargaining process occurred, they were to be settled through labor courts and tripartite tribunals, in which representatives of workers, owners and the government would arbitrate disputes. Over the subsequent 40 years workers won a series of gains in income, job stability, and their right to participate in the debates over working conditions. Unionization spread beyond miners and factory workers to include such middle-class groups as teachers, clerks, and government employers. In 1967 rural workers who were employed on large estates were granted the legal right to organize. By 1970 over 24 percent of the work force was unionized; by 1973, 35 percent.

Unions in Chile generally had a relatively low level of bureaucracy. While their links to political parties were strong, the ties between the government and unions were less direct than in other Latin American countries, for example, Mexico, where a single dominant political party or ruling coalition controls the labor movement. In Chile political parties vied for leadership within the union movement. The Christian Democrats, Communists, and Socialists were almost equally strong among the unions, and therefore if leaders with ties to one party were not accountable to the rank and file, they were likely to be voted out and replaced with leaders affiliated with another.

Federations — most importantly the *Central Unico de Trabajadores*, or CUT (which incorporated two-thirds of all unions) — functioned as a sounding board for relatively decentralized unions and federations in a particular industry. They channeled worker input into national development strategies. Through their strong ties to political parties, organized workers participated in national debates over questions of employment and social policy, regularly defending the unorganized majority of urban workers.[3]

Prior to the military coup, then, the role of labor unions in Chile resembled that in most developed European countries: unions were respected organizations that participated fully in national decisions, insured stability and discipline in the work force, and received a share of the benefits of economic growth. Unions were fundamental vehicles for widening participation in the political process and making economic development more equitable.

The Wages of Fear

"Fear was the great ally of the military regime," explained Manuel Bustos, a textile worker and after 1988, the head of the revived CUT.[4] Workers bore the brunt of repression during the coup and throughout the Pinochet regime. The Armed Forces viewed workers — and the level of organization they had accomplished under previous governments — as the greatest threat to the traditional power structure. In the last year of the Popular Unity administration, workers had taken over numerous factories and conducted experiments in workers' control that were bold, although economically unsound, at least in the short term. Unions had forged close ties to organizations in working class neighborhoods that seemed determined to defend the constitutional government. Yet, in spite of the level of popular organization and the rumors of proletarian and guerrilla armies (often fanned by the military), workers put up little effective resistance to the coup, even when the military occupied the country's principal factories. In order to justify the human rights abuses they committed, the military still insist on referring to a "civil war" they waged against "the communist left."

Nowhere was the "enemy" seen by the coup makers as more omnipresent than among labor unions. Armed troops went after workers in general — and their union leaders in particular — with a virulence far exceeding the "class hatred" they claimed to be stamping out. Even union leaders affiliated with the Christian Democratic Party (which initially backed the coup) were rounded up to spend weeks in the national soccer stadium (a makeshift detention center) or in clandestine jails. Many union activists went into exile to avoid being apprehended. Workers who had participated in Popular Unity committees within factories at the very least found themselves without jobs after the coup.

The numbers detained, fired, murdered, imprisoned or exiled are only now beginning to be documented. One gets an idea, however, from a survey in 1975 of 16 Chilean organizations attending a meeting of the International Labor Organization in Switzerland. According to the survey, in the aftermath of the military coup, at least 2,200 union leaders were fired, 110 killed, 230 jailed.[5] The Rettig Commission set up by President Aylwin to investigate human rights violations under the Pinochet government found that workers had been the part of the population by far most targeted by government repression.[6]

In the wake of the coup, factory owners gained absolute control over their workers and could fire any worker without cause. From 1973 through 1978, practically every labor right for organized and unorganized workers was suspended. All the tools of collective bargaining, including of course the right to strike, were outlawed. The tripartite commissions functioned only sporadically and in a non-binding, advisory capacity; no other intermediary institutions were permitted. Employers could count on the certain backing of the military government in any conflict with workers.

Union leaders, who previously had been exempt from firing for a period after holding office, were dismissed on the basis of legal technicalities.[7] Most labor federations were dissolved and their offices confiscated. Virtually all rural unions were abolished. Within the unions that survived, elected leaders were automatically replaced by the most senior workers available and meetings required special permission from the government.

In October of 1978, bowing to internal and international pressure, the government issued a surprise call for internal union elections — to be held four days later, without nominations or slates, and excluding from office any member who had held a union office or had been affiliated with a political party in the previous 10 years.

In spite of the repression and the many legal restrictions, within two years of the coup workers were attempting to organize nationally to oppose the regime and support broad social demands. The most important vehicle of worker demands was the "Group of Ten," which included many of the non-left union leaders who held office before the coup. In 1977 they publicly denounced the government's economic policies. On May Day, 1979, leaders of the Group of Ten celebrated Labor Day for the first time publicly since the coup and declared, "The capitalist and powerful classes. . . have reconquer[ed] all their privileges [in a] profound revolution for the benefit of the rich," while "workers are currently managed with repression and the fear of unemployment."[8]

The military government responded to such declarations by jailing labor leaders, exiling them abroad, or "relegating" them into internal exile in small rural communities in the far north or south of Chile. And when "La Coordinadora" — a loose coordinating body of labor unions that replaced the Group of Ten and included union representatives from the left — called for the first national gathering of labor leaders in 1980, the government responded by shutting down the meeting and putting two of its most prominent members, Manuel Bustos and Hector Cuevas, on airplanes out of the country.

Such heavy-handed violation of organizational rights often backfired. Internal exile, we were told by various of its victims, helped to forge unexpected alliances between opposition leaders from different regions. In Europe, Manuel Bustos was received by heads of government and the Pope, and the plight of Chilean workers received considerable international notoriety. Even after the implementation of the Labor Code, however, as late as 1988, when a new CUT was formed to unite all national unions into a single confederation, its principal organizer, Bustos, was again sent by the government to live in a small rural town in Chile for 18 months.

The Trauma of Unemployment

Fear of repression was an essential element in the implementation of a free labor market, but far more pervasive was the fear of unemployment.

Traditionally, the manufacturing sector had provided stable jobs, and good wages assured a mass market to consume the products produced. Manufacturing also provided direct links throughout the economy that the export of primary products such as those of mining or forestry had not. And in times of international crisis (such as the global depression of the 1930s) the manufacturing sector played a counter-recessionary role by creating employment and producing goods that could no longer be imported. There were, however, serious problems. Domestic manufacturers were overly protected and pampered by tariffs and interest rates lower than inflation. Most had failed to innovate and compete with international products, and they had not developed much of an export market. Among the results of the traditional policies were high-priced, poor-quality products.

In the aftermath of the military coup, many traditional manufacturers expected to retain their protected markets and governmental investment subsidies. They also expected as an added bonus that the labor movement would be kept in tight check. They soon discovered they were only half right.

Chile's Chicago Boys were determined to give their country a radical initiation into free trade and the meaning of unfettered market forces. If in an environment unprotected from foreign competition investors abandoned manufacturing, their thinking went, they would surely go into more productive enterprises. Tariffs on imported goods were dropped from generally over 100 percent in the mid-1970s to an across-the-board 10 percent by 1980. And, as also previously discussed, the country was flooded with cheap imported consumer goods, thanks to the government's over-valued peso; many Chilean producers could not compete.

Alberto Martinez, vice-president of the Chilean Textile Institute and a graduate of the University of Chicago, described this chastening experience for the manufacturers in Darwinian terms: "The military government came up to the pool side and pushed us in. Some sank. Some swam. In other countries industrialists wanted to just fool around, stick a finger in first and get it wet. This never works."

Other members of Chile's traditional economic elite, faced with foreign competition and dwindling profits, went heavily into debt to remain afloat. Contrary to free-market theory, others moved their capital from production into highly speculative areas which were being favored by government policy — finance, commerce, or real estate. Between the years 1979 and 1982, in the middle of the touted "Chilean miracle," more than a fifth of manufacturing companies failed and manufacturing employment dropped by over one fourth.

What happened to these workers? According to one calculation for the decade before 1981, "out of every 26 workers released by the manufacturing sector, 13 joined the lines of the openly unemployed, five became members of the urban informal sector, and eight had to work for $30 a month in a government emergency employment program."[9]

When the bottom fell out of the economy in 1982, the trend toward bankruptcy accelerated and expanded to all sectors of the economy. Chile's GDP plummeted 14 percent in one year. Manufacturing and construction were particularly hard hit, with production down by 19 and 28 percent respectively. In the textile industry alone, an estimated 35 to 45 percent of companies failed.[10]

In spite of the "sink or swim" rhetoric of the Chicago Boys and the after-the-fact boasting of some survivors, government policy shifted from its previous doctrinaire position of unprotected markets and monetarist purism: tariffs were raised from 10 percent to between 20 and 35 percent, and the peso was drastically devalued, providing a substantial level of protection against imports.

Some business owners responded to the crash by "rationalizing" their production processes: a few purchased new machinery and technology to improve efficiency and quality; some employed new marketing techniques; some imported more of the components of their products. By far the most important rationalization was the lowering of labor costs. This was accomplished through massive layoffs, by intensifying the work of the remaining employees, and by pushing wage levels down well below historical levels. For example, through a combination of new machinery, layoffs, and work speedups, Sumar, a textile company, cut its labor force from 2,600 workers in 1970 to 1,800 in 1988, while maintaining the same level of production.[11]

Layoffs created a virtual army of Chileans looking for work. Unemployment levels officially averaged 20 percent from 1974 to 1987. Chronic high levels of unemployment afforded employers considerable leverage in setting working conditions and wage levels. By declaring bankruptcies, companies could fire senior workers without any compensation, reorganize, and then hire them back at much lower wages.

The stream of bankruptcies during the first 10 years of Pinochet's government terrified workers. Those who lost their jobs were forced into unemployment or, at best, into temporary or casual work. A factory worker who became unemployed at age 30 feared never to be employed again. We came upon many former factory workers driving taxis in Santiago, or working on fishing boats in southern Chile. Not surprisingly, under such circumstances those workers who managed to hold on to their jobs were willing to make repeated concessions to employers, or in order to get a job, workers often submitted to onerous terms.[12] In some industries — primarily export industries such as fresh fruit, forestry and fishing — accelerated expansion after 1984 was largely based on hiring large numbers of impoverished workers and their families at low costs and on a temporary basis.

Most Chicago Boys endorsed the use of military force to rein in the union movement and showed little concern for the fears and social costs of widespread unemployment. At the same time, they realized that instilling fear alone would not long suffice to assure the cooperation of workers. Instead a new institutional framework was needed that, while providing certain "freedoms" to buy and sell labor, guaranteed that workers would not be able to raise issues of work conditions or broader social issues when negotiating their position in the labor market.

The Labor Code

After over thirty years as a waiter in the downtown Santiago restaurant *El Nacional*, Joaquin still takes enormous pride in his work. Even so, working conditions, he says, have changed for the worst. As with many older workers, the rights and status achieved through the labor movement before 1973 are benchmarks by which he measures his present situation. "You know, the new labor laws have taken away 142 of the rights we workers had before." Many workers share Joaquin's sense of bitterness over hard-earned and tangible rights taken away.

The new Labor Code was decreed six years into military rule, largely in response to increasingly open opposition by workers as well as to international pressure. Perhaps the most urgent of the regime's concerns was the threat to impose a boycott on Chilean products in the United States, led by the AFL-CIO during 1978 and 1979. In spite of Pinochet's grumblings of an international "communist" conspiracy, even multinational corporations (which relished the iron-fisted guarantee of labor peace in Chile) were squeamish about investing in a country that restricted worker organization by force rather than by law, much less investing in a country threatened with a boycott.

In a few short months in 1979, a small group of businessmen and U.S.-trained economists in the Ministry of Labor hammered out a Code on labor relations. The purpose, in the words of minister Piñera, was to "introduce democracy into the world of Chilean unions and resolve problems that for decades had been obstacles for the progress of workers." In spite of this populist language, the Labor Code's intent was clearly pro-business: to maximize an employer's flexibility and to keep any eventual elected government from intervening on behalf of labor in negotiations between employers and employees.

A series of radical breaks with past policies gave employers the legal flexibility they felt was necessary to modernize Chilean industry. The new Labor Code facilitated shifting workers from one position to another within a firm, and more importantly, allowed employers to fire workers at will, individually or *en masse*, for "business necessities." This, according to the architects of the Code, eliminated the "monopoly" many workers had on their jobs. It became possible for employers to hire or lay off workers not only during economic recessions, but from one month or season to the next; labor costs were thereby reduced to the level determined by supply and demand, plus training costs.

Many workers in different industries described to us how they had received a layoff notice in their pay envelope, without explanation. "It is really simply a question of dignity to know the reasons why you are being laid off," we were told by a middle-aged taxi driver who had been a steel worker. Moreover, the Code limits indemnities given to laid off workers. Temporary workers, of course, received nothing, and permanent workers received the traditional one month's pay for every year they had worked, up to a maximum of five months' pay for five or more years of service.

Organizing in the free market

Widespread unemployment and a high percentage of jobs in small-scale commerce and services have created a labor force that is more fragmented, and less engaged in society-wide issues. Nevertheless, the free marketeers took no chances by designing regulations that would limit opportunities for workers to organize.

"The basic pillars of the law of union organizations," explains Piñera, "are the values of democracy and liberty."[13] More likely, however, the Chicago Boys had other objectives in mind when they crafted the Labor Code's regulations governing workers' organizations: to assure the political neutrality of unions; to clearly delineate the issues for which unions could negotiate; and finally, to reduce the likelihood of strikes and conflicts.

In early 1990 we visited the headquarters of the national labor confederation, the CUT. Re-formed during the political liberalization that preceded the plebiscite over Pinochet's continued rule, the confederation had improvised tiny offices from a warehouse in one of Santiago's oldest working class neighborhoods, a long walk from the seat of economic and political power. The CUT's modest circumstances seemed emblematic of how altered the status of labor unions is in free-market Chile.

Under the new Labor Code, not all workers were granted the right to organize. The Code extended organizational rights only to workers employed for at least six consecutive months. Seasonal and temporary workers — indeed, an overwhelming majority of workers in agriculture, forestry, construction, many service industries, and in the informal urban labor market — were and remain excluded. Laborers in these areas can organize only if employers consent, and of course, they almost never do.

Permanent workers, the Labor Code concedes, can form a union if at least 25 workers and 10 percent of all employees agree. (In companies that employ fewer than 25, at least eight workers and more than 50 percent must join.) Unions are prohibited during the first year of a business's existence. The closed shop, in which a single union dominates a particular work place, is forbidden, so a single company can have several unions, or have a non-unionized majority. According to the neo-liberal architects of the Code, this maximizes the choices that workers enjoy. In practice, it invariably divides the labor force of a particular company between rival unions or, more commonly, between those organized and those not. Benefits negotiated for one group are not automatically extended to other workers. As a result, the size of the average union in 1985 was half what it had been in 1970.[14]

One labor organizer explained that under these conditions, union membership hardly guaranteed a better wage. He offered the case of the Goodyear tire factory as an example: "Non-unionized workers often get better wages than those fifteen percent of workers who are members of the union." In fact, multinationals can often afford to pay higher wages to guarantee a non-union environment. "In such a situation," he went on, "there are no clear benefits to joining a union except worker consciousness and solidarity." Another union leader told us that in his textile factory, when layoffs were made, the manager fired unionized employees first. During the eighties, he recalled, many union leaders — still protected from firings in the new Labor Code for two years after holding office — watched impotently while rank and file were fired, decimating the union into dissolution. "It's no wonder," he explained, "that many workers are still afraid to join unions."

The Labor Code included provisions designed to isolate unions from government, political parties, and each other. One such provision was that internal union elections had to forgo formal nominations or slates of candidates. Instead each member votes on a blank ballot for whomever he wishes. The name that appears most often wins. This requirement was intended to eliminate "party tickets" characteristic of traditional union elections. In addition union funds must come only in the form of voluntary contributions from members; dues cannot be automatically deducted from paychecks, nor can union contributions come from the employer. Both provisions broke with previous laws and severely undermined the financial viability of unions.

A key provision of the Labor Code limits collective bargaining to workers and employers of a specific workplace. Federations that might effectively represent large sectors of the economy or regions are not allowed to enter negotiations with employers. To reinforce this fragmentation, the Pinochet government shuffled the country's companies into alphabetical order and assigned them the date on which they were required to negotiate a new employee contract. As a result, the collective bargaining process of one factory never coincides with that of a related factory, and the possibility of workers joining forces to negotiate collectively or to threaten a nationwide strike was greatly diminished.

The Labor Code restricted collective bargaining to only one issue: wages. Other areas of concern to workers, such as the size of work crews, the technology used, or mechanisms for internal promotions, were expressly excluded from the collective bargaining process.[15]

Even in negotiating wages, workers were stripped of any guarantees that might, in the language of the free marketeers, "distort the true value of labor." When we asked workers what was their greatest objection to the Labor Code, they invariably mentioned

Decree 18.134. This decree, imposed in the wake of the economic crash of 1982 as an amendment to the Labor Code, eliminated the "floor" (*piso*) for negotiated wages. Previously an established "floor" guaranteed that wages couldn't be negotiated downward, and would at least keep pace with inflation.

As Benito Gallardo of the textile workers' federation (CONTEVECH) explained: "Before when you negotiated a contract, you could not get a worse deal or lower salary than that of the previous contract. Now, you can actually come out of the negotiations with a lower salary. This puts enormous pressure on union leaders, since a bad deal can be disastrous." Decree 18.134, which transferred much of the burden of recovery and profitability to workers, became central to the recovery in Chile throughout the rest of the decade.

By giving every advantage to the employer, the new Labor Code made the strike — or even the threat of a strike — an ineffective bargaining tool for workers, since employers could resort to lockouts, hire strikebreakers, and negotiate individually with striking workers. Strikes are now legal only if no new contract has been signed at the end of an existing one, and only if a majority of union members support the strike. Strikes are restricted to a single factory. The Code no longer allows for government mediation. "The ability to strike is another joke because strikes are limited to a maximum of sixty days, and during that time management is free to hire other people. Furthermore, after 30 days the striking workers themselves are entitled to negotiate individually with the plant," was how textile workers' leader Bustos summarized the strike provisions of the new Code.[16]

High unemployment levels further strengthened employers' leverage over workers. For example, when 300 workers from the Madeco company went on strike in 1983, seven thousand unemployed people responded to the company's call for replacements. The strike quickly failed.[17] Given the labor regulations and the high unemployment levels that characterized Chile throughout the Pinochet years, strikes proved to be at best symbolic, and at worst, suicidal. It is not surprising then that during the period 1984-85, fewer than 3 percent of collective negotiations resulted in a strike.[18]

In his memoir of this period, former minister Piñera muses over the irony of a military government imposing union democracy. The government, he claims, "recreated the debate that would have taken place in a democracy" among the U.S.-trained economists in the labor ministry (particularly Piñera and Hernan Büchi), Pinochet, and the other generals of the junta.[19] Some labor leaders were granted individual audiences with Piñera, but when some of them attempted to gather together all labor representatives from throughout the country to discuss the Code, the government disbanded the meeting and sent its organizers into exile.

The potent combination of repression, pervasive unemployment, and the new Labor Code drastically changed the face of organized labor. By 1987, union membership accounted for only 11 percent of the labor force, less than a third of pre-coup levels.[20]

Yet organized workers have not been as impotent as the Labor Code would have them. Wherever possible, workers contested the terms of the Labor Code, sometimes managing to turn some of its restrictive provisions in their favor. For example, the Code's architects intended to exclude and fragment political factions to keep them from holding union office. Instead the absence of ballots favored those groups within unions that were most organized, often as a result of affiliations with political parties traditionally rooted in the labor movement and opposed to the military regime. Also, workers from individual factories bypassed the Labor Code's prohibition on sector-wide collective bargaining by using federations to manage informal coordination of demands.[21]

Denied a forum to bargain for anything but wages, unions ventured into the public arena with their concerns over broader social and political issues. After 1980, union federations overwhelmingly opposed the military regime and took aim at specific social and economic policies, including the privatization of public enterprises. During the mid-eighties, unions were fundamental to organizing the national protests that led eventually to negotiations for the 1988 plebiscite.

Working conditions

For those who remain employed, the work pace intensified and the work day lengthened. The maximum time an employer could demand of a worker without overtime pay was raised from 8 to 12 hours, and even longer hours were allowed in some "low intensity" jobs (for example, theater attendant). Extended days became commonplace in commercial shops and service industries. In 1990 many restaurant and hotel employees worked 12 hour days, 72 hours a week, according to the Federation of Hotel and Restaurant Workers. In Santiago most restaurant workers are let off for a couple of hours without pay during the dead period in the afternoon between lunch and dinner. "But what can they do for two hours?" asked Antonio Gonzalez, an official of the Federation. "They don't have the time or money to visit their homes in the *poblaciones*, so they go to the "flippers" (video arcades) or the 'topless' bars which line certain streets in downtown Santiago." Such hours and diversions, he added, put a terrible strain on family life and create real social problems.

Although the legal work week in other types of employment is not supposed to exceed 48 hours, many Chileans work far longer without being paid for overtime. Even free-market celebrants Lavín and Larraín admit that working extra and unpaid hours remains a serious problem.[22] Abuse is made more likely since the minimum wage is set per month rather than per hour. It is commonly assumed that employees will work overtime without pay, or else. Or else what? Typical is the case of a man we spoke to in the *población* of La Pintana, where jobs are scarce and coveted. After working for a month as a driver from 7 a.m. to 10 p.m. daily, he demanded to be paid for his extra hours. Instead, he lost his job and didn't receive pay for the extra hours.

In manufacturing, employees are commonly paid by the piece rather than for a given number of hours. This is typically the case in large factories, and almost universal in the informal sector's semi-clandestine shops. In one typical small sweatshop we visited, the four (women) workers were paid 50 pesos for each dress they sewed, dresses that sold in the stores for ten thousand pesos, about 30 U.S. dollars. By sewing 20 dresses during a 12 hour day, a worker could perhaps eke out the minimum wage.

Similarly, in the fruit industry, workers are paid by the box picked and/or packed. This type of payment often imposes a brutal step up in the pace of work, one that few workers can sustain for very long (or over very many years).

Companies in general and service industries in particular pare down their permanent staff to a minimum and regularly bring in temporary workers, who are by law non-union and therefore often have much lower wage and benefit levels. Another common practice is to contract out work once performed internally, often to a smaller business or intermediary that pays substandard wages. Even when large companies contract out jobs to third parties, responsibility for abusive wages and work conditions is that of the intermediary.

A worker in the Federation of Hotel and Restaurant Workers spoke to us of the Hotel Carrera, Santiago's traditional luxury hotel. In the years after the Labor Code was implemented, he recalled, the hotel's permanent staff was cut from 440 to 200 workers. This was accomplished by contracting work out and employing temporary workers on weekends. Employers insist such reductions are necessary to reduce costs and raise efficiency, but many hotel and restaurant workers complained to us that with these changes, their jobs had become de-professionalized. They had lost all input into decisions, they complained, and because of the reductions and the intensity of work, they could no longer provide the same level of service.

In manufacturing the pattern is similar. Alejandro Olivares, a CUT officer responsible for organizing workers in the informal sector, described in a 1991 interview a typical example of the new organizational innovations: "Take the Jarmin shoe factory. Before the crisis of 1982-83, the factory produced four thousand pairs of shoes a month. Now they produce thirty thousand." This was possible, he explained, because now the workers only cut shoe pieces in the factory which then are distributed through intermediaries to be assembled, for 30 pesos a pair, in people's homes. The pattern resembles European production systems of the mid-nineteenth century, standards which were raised only by the interventions of labor unions and reform-minded government.

Business interests argue that subcontracting has helped create a vibrant informal economy. But subcontractors tend to pay sub-minimum wages, employ minors, and force employees to work under dangerous conditions and excessive hours. As CUT organizer Olivares insists, "A system of contracting out work depends upon the existence of an army of unemployed and underemployed. And how do you organize or protect those working for subcontractors, since they are no longer working together, and don't even know who their real employer is?"

It is almost impossible for the government to regulate smaller firms for abuses, even if the Ministry of Labor had sufficient will and staff to do so. Sweatshops and firms sub-contracting services disappear at the first sign of regulation or financial troubles, often springing up again under a different name.

With the neo-liberal changes, remuneration has been reduced to the wage, ending most benefits that workers had gained over the years. Moreover, the privatization of such services as health care and retirement security was two-edged: not only were these services handed over to private businesses, but the costs are now taken entirely from employee earnings. The employer contribution to the costs of retirement security — a hallmark of twentieth century capitalist reform — went the way of many other social gains.

In the first years after the coup, wages dropped precipitously. But during the first couple years after the implementation of the 1979 Labor Code, wages rose with the economy buoyed by the over-valued peso and massive infusions from international borrowing. By 1981 the average wage was only four percent less than it had been in 1970. Wage recovery also occurred because the new Labor Code reinstated the traditional automatic adjustment for inflation.

In 1982 in the face of an economic collapse that threatened the viability of the entire free-market experiment, something had to give, and the Chicago Boys decided that it would be wages. Wages, they explained, should be allowed to find their natural level, free of distorting guarantees against wage cuts or inflation (Decree 18.134).

During the years of severe economic crisis (1982-84), employers systematically forced workers to accept wage reductions, often under the threat that large-scale layoffs were the only alternative. And wages stayed low even as the economy began to recover. Low wages were key to the celebrated "miracle" recovery. From 1984 to 1989, GDP in Chile grew an average of six percent annually. By 1987 Chile had recovered the production levels of 1981, and by 1989 production levels exceeded 1981 levels by 10 percent. The average wage, by contrast, was 5 percent lower at the end of the decade than it had been in 1981 — almost a tenth lower than the average wage of 1970.[23]

The drop in the minimum wage was even more drastic. Free marketeers strongly pushed for the elimination of the minimum wage on the grounds that it too prevented wages from finding their true price. If wages were set through government intervention, they argued, the result would be less overall employment than if wages were determined entirely by the market. But public discontent during the years of economic crisis made it politically inopportune to eliminate a minimum wage; instead, it was allowed to erode steadily in the face of inflation. By 1988, it was 40 percent lower in real terms than it had been in 1981, the equivalent of 43 dollars a month. In that year, 32 percent of the workers in Santiago earned the minimum wage or less.[24]

A 1987 study by economist René Cortázar (later Aylwin's Minister of Labor) estimated that the minimum wage could be raised 50 percent without significantly affecting employment levels, and at least some entrepreneurs acknowledged that they could pay higher wages.[25] But many employers were unwilling to give workers a greater share of profits, insisting that wages should be determined by national and international labor markets. When in 1990 we suggested to Alberto Martinez of the Textile Institute (which represents the country's major textile companies) that the textile industry was now stable enough to afford to pay higher wages, he claimed that Chile was no longer competitive in textiles. Textile wages were well above those of much the world, he insisted.

The examples of numerous industrialized countries show that no industry can remain competitive based purely on low wages for very long — there will always be a country that can provide cheaper labor. Lasting competitiveness must come not from cheap wages, but from technological innovation, the development of human resources, and a certain amount of government intervention that ensures both.

The relationship between wages and unemployment in Chile is complex and important. When the Labor Code was first outlined publicly on May Day, 1979, Minister Piñera referred to "our struggle against unemployment, which is the first priority among the social objectives of this government."[26] Such declarations should have left listeners wary, since the Chicago Boys clearly subordinated social objectives to economic ones. The solution to the social problem of unemployment, according to neo-liberal econo-mists, is to subject wage levels to the rigors of the free market: wages may initially be lower, they claim, but more people will be employed.

But Chile's free market has been slow to create jobs. During the 1960s, unemployment hovered around 6 percent; by contrast, the unemployment level for the years 1974 to 1987 averaged 20 per-cent of the workforce. Even in the best years of the "boom" (1980-81) it stayed as high as 18 percent. In the years immediately following the 1982 crash, unemployment peaked at 35 percent of the work force.

The government emergency work programs were a concession to bad economic conditions. The government was forced to break briefly with free-market ideology, creating in 1983 the Program of Minimum Employment [PEM] and later the Program for Employment of Heads of Households [POCH]. These two pro-grams gave work to 12.5 percent of the workforce in 1983, typi-cally planting trees or sweeping streets and subways, jobs with no stability or benefits and paid at far less than the minimum wage.[27] Many of the Chicago Boys denounced such projects as contribut-ing to the "distortion" of wage levels and delaying recovery.

By 1989, after five years of recovery and growth, official unem-ployment had dropped to 8 percent and emergency work pro-grams were eliminated. On the surface this appears a considerable drop from 1983, but official statistics grossly underestimate the real level of unemployment among the population. "The INE (National Statistics Institute) employment surveyors go around and ask if you worked one day in the last week," Alejandro Olivares of the CUT labor confederation explained to us. "If you worked one day cutting grass or selling something in the street, then you are counted as employed." Independent surveys (conducted by a respected church-sponsored institute on employment) in which respondents are asked to define themselves as employed or unem-ployed, revealed unemployment figures in Santiago to be as high as 21 percent in 1988, dropping to 17 percent in the following election year (when, contrary to the free-market principles, the government pumped up the economy).[28]

Those Who Work

Much of the growth in jobs after the 1982-83 crash came in economic sectors characterized by seasonal employment — most importantly, agriculture, fishing, forestry and construction. All of these industries are notorious for low pay, long hours and high turnover during certain seasons of the year. In agriculture, for example, three-fifths of the work force is temporary, usually employed no more than three or four months of the year.[29] As a result, over 30 percent of agricultural workers live in urban areas and commute, either daily or seasonally.

Many Chileans have been permanently pushed into the informal sector. The jobs in the underground economy are usually unstable and poorly paid, and by definition lack the benefits or security (however limited) of the formal sector. In 1989, over 30 percent of the jobs in the Santiago metropolitan area were in this category. The majority of those in the underground economy simply sold imported bric-a-brac on the street, performed services such as washing cars, worked as maids in upper-income homes, or sewed in sweatshops. The incomes these jobs provided in 1990 were less than half the average of those in the formal sector.[30]

The deregulation of workplace safety and health standards has also had tremendous consequences. Chile's 1968 Law of Occupational Health and Accidents had been considered one of the most advanced in the world, but under the Chicago Boys, Pinochet decreed modifications, and lax enforcement made a mockery of what remained. Longer workdays and a stepped-up pace of work heightened the likelihood of accidents and sickness. Workers who are paid by the piece, or office workers who are paid by the words and numbers they input, are subject to painful tendon ailments that result from sustained repeated movement. The limit on loads to be carried — which at 175 pounds was already three times the U.S. limit — was eliminated entirely. And in 1984, the regime lifted numerous health and safety regulations regarding lighting, ventilation, the size of workspace, and the maintenance of equipment. From 1982 to 1985 (the only years for which we have data), the number of reported workplace accidents almost doubled. Public health experts estimate, however, that over three quarters of workplace accidents go unreported to the labor ministry, in part because over half of the workforce is without any kind of accident coverage.[31]

The maximum allowable levels for worker exposure to chemicals and radiation that might have been acceptable for an eight-hour work day quite conceivably become dangerous when applied to the widespread twelve-hour day. In 1983, pesticide exposure limits were suspended altogether, resulting in an immediate rise in the incidence of poisoning among farm workers.[32]

Workers have little recourse but to accept such conditions. In any business employing more than 25 people, the employees have a right to form — with management — a health and safety committee. But according to public heath worker Soledad Ugarte, "In practice these committees almost don't exist, as much because workers don't know about the possibility as because they are afraid to participate, since those who participate are given no protection from firing." It is not unusual for an employee who develops a work-related ailment to be fired "because of the necessities of the firm."[33]

The Fruits of Labor

Free marketeers argued that free trade would benefit all Chileans through access to cheap imports. During the import boom of 1979-1981, as previously mentioned, consumption patterns did improve for the vast majority of Chileans. Mercedes Benzes and cheap foreign electronic goods flooded the market. In *poblaciones*, imported televisions became commonplace, even where food was lacking. As economic growth resumed in the mid-1980s after the crash of 1982, stagnant wages and the unequal distribution of income severely curtailed buying power for most Chileans.

A 1988 survey showed that fewer than half of the families in Santiago earned enough to buy what was considered a basic "basket" of necessary goods and services. This was almost double the percentage in 1969.[34] Diets in the *poblaciones* tend to be heavy in bread, tea and rice.

A good indicator of consumption patterns among the majority of the population is the annual purchase of stoves, which numbered over 200,000 in 1970, and had recovered to the same level by 1981. However, five years into the recovery from the 1982-84 recession, the purchase of new stoves remained at barely a third of its 1970 level.[35] In many houses in *poblaciones*, cooking is done over tiny and dangerous jars of paraffin, either because families can't afford the stoves, or, if they have one, can't afford the cost of a tank of liquid gas.

The distribution of income in Chile in 1988, after a decade of free-market policies, was markedly regressive. Between 1978 and 1988, the richest 10 percent of Chileans increased their share of national income from 37 to 47 percent, while the next 30 percent of middle-income households saw their share shrink from 23 to 18 percent. The income share of the poorest fifth of the population dropped from 5 to 4 percent.[36]

Claiming a strong economy as his legacy to the ungrateful majority who had voted against him and the Chicago Boys, Pinochet surrendered the presidential sash in 1990. Yet in that year, five million Chileans (almost half of the population) lived in poverty, far more in absolute and relative terms than any time since 1964.[37] Free-market policies in the late 1980s provided growth, but little equity.

Conclusion

By forcefully intervening to impose strict limitations on labor organizing and collective bargaining, the Chicago Boys sought to reduce the negotiation of the labor contract down to its smallest unit — preferably the individual worker and his or her employer. Attempts by organized workers to protect themselves from the vicissitudes of the market, or to influence economic and social decisions during a period of dramatic restructuring, were either prohibited or made extremely difficult by free-market policies and the structures of enormous power inequalities imposed by the regime. In the design of the Labor Code, as in other areas, we see the contradictions between the rhetoric of freedom and the authoritarian imposition of rules that clearly favored business.[38]

Many workers feel that the impetus for a new social pact between labor and capital must come once again from the government.[39] Labor economist Jaime Ruiz-Tagle points out that by having removed the broader political and national dimensions from labor conflicts, "social classes confront each other directly, without any mediation by the state."[40] By eliminating government mediation, the new rules for labor relations reopen the prospect of violent confrontation between workers and business, such as the bloody episodes that occurred regularly in Chile before 1930.[41] In spite of workers' traumatic experiences over the past two decades, a resurgence of class conflict could eventually occur if employers continue to defend the unfair advantages they received from the Labor Code. In the first year of civilian government in Chile, the number of strikes increased by 50 percent, and the participation of workers in strikes grew by 20 percent.[42] At the same time, most union leaders realize that there is not mass support for the confrontational and ideological positions of the 1960s and early 1970s and that labor unions must adapt to the de facto export orientation of the economy and the new patterns of economic concentration within Chile. The development of a genuine democracy in Chile depends largely on the willingness of employers and politicians to incorporate workers and their organizations into workplace decisions and national discussions of economic and social policies.

PART THREE:

SOCIAL POLICY

8

Marketing Health

At international conferences, where Pinochet's human rights record invariably came under attack, defensive Chilean officials would boast of Chile's falling infant mortality rate (IMR), which since the 1970s had become internationally recognized as a key indicator of socially positive economic development.

In Pinochet's Chile, the number of infant deaths in fact was plummeting. Of every 1000 born, the number who died before reaching their first birthday fell from 65 in 1974 to 20 in 1986 to 17 in 1989, a level comparable to that of some economically developed countries. Citing the infant mortality rate and other indicators such as life expectancy, Lavín and Larraín boasted in 1989 that Chile, thanks to free-market policies, enjoys "the health profile of a developed country."[1] The number one cause of death had become, they noted with pride, cardiovascular disease, followed by cancer. Such a ranking they hail as "the failure of success."[2]

The Chicago Boys assert that these health benchmarks have been achieved at the same time their policies have allowed the government to sharply reduce its outlays on health. They charge that for decades politicians had promised, especially in election years, so many government health care programs that costs skyrocketed, driving up fiscal deficits and thereby fueling inflation.[3]

But conversations with middle-class as well as poorer Chileans certainly evidenced widespread resentment and even outrage over free-market health policies.

A Healthy Legacy

Chile was the first country in the Western hemisphere to develop government health insurance for non-military public workers when employees of the publicly owned railroad began receiving free or low-cost medical care in 1918. For generations, Chile continued to pioneer on the road toward equal access to health services for all.[4]

Historians point to the influence of European social programs, notably those of Bismarck in 1880s Germany, which developed health care reforms in order to undercut the powerful appeal of socialist labor and political organizers, as well as to provide a healthier labor force.[5] In Chile, as in Western Europe, strong labor unions and allied political parties pressed for sickness and disability insurance for unionized workers and their dependents with the financing shared by government, employers and workers. One of their landmark achievements was the 1924 (Blue-collar) Workers Insurance Law which, among other things, introduced the right to maternity leave for 45 days before and 45 days after delivery for all working mothers. Another breakthrough in 1956 extended the coverage for blue-collar workers' children to the pre-natal period, thereby helping promote pre-natal medical care.[6] In 1959 the right of working women to maternity leave after birth was extended to a total of 90 days in order to encourage breast-feeding.[7]

For decades Chile led the way among Latin American nations in public health. Some of the older health professionals we interviewed gave part of the credit to public health ideas fostered through scholarships for Chilean health professionals funded by the U.S. government and the Rockefeller Foundation for the leading schools of public health in the United States. The School of Public Health established in the 1950s, the first in Latin America[8], developed into one of the most respected public health research and training institutions in the world.

Chile also stood out in medical training. Free or low-tuition training was combined with scholarships for specializations that rewarded young doctors for tours of service in rural areas and poor urban neighborhoods. Chile was known internationally for medical training that highlighted the socio-economic factors in health. "Social health" courses formed part of the training for all students in the health sciences.

Through the 1930s and 1940s, the Chilean Congress, with the support of diverse political coalitions, established more than fifty agencies and programs to oversee preventive and curative health services. In 1952, in fulfillment of a presidential campaign platform and inspired by the establishment of a national health service in Britain by the Labour Party, the National Health Service (SNS in Spanish) was set up to better coordinate the unwieldy array of government health programs and policies. (The legislation for the SNS was introduced by then Senator Salvador Allende, one of a number of physicians over the years elected to the Chilean Congress.) Most charities, mainly founded by the Catholic Church, also were brought under the direction of the SNS. The SNS improved services for blue-collar workers and expanded coverage to include indigent people. By the mid-1950s, the SNS was providing free health care for 65 percent of all Chileans.[9]

In 1968 President Frei's Christian Democrat administration created the National Medical Service (SERMENA) for white-collar workers and their dependents. SERMENA was a government-administered health insurance plan that brought together the multiple organizations serving white-collar employees and their families, an estimated 20 percent of the population. The health services provided were financed by a mix of government contributions, modest withholdings from employees' paychecks, employer contributions, and co-payments by the beneficiaries for services received. Co-payment opened the door for beneficiaries to "freely choose" private health care providers.[10] (The white-collar beneficiaries of SERMENA were allowed to use SNS hospitals and clinics, perhaps thereby overburdening these public facilities.)

Also in 1968 Chile became probably the first country in the Third World to legislate mandatory insurance for work-related accidents and illnesses. Premiums were paid entirely by the employers and set according to a schedule weighting the risks of particular industry and occupation, thus building in an incentive to employers to lower the risks.

By the end of the 1960s, then, government-administered and (in part) publicly financed programs guaranteed the health needs of 85 percent of the population, while allowing white-collar workers the option of private medical facilities. In the 1970 election, the

Popular Unity government proposed a unified national health system providing uniform and comprehensive services independent of worker status. President Allende did not succeed in pushing through the Congress health care reform legislation, aimed at making governmental health care programs more egalitarian, before the military coup toppled his government. Nonetheless, the government's health budget was substantially increased during the Allende years, with emphasis on preventive programs such as infant feeding supplementation and school lunch programs ("half liter of milk for every child" being one of the Popular Unity's most-remembered slogans).

One doctor on the staff of a Santiago public hospital shared with us another memory of the Popular Unity period. "In the final months of the Popular Unity government there were shortages in this hospital but not as bad as now. Yet I have to confess the Popular Unity was very irresponsible. When we in the health sector needed something we were told, 'Just go ahead and get it.' We had no idea what something cost — we didn't care. One thing I have to admit about the impact of the Chicago Boys is that they have made us all economists. We now know that things have to be paid for and what they cost. We've all come down to earth, and that's good."

Repression

At least one thousand doctors and hundreds of other Chilean health professionals who worked in the SNS, medical schools, hospitals, clinics, research institutes and private practice fell victim to the reign of terror in the aftermath of the 1973 military coup. Any health worker suspected of having actively supported or simply of being sympathetic to the Popular Unity government or to have opposed the coup even by giving emergency medical treatment to anyone wounded by the military was targeted.[11] Those health workers so suspected could count on being "relieved" of their positions and losing retirement benefits for themselves and their families. Many were detained, imprisoned, tortured and driven into exile. Twenty-two doctors were executed or "disappeared."[12] Doctors who had not joined the medical strikes were singled out; at sham trials they discovered themselves accused of abandoning the sick, eating the food of patients, arguing with colleagues, etc.[13]

Official persecution of health professionals did not end with the reign of terror in the days and months following the coup. When in the 1980s individual doctors and the Medical Association protested the neo-liberal changes in health care policies, numerous health professionals were attacked, detained, interrogated and relegated to internal exile. An issue of the magazine of the Medical Association published photos of a march of white-smocked doctors in downtown Santiago on the annual Doctor's Day being tear gassed by legions of police.

Authoritarian repression took additional forms. For 10 years the health ministers were military generals and admirals with no previous experience in health policy. All decisions were handed down without any participation by autonomous organizations of health professionals, let alone the general public.[14] The National Health Advisory Council, which for years had advised the government, was abolished, and the Medical Association, which previously had legally sanctioned input in health policy matters, was reduced to the status of a "voluntary organization." (Ironically, the Medical Association had been one of the first professional organizations to call for the resignation of President Allende, one of its founding members.[15]) Throughout the period of sweeping health-policy decrees, doctors and other health care workers were explicitly prohibited from meeting to discuss non-clinical business in public facilities, even after working hours.

Many of the Pinochet regime's other policies also jeopardized the health of the Chilean population. The Chicago Boys' "shock treatment" spawned widespread unemployment and drastically cut wages, thereby widening and deepening poverty and malnutrition. More people worked "informally" and for subcontractors in the deregulated business environment which increased occupational health and safety risks. Deteriorated living and working conditions made millions of Chileans more vulnerable to health crises and therefore more in need of access to health services.[16]

In 1989 medical researchers estimated that 2.5 million Chileans suffered from one or more serious mental health problems, ranging from mental retardation to psychosis to excessive drinking.[17] Much of the considerable increase in mental health problems can be linked to dehumanizing unemployment and underemployment, overcrowded living conditions, destruction of networks of support, and political repression.[18]

Dismantling Public Health Services

In Chile, access to health care is now based on income. Between 1979 and 1985 the government issued a series of decrees that sharply reduced governmental and employer contributions to health care services, passing more and more of the bill to users through wage and salary withholdings and co-payments. These changes fostered the rise of private for-profit providers of health services.

The theory is attractive enough. Thanks to "reforms," consumers now may "freely choose" from among a greater number of health care systems (both public and private) at various prices. The changes, according to the neo-liberal proponents, generate competition in the medical marketplace, forcing providers to give better care and to keep costs down. Moreover, as already pointed out, less comes out of the public purse for health services. Last but not least, eliminating employers' expenditures for health benefits should help them hire more workers and make Chilean industries more competitive on the world marketplace.

How does the new setup work? Seven percent of the gross pay of every formally employed person is withheld for health care. The employee can choose where this deduction goes. Since 1981, one option is to choose one of the "plans" or contracts offered by an "ISAPRE" (Instituto de Salud Previsional), one of the competing health insurance companies modeled after HMOs in the United States. Depending on the employee's income (and thus how much money the 7 percent withheld amounts to), the plan may require additional premiums and/or co-payments for actual services. (More on the ISAPRES later.)

Another option for the 7 percent withheld is the public sector's FONASA (National Fund for Health). There the employee can further opt for what amounts to a government-run ISAPRE, giving him/her "free choice" (*libre elección*) from an approved listing of doctors, clinics, hospitals and other providers of health services. Depending on the absolute size of the 7 percent withheld, the employee may be required — most are — to make co-payments for actual services. Also determining what the co-payment will be is the "level" of the health professional chosen; of course, officially all health professionals are competent but differ in terms of experience, specializations, reputation, location, office amenities, and so forth.

Or the employee can opt to receive medical services through the public health care facilities, the remnants of the old SNS. For reasons soon to be detailed, few choose this option. However, if one is laid off or working in the so-called "informal" sector or is otherwise hard up, one is stuck with the public institutions.

To recap so far: The vast majority of Chileans are either in the private or the public system of health care coverage. The private system is in the hands of competing for-profit companies, the ISAPRES. The public system has two different tracks, one offering — for a price — a choice of private providers of health services and the other, only publicly owned facilities.

True to the ground rules of the marketplace, the actual determining factor is not "choice," but one's ability to pay. With the new setup, a wider range of service providers offering an array of options is *available* to each person; they are not, however, necessarily *accessible* to that person.[19] This fundamental real-world distinction becomes even clearer with a closer look at the system's "options," and who takes advantage of which.

First, let's look at the breakdown of how many Chileans are with each system. As of 1990, only 15 percent of Chileans were with one of the much-touted ISAPRES. (This figure includes dependents of subscribers who generally are also beneficiaries.) About 70 percent of Chileans are with the public system. Of those, somewhat fewer than half are with the "free choice" FONASA plan. That adds up to 85 percent of the Chilean population. What about the remaining 15 percent of Chileans who are in neither system? They are mainly the 600,000 members of the Armed Forces and the National Police and their dependents — we'll come to them in a while — and those few who are self-employed or rich and opt simply to pay for whatever services they need or want.

As one might expect, the ISAPRES have captured most of the high-income Chileans and the public system has wound up with all the low-income Chileans. Almost three-quarters of the ISAPRES' clients are in the top 30 percent of Chileans by income, while 41 percent of those in the public system are in the bottom

30 percent by income.[20] The average income of an ISAPRE client is about seven times that of the average wage earner in the public system.[21] In 1989, 21 percent of the users of the public system — over two million people — were too poor to have withholdings or make co-payments.[22]

Even if an employee's salary is in the middle-income bracket, the 7 percent deduction for health care might well amount only to enough money to qualify for a private plan with steep supplemental premiums and co-payments and other "catches." Most ISAPRE plans set premiums according to the age and gender of the subscriber as well as of any dependents on the plan, with the heaviest premiums by and large charged for elderly persons and females. An ISAPRE, moreover, has the right to reject would-be subscribers of any income if he or she is judged high-risk. Moreover, subscribers can be dropped if they develop an "expensive" disease like cancer during the one-year contract (most contracts don't cover cancer if it is judged "undeclared pre-existing"). In the words of a Medical Association board member, "The ISAPRES select out, and monopolize, the revenues from, the rich, young and the healthy."[23]

And the poor, old and infirm? By default, the public system winds up with them. Given the country's highly polarized income distribution at the end of the 1980s, over two thirds of Chileans remain in the public system despite the much-advertised glories of the health care services offered by the ISAPRES.

Not only does the public system carry the burden of those Chileans whose payroll deductions for health insurance don't amount to enough for them to be attractive to an ISAPRE, but in compliance with its neo-liberal dogmas the government has sharply cut back its contribution to the public system. On a per-person basis, the government's contribution to health has been cut by 43 percent between 1974 and 1989 (from 3910 pesos to 2228 pesos in 1986 pesos).[24] Nevertheless, it is this financially beleaguered public system that is supposed to attend to the health needs of 70 percent of Chileans, not to mention 100 percent of the nation's public health costs (environmental health, sanitation control, occupational safety, etc.).

Beware of the Chicago Boys' misleading terminology. They prefer to talk not about the actual line item in the government's budget for the public health care system but about what they call the "public expenditure in health," lumping together under that phrase not only the government's expenditure but also the health withholdings from those in the public system and the co-payments made by the users in the public system.

The public health services system is grossly underfunded. Between 1973 and 1988, the number of employees in the public health services system was slashed from 110,000 to 53,000, even though the number of people dependent upon it grew by one million during the same period.[25] The remaining employees have seen their real wages fall while they are assigned ever greater workloads in deteriorating working conditions.

Investment in equipment and facilities has been even more drastically cut. Expressed as a percentage of the public system's budget, investment declined from 9.7 percent in 1974 to 3.3 percent in 1987.[26] By 1983, the investment in public health facilities had been cut to only 11 percent of what it was during the last full year of the Popular Unity government.[27] Through the 1980s an average of less than $1 million per year was spent maintaining and building public health facilities.[28] With so little investment in equipment and facilities, any number of health professionals commented to us that the public system has survived (but barely) off the legacy of government investments in health before the Chicago Boys. Of course, not only does equipment run down and break down, but advances in medical technology demand ongoing and, in all probability, increased investments. One analysis in 1990 put the backlog of urgently needed investments in public health facilities at $800 million.[29]

Chile's public hospitals and other health facilities are visibly deteriorated. Many of the buildings have badly peeling paint, missing light bulbs, and outmoded equipment and (we were told by the staff professionals) lack adequate medical supplies. Wards are often so overcrowded that patients are stuck in the hallways. One seasoned doctor (who would speak only on the promise of confidentiality) at Santiago's Central Emergency Hospital — which attends to 40,000 patients a month — told us in a hushed tone, "We used to be technologically three to four years behind the U.S. Now we're twenty. Equipment here is so old that anywhere else they'd throw it out." Not one public hospital in Chile has a CAT scanner, even this emergency hospital with at least 500 patients with head concussions every month.

It's not only expensive equipment that the public hospitals lack. The doctor at the Central Emergency Hospital admitted, "We don't even have enough sheets. We have to tell patients' relatives to bring sheets, syringes, medicines. It's embarrassing and it's demoralizing to work now in a public hospital." With a look of genuine agony, he continued, "The patients we see here and their families — they have to sell everything, their furniture, everything, to afford the medicines. Sometimes it's better not to tell them that, yes, we could do something to cure you or your loved one because you know they won't be able even with the help of relatives and friends to come up with the money for the medicines."

Several private hospitals have CAT scanners, as does each one of the military hospitals. "We have two kinds of medicine today in Chile, with different results," the doctor told us. "And everyone knows it." He recounted a visit he made two years earlier to a private hospital at its inauguration. "It was fantastic. It had everything. I asked how much it all cost. Fourteen million dollars. Well, we spend $24 million for the cheapest plane for our Air Force."

Another older doctor reported that the public sector in health care is looked down on today. "Twenty years ago a doctor would have been ashamed not to be associated with a public hospital. People would have wondered what was wrong," she explained. "Everyone knew that the hospital was where you really learned, participated in seminars with your colleagues on interesting cases, kept up to date."

This doctor observes a difference between her colleagues who are products of the "new order" and those of earlier generations. "Now a new doctor, 25 years old, married and loaded down with school loans to pay off, can't possibly afford to work in the public sector. Before, working in the public sector you could also study, reflect, have a family, have dignity. That's a big difference." She continued, "Since the free-market mentality has made medical school expensive for the students, a young doctor doesn't feel any obligation to the public. We thought that we had a debt of gratitude to the nation, to the Chilean people."

Doctors nevertheless are more likely to work in the public sector than are nurses, orderlies, and technicians, all of whom, as a result, are in especially short supply in the public system. Doctors, in contrast to nurses and others, can work part-time and therefore have a private practice on the side — one tradition not changed by the Chicago Boys. Nurses in the private sector earn three times more than in the public sector. The medical schools are associated with the public hospitals. "The public system subsidizes the private sector," a public hospital administrator commented. "We train everybody and then out they go, sucked right out by the private sector."

Ministry of Health statistics reveal that the 1980s saw a serious drop in the number of hospital beds per 1000 inhabitants, from 3.3 in 1983 to 2.6 in 1987 to 1.95 in 1990. In Santiago's San Juan de Dios Hospital, despite its official 120 percent occupancy rate — that is, considerably more patients than beds — entire wards are sometimes closed off because of a shortage of nurses and orderlies.

The sharp curtailment in government funding for health care plus the flight of higher-income people from the public system have made for more inefficiencies. A patient forced to remain in the hospital seven days waiting for an x-ray takes up space and other scarce resources. Excessive waiting periods mean many patients wind up in emergency care, not only placing their lives in extra jeopardy but using up considerably greater resources. The minimum wait for specialized treatment is six weeks and once the appointed day comes the patient must wait until a bed is free.[30] One hospital administrator told us that an ulcer is likely to be unattended until it bleeds, then be treated as an emergency at a much greater financial cost. Public sector statistics document that between 1974 and 1987, of all categories of medical treatments, "emergencies" showed the greatest increase, accounting for 40 percent of the total.[31]

In a public hospital in Talca in 1990 we found new x-ray equipment but no specialist to operate it. An older doctor attributed this to the elimination of government-funded scholarships which gave the health ministry the leverage to plan sensibly what specialists would likely be needed. One longtime public hospital administrator complained that the government's contribution covers only 9 percent of hospital costs. She expressed her frustration at the Chicago Boys' doctrine that public hospitals should be "self-financing;" even with enormous efforts and grossly inadequate conditions, she said, her hospital runs a roughly 20 percent deficit each month. "When things get really desperate, the director goes to the Ministry and cries."

We also visited two Santiago private hospitals, Santa Maria and Las Condes. It was as if we had journeyed to another country. They're spiffy, especially the foyer of Clínica Las Condes, located in Santiago's toniest neighborhood. Both looked and felt not only like hospitals back home, but *upscale* hospitals at that. No shortages or beds in the hallways here. And, yes, a patient does have choices — individual room with shared bath, or a small room with half bath, or a large room with full bath, or a small apartment. A sign in the reception area explains it all: to be admitted one needs "a blank check and an American Express or Diner's Club card."

In 1990 three of the six largest ISAPRES were pulling together the financing (possibly with World Bank support) for yet another private hospital in a wealthy neighborhood.[32]

We also drove by two of the several medical complexes of the Armed Forces and of the National Police. By all appearances and reports, the military's medical facilities testify to the fact that "public" doesn't necessarily mean antiquated and shabby. As one doctor whose father is a military officer told us, "The Armed Forces have socialized medicine — good facilities and service and no free choice." No data about the military and police health system are publicly available, as a number of studies of Chile's health sector pointedly note.

Shifting the Burden

Stepping back and looking at the net impact of health care privatization — the tremendous shrinking of the role of the government — we see that it has shifted most of the cost of health services on to the consumers. In 1989, over 81 percent of all health expenditures in Chile came from the paychecks and wallets of the consumers of health services (up from 19 percent in 1974). The government contributed only 17 percent (down from over 61 percent in 1974). Employers were off the hook, contributing only 1.6 percent, and by and large voluntarily at that; by contrast, in 1974 their mandatory contributions had amounted to over 19 percent of total health expenditures.

Such a sweeping reduction in the roles of government and employers in citizen health care has landed Chile a world record. Only Switzerland, a country where personal income is typically very high, comes close; there the direct contributions of consumers account for 71 percent. Excluding Switzerland and Chile, the contribution of consumers for most countries runs between 0 percent (Canada and Denmark) and 46 percent (Austria).[33]

This shift in burden, however, does not fall evenly on all Chileans. Middle-class and even poorer Chileans have seen dramatic increases in what they must pay for health insurance and services, while many higher-income Chileans are likely to be paying less. "Middle-class" wage earners in the public system, from the deductions from their paychecks as well as increasingly stiff co-payments, are being forced to pick up the lion's share of the tab. In 1989, the government covered only 38 percent of the budget of the entire public health care system, with employers contributing nothing.[34] Since those 15 percent of Chileans with higher incomes who are with ISAPRES contribute not a peso to the public system and the government by the late 1980s was paying for only 38 percent of the public system's budget, it is the comparatively low wage earners in the public system — mostly already hard-pressed lower middle-class Chileans — who heavily subsidize the health care of over two million poor Chileans. In the words of Dr. Raul Donckaster, of the Medical Association, "*Son los pobres que ayudan a los más miserables*" — It's the poor who help the poorest.

Moreover, while the total spent by the nation as a whole on health services was still about the same percentage of the GDP in 1990 as in 1973 — 4 percent — the reduction in the government contribution and the creation of the ISAPRES have markedly redistributed those resources. In the words of a major analysis of the changes in health policies in the 1980s: "Now there are more funds for the health of the high-income groups, while the other 85 percent of Chileans pay more and receive less."[35]

A Free-Market Paradigm?

The ISAPRES, selling health insurance and care, showcase what happens when the private sector is given free rein. Here are the main things we see:

(1) *With the free-market model, income is what determines access to medical care.* ISAPRES find a certain historical precedent in Chile in the *"cajas de previsión"* (security funds) which from the 1930s until the neo-liberal reforms of the early 1980s operated as prepaid medical programs for the employees of certain private and government firms. The fruit of years of labor organizing, a *caja* offered a firm's employees an alternative to crowded and otherwise less attractive public facilities. A *caja* was financed by employee wage withholdings and employer contributions; as already noted, the employer contributes nothing for an employee's ISAPRE. An even more crucial difference is that in a *caja* every employee of the firm was on equal footing. According to Donckaster of the Medical Association, "In the *cajas* there was solidarity — no discrimination from the office boy to the top guy. Every employee got the same medical attention. Now the medical attention you get is entirely based on your income — how much your 7 percent withholding amounts to and how large are the co-payments you can afford."

Once income becomes the medical services gatekeeper, it follows that oodles of resources may be dedicated to prolonging the life of one high-income old man while the majority of people can't obtain even basic medical care. Such is the logic of the market.

For many Chileans, the whole concept of medical care has been changed, and they are terribly uncomfortable with the new concept. One teacher complained, "Now you have to demonstrate you can pay before you can get treatment." Several doctors commented that the market model had made the doctor-patient relationship into the doctor-customer relationship. A taxi driver, after we explained we were in Chile to understand the impact of the free-market model, told us that a few nights earlier he rushed a woman in labor to the nearest hospital only to be turned away because she did not have an ISAPRE. "I couldn't believe it," he mumbled over and over. Others told us of a newspaper account that had scandalized many Chileans of a badly hemorrhaging woman thrown out of a hospital because she could not pay.

(2) *The essence of the profitability of an ISAPRE is discrimination.* Most of the 30-odd ISAPRES don't themselves operate health services facilities but sell health insurance. In any case, the profit-seeking logic of the marketplace is to sell coverage only to those least likely to need it.

Most ISAPRES screen out those with certain congenital diseases or pre-existing cancer and those who are thought to be at high risk of AIDS. They refuse applicants over 60 or 65 years of age or charge them very high premiums; by 1990 only two percent of ISAPRE subscribers were retired. Renewing an ISAPRE contract might require dropping coverage for an aging dependent mother. Cancer is unlikely to be covered until after five years of premiums have been paid. Psychiatric and dental care are rarely covered. Contracts are loaded with "fine print." The ultimate "out" for the ISAPRES, as already noted, is that customers who have proven costly over the course of a single year will have their premium substantially hiked or be dumped, with little prospect of buying coverage from another ISAPRE.

Individuals in rural areas, where there are too few potential customers for the system to operate profitably, are also often unable to buy health coverage. The logic of market-driven health services, in contrast to the efforts previously of the national health system (SNS), has drawn doctors and other health workers out of the rural areas and into the principal urban areas.

ISAPRES initially rejected women of childbearing age, or minimally required women to certify they were not pregnant. This ran against, observes health policy analyst Joseph Scarpaci, "a long tradition in Chile of extremely progressive medical care coverage for women."[36] It also generated a lot of adverse reaction in the upper-income strata to the ISAPRES, as evidenced by articles and letters to the editor in the establishment newspaper, *El Mercurio*. As we detail below, the government came to the rescue of the ISAPRES.

(3) *Government interventions have consistently favored ISAPRES to the detriment of the public health system and the public purse.* From their legal authorization in 1981, ISAPRES had a slow take-off. The government therefore intervened to expand the market for the ISAPRES. In 1983 it increased mandatory health care withholdings from 4 percent of wages and salaries to 5 percent, then to 6 percent in 1984, and to 7 percent in 1986. Such rapid increases meant that the withholdings of a greater number of Chileans would amount to enough money to make them potentially profitable customers for ISAPRES. Moreover, the government decreed that employers may add a voluntary 2 percent contribution to the 7 percent withheld from any employee's earnings and get a tax write-off but only for employees in ISAPRES and not the public system; since such employers are eligible for a corresponding tax write-off, this decree amounts to yet another public subsidy for the private insurance companies.

Perhaps even more vital for the ISAPRES was the 1986 Health Law decree that mandated that the public system (FONASA) take on the payment of all medical and maternity leaves and of neo-natal care for those insured by ISAPRES. Similarly, it was also decreed that FONASA reimburse wages lost by ISAPRE subscribers due to illness beyond the tenth day of absence from work and during the ninety days of maternity leave. The ISAPRES were thereby relieved of a potentially bankrupting burden and enabled to view fertile women as potentially profitable customers. Here again the majority of Chileans who are lower middle class and lower income wind up subsidizing the higher-income minority: since ISAPRE members tend to be distinctly higher earners, it is much more expensive to cover their leaves than the leaves of those who are not with an ISAPRE; yet, as we have seen, any funds expended by

FONASA come mainly from the pockets of the middle 40 percent of Chileans and from tax revenues largely drawn from these same middle classes.

As the Chilean population rapidly ages, and absent a more equitable distribution of income, the future of the ISAPRES is shaky. Of course, there's always the possibility of more government interventions to rescue them. Some experts charge the financial holding companies have started up new ISAPRES for healthier younger clients while letting the older ISAPRES they own, as they grow ever less profitable, declare bankruptcy — a ploy perfectly legal in free-market Chile.

Of course, paving the way for the higher wage and salary earners to withdraw from the public system further drains financial resources from the public system, making it less desirable.

(4) *Yet another way those paying into the public health care system subsidize the profits of the ISAPRES is by allowing ISAPRES the use of public facilities.* By using public facilities for emergency cases and especially for very major procedures such as heart and brain operations, ISAPRES can avoid undertaking costly investments in such facilities.

(5) *Private medical care insurers by their very nature do not invest in preventive health care.* Since contracts are for only one year, subscribers can easily switch to a competing ISAPRE. Free-market champions might say that's good for promoting marketplace competition, but it also destroys any economic incentive for an ISAPRE to invest in preventive care. In fact, a 1987 study found that a mere 1 percent of what ISAPRES spent on health services went for preventive care.[37] Most ISAPRES treat patients as relatively expendable customers who, as we have already pointed out, can be dropped if they are not profitable.[38] (By contrast, the few ISAPRES that are "closed" — that is, open only to the employees of a particular company — tend to spend significantly more on prevention; keeping their stable pool of clients healthy is key to their profits.)

(6) *Advertising and sales expenditures are a major part of the "costs" of privatized medical care.* Given Chile's highly skewed income distribution (in part, the product of free-market dynamics), already by the late 1980s the pool of potential ISAPRE customers had stagnated. An ISAPRE's new clients are mainly dissatisfied clients of a competing ISAPRE wooed away.

In 1989, on average, ISAPRES spent one in six pesos on advertising, sales and related administrative expenses. Many ISAPRES spent more than that, some over one peso in three. The most profitable ISAPRE that year (Banmédica) spent the most on advertising, more than twice the industry average.[39]

(7) *The privatized free-market system generates an excessive demand for high-amenity, high-cost medical services and an upward push on prices for all medical services.* Lavín and Larraín celebrate the "medicalization" of daily life, attributing to the ISAPRES that "medical consultation has become part of daily life and no longer an exceptional event."[40] The low co-payments charged in most ISAPRE plans combined with the good incomes of the subscribers undercut much of their incentive to monitor the quantity, quality and price of the treatments (not to mention their likely medical naiveté). As a result, service providers tend to push with abandon multiple referrals, superfluous laboratory tests, unwarranted surgical procedures, and so forth. ISAPRE clients visit a doctor an average of 4 times a year, while those obtaining free service in the public system go on average 1.7 times a year. The most frequent reason for ISAPRE clients to visit a doctor is the common cold.[41]

The tendency, then, is for ever more costly expenditures on the health of the small minority of Chileans who are economically well-off.

(8) *ISAPRES certainly can be profitable.* The dismantling of public health services and the fostering of private health insurance companies launched a lucrative industry. Reported

profits in the late 1980s for the more successful ISAPRES ran about 15 to 18 percent. The money-making opportunities in health care insurance have attracted several multinational corporations from the United States and Spain. Cigna International Financial Service based in Philadelphia, for instance, fully owns Cigna Salud which in 1990 took over ISAPRE Luis Pasteur.[42]

(9) *It is meaningless to argue that ISAPRES give "more efficient" or even "better" health care since they have so many more resources than the public system.* In 1989 the ISAPRES had 6.5 times more financial resources per person than the public system.[43] ISAPRE clients consume 70 percent of the total deductions for health care, even though they are less than 15 percent of the national population.[44] Such is the "natural" dynamic of the free market, but the system should not be heralded as an efficient allocator of resources, especially in the face of how vital health services are for many people. It is entirely likely that with the public system so run into the ground most Chileans today would choose to be in the private system (if they could afford to do so). But what does that prove?

Laissez-faire

There's another face to the private health sector. *A Quiet Revolution,* Lavín's celebration of free-market Chile under the rubric of "The New Businesses of the Private Sector," opens with a description of "the amazing world" of private health services: "Nothing could be better than walking down the first three blocks of Avenida Salvador, in Santiago, which have become a 'medical district.' In less than 400 meters, seventeen companies compete in a very wide range of services: from x-rays, laboratories and computerized tomographies, to plastic surgery."

Never mind, as by now is clear, that what's available in this "supermarket of medical entrepreneurship" is not accessible to the majority of Chileans. But Dr. Donckaster of the Medical Association's board of directors raises an additional concern about what the free market means for medical services. "People with money just rent a house, move in furniture, contract some doctors and nurses and call it a medical center," he said. "There's no real regulation in neo-liberal Chile. Anybody can open a clinical laboratory. The Chicago Boys say that the market is the best regulator, that people won't come back to a medical center if they die from a treatment there. That would be reassuring except that it's not the patient who learns but his grieving survivors. They also say you have to put the sardines and the sharks in the same tank. Both the sardines who learn to escape the sharks and the sharks who learn to eat the sardines will prosper. Well, I say before long there won't be many sardines."

Obviously perturbed, Dr. Donckaster went on to explain that because the free-market government is ideologically opposed to regulating private business, there's no effective oversight of medical credentials in privately owned health businesses. "Just put whatever specialization you want up on the board by the reception desk."

The owners of many medical centers, he charged, exploit the unemployment and underemployment of doctors resulting in part from the reductions in employment in the public sector. A medical center can collect, say, 3,000 pesos for a visit to one of its doctors but pay the doctor only half of that or less.

Decentralization

In the name of decentralization and community participation — "bringing health services closer to the needs of the people" — national health clinics have been transferred to management by the municipal governments. The transfers were carried out in three waves, starting in 1981 mainly with the better-off municipalities (whatever be the logic of testing a social services program through the experience of the well-heeled!). An outside evaluation carried out in 1983 for the Ministry of Health of the municipal clinics in Las Condes concluded that, because the funding from the national government was insufficient, "under the present circumstances there is no possibility that the municipal administration of health [services] is able to finance itself without a deterioration in service delivery."[45] Mind you, Las Condes municipality is as wealthy as they come. Nevertheless, faithful to the decentralization-is-good dogma, neo-liberal policy makers plowed ahead with municipalization until virtually all clinics (92 percent in urban areas and 100 percent in the countryside) were handed over to the municipalities by April 1988,[46] reducing *several fold* the financial contribution of the national government.

Municipalization might contain the seeds of much-needed community participation in primary health care, but in the context of an authoritarian government in which every municipality's mayor is designated by a military dictator and given almighty powers, only the naive could expect participation even by the professional staff, let alone the community. Several health professionals told us that the regime viewed community participation in identifying local health needs as "political activity." In one clinic a doctor we visited who asked not to be named commented, "We work at the pleasure of the smile of the mayor." The mayor of that municipality, a member of the neo-Nazi party before the dictatorship abolished political parties, regularly handed down quotas of how many doctors and other employees at the clinic had to attend pro-Pinochet rallies. Joseph Scarpaci in his research found, "Physician directors are routinely dismissed who engage in community outreach activities that address the real needs of shantytown dwellers such as impetigo, body lice, respiratory infections. . . ."[47] He suggests that recognizing these needs would indict the public health system which is so underfunded it could not attend to them.

True to free-market notions about efficiency, central government funding for the transferred clinics was based not on past budgets before municipalization but on a reimbursement payment to the municipality for each treatment actually provided. A municipality could make capital investments in the clinics either from its general tax revenues or by lowering operational costs and thus netting revenue from the government per-treatment payments.

Since obtaining central government funding now depends on the number, and not the quality, of treatments there is pressure to speed up each treatment. As a result, many charge, the quality of care is often sacrificed. The Ministry of Health, in its "normative role," set the standard of five treatments per hour,[48] but in the two clinics in poor municipalities we visited we found higher and apparently stricter norms. In one, for instance, doctors work six-hour shifts. If they do not see 36 patients during a shift, then the clinic is docked by the municipality. At times, we were told, the staff has gone into the streets to try to scare up patients.[49]

Since the Ministry of Health has assigned different reimbursement values for each specific treatment performed by the municipal primary health clinics, the clinics tend to perform whichever primary care procedure is most profitable, that is, whichever gets the largest payment and can be performed in the shortest time. Preventive health care services such as vaccinations and checkups are not eligible for payments from the central government. (TB specialists charged that the increase in TB cases in 1989 could be attributed in part to fewer examinations for TB.[50]) Thus the market-oriented approach to the delivery of health services, on top of the pressure on each clinic to be "self-financing," has not fostered decisions based on what community members could most benefit from.

After initially allowing for an unlimited number of treatments that a municipal facility could claim for reimbursement payments, the Ministry of Health placed a ceiling on total payments for each facility. The formula for deciding these limits was never explained. The ceilings combined with the reduction in the amounts paid by the government for most treatments (reduced also without any justification offered by the Ministry) has meant that the municipalities have had to scramble to cover growing operational deficits — averaging 26 percent of total costs in 1987. Of course, this is far more possible for the better-off municipalities. Perversely, the municipalities with the greatest percentage of citizens who must depend on the public sector health services are the very municipalities with the least revenues. Virtually all municipalities have had to cut their investment budgets drastically, down to an average of only 2 percent of total budget. The truth is that Chile's decentralized primary health services facilities are surviving off a legacy of facilities and equipment from the past and its model of a centralized redistribution of resources.[51]

As with hospital and other higher-level health services, all patients except those who demonstrate they are indigent must pay either 25 or 50 percent of all fees for primary health care, depending on household income. As of 1986, all users of the public system health facilities must carry employer-certified income cards. Households whose income in 1990 exceeded the very modest sum of approximately $120 per month were in the highest category. As one veteran health professional told us, "With a salary of only $160 a month, I'm in the same boat with the richest people in the country."

Pobladores we spoke with complained that to receive non-emergency primary medical attention at the municipal clinics they had to line up early in the morning, lines often quickly building to 200 or more people — and that to get an appointment a month or more in the future. In one working-class *población* (Lo Prado), we were told it takes three to four days to get an appointment for a blood or urine test and 30 to 40 days for an x-ray. Medicines are in particularly short supply. One health professional estimated that for every ten drugs prescribed only two or three are available. In a survey of 253 doctors in public clinics 84 percent indicated that there is a shortage of medicines.[52]

Staff morale at the clinics is particularly low. The just-cited survey found that most doctors in the public clinics complained about lower real wages, poor working conditions, and too many patients per hour. This cannot help but tend to affect negatively service to the patients. Many doctors and other health professionals see themselves as particularly victimized by municipalization. No longer employees of the Ministry of Health, they have lost many benefits to which public employees are entitled such as cost-of-living adjustments, in-service training, job security, paid vacations, etc. Now they are simply private contractors with a municipality. Not surprisingly, the Medical Association opposed municipalization. Social workers attached to neighborhood clinics have been particularly decimated, even though social health problems such as alcoholism, drug abuse, teenage pregnancies, and domestic violence are epidemic in many *poblaciones*. Overall there has been a 50 percent reduction in the number of social workers in the public sector.

The very reduction in the quality of health services in the public sector, as sociologist Pilar Vergara observes, contributes to the achievement of the neo-liberals' stated goal of focusing the remaining public resources for health services on the poorest Chileans. Anyone who possibly can escape the public sector and buy better services on the marketplace is ever more likely to do so.[53]

Targeting

In line with neo-liberal doctrines, the Chicago Boys "focused" much of the government's sharply reduced budget for health services on primary health care and particularly for impoverished infants and pregnant mothers. Focusing resources on primary health care for the "truly poor," especially infants and pregnant mothers, they tell us, fits the government's "subsidiary role" since it is an area not likely to be of interest (i.e., profitable) to the private sector. (Moreover, a little money should go a long way by boosting indicators of infant survival.)

The public purse thus has funded, and even stepped up funding for infant immunization campaigns and supplemental feeding programs for infants and pregnant mothers. Nevertheless, the neo-liberal policymakers took existing nutrition programs and targeted them more narrowly. For example, during the Popular Unity government, all children under fifteen qualified for the National Supplementary Feeding Program; since 1974, the program has been limited to children under six and to poor pregnant and nursing women. Left out are other vulnerable groups such as needy older children, elderly people and young teenagers not in school and unable to benefit even in theory from the School Feeding Program.

The military government repeatedly refined its "targeting mechanisms" in its relentless drive to limit feeding programs to the poorest and neediest small children and mothers.[54] Since 1980 an index system based on socioeconomic surveys has been used to limit the beneficiary populations of the social programs administered by the municipalities or the central government. Food distribution through workplaces and welfare offices was replaced with distribution, more tightly controlled, through public sector health facilities where children's weight could be monitored.

In addition to nutritional programs, other public sector health services affecting the well-being of infants and mothers were increased, helping to lower the number of infant deaths. Maternity visits in the public sector were increased 100 percent between 1973 and 1979. Over the same period the percentage of births with medical assistance, already at 85 percent, increased a further 6 percent.[55]

Perhaps the most striking targeting of mother-infant health care, however, has been the Corporation for Infant Nutrition (CONIN). Created in 1975, on the basis of a government-funded pilot program, as a not-for-profit agency ("private" yet 80 percent funded by the government), CONIN constructed 30 Nutritional Recuperation Centers (with 40-60 beds each) where between 1975 and 1982 over ten thousand of the most severely under-nourished infants stayed an average 160 days receiving rehydration, special feeding and physical and mental stimulation along with education programs for the mothers. The average cost of this care was $1,200 per infant, many times the per person governmental expenditure on health care.[56] Obviously, such intensive emergency care of infants who otherwise most likely would die, keeping them under medical attention for an average of almost six months, should lower the number of infant deaths, that is, improve the IMR. But what will happen to them after they are "released" to return to squalid, overcrowded housing with parents struggling catch-as-catch-can for survival?

The declining IMR

The declining infant mortality rate so celebrated by the dictatorship is attributed by its neo-liberal policymakers as proof that focusing the government's health care resources "works." But they gloss over the fact that, in the face of the deterioration in living conditions of so much of the population due in no small measure to free-market economic policies, major *governmental* efforts were mobilized to insure that more infants did not die. As Clara Haignere concludes from her study of health and free-market economics in Chile, ". . . infants from low-income families have been kept off the coroner's books not by 'sound capitalistic economics' but by expanded and new 'socialistic' maternal and child health care programs."[57]

The government's focusing of its reduced health budget on impoverished infants and mothers is only one of several important factors in the decline in infant mortality.[58]

Most fundamentally, many health experts who have analyzed the decline in infant mortality in Chile during these years view it as part of a long-term trend since the 1920s (especially rapid during the years of the Frei and Allende presidencies). They attribute this trend primarily to the expanding coverage of health services, free for blue-collar workers, that is, to the legacy of government-supported interventions highlighted earlier in this chapter. They point also to the tradition of publicly funded universal basic school-ing, even suggesting that the effectiveness of the neo-liberal govern-ment's stepped-up programs targeted at poor mothers was greatly boosted by the legacy of public schooling among poor women and of a network of publicly financed health services facilities.

Another factor in Chile's declining IMR was that in the 1980s in Chile (as in so much of the world) there was a baby boom among the yuppies which would tend to improve the infant mor-tality figures since a greater portion of babies were being born to families with significantly better incomes and therefore healthier living conditions.

Some of these health experts also call attention to the fact that from 1983 on infant mortality virtually ceased to decrease. This underscores, they argue, the limits of narrow technical interven-tions that address the most glaring symptoms of impoverishment rather than its roots in the inequitable distribution of economic resources.[59] These underlying causes are pointed to by the fact that, despite the focusing of publicly funded health services on the poorest infants and their mothers, the infant mortality rate near the end of the Pinochet regime (1989) was more than three times higher in Santiago's poorest neighborhoods than in the ritziest. For instance, the rate in Cerro Navia was 23.1 while in Providencia it was only 7.5.[60]

Targeting. . . What is Missed

A number of the health professionals we spoke with charged that the proponents of infant-mother targeting seem willing to sacrifice everything else. Luz Ramirez, a social worker for 13 years attached to the public clinic in the *población* of Lo Prado, in the course of giving us an overview of the serious health problems of the neighborhood exclaimed, "What we've been through here is excessive targeting! They targeted infants and low-weight pregnancies but abandoned the old, the chronically ill, the well. No preventive care. No dealing with the rampant alcoholism even among the young. They're interested only in small children and only once they are sick. This isn't health care; it's just recuperation."[61]

Children only somewhat older than the infants who were the focus of the government's nutrition and medical care programs (children aged one to four) failed to show a comparable decline in mortality rate and suffered from increased illness.[62] Accidents and poisoning during this period emerged as leading causes of death for children, greatly increasing for small children; this is due, some researchers think, to a wide range of heightened "hazards confronting children in poor families — unsafe neighborhoods, increased alcohol and drug abuse, overcrowding, fragmented families, family violence."[63] A new phenomenon has been the death of young children, locked in their houses by parents working or looking for work, from fires and other accidents.[64]

As will be discussed below, while the public sector in health services suffered severe cutbacks and the focus narrowed largely to infants, many infectious diseases in Chile showed marked increases, especially those diseases against which there is no "one-shot" immunization but are engendered by the severe deterioration in nutrition and living conditions suffered by so many Chileans.

Manifestly what is not the case is what the Pinochet dictatorship and its free-market cohorts would have the world believe, namely, that the decline in the percentage of infants dying demonstrates that the Chilean people have benefited from the neo-liberal approach to health care. What is demonstrated by the experience of Chile is that it is a mistake to use infant mortality as the sole yardstick to measure a nation's health services let alone its people's well-being.

Will the Private Sector Guard the Public's Health?

Dr. Catterine Ferreccio, of the Ministry of Health's department of communicable diseases, showed us two graphs that dramatized the impact of free-market policies on public health.

INCIDENCE OF TYPHOID FEVER IN GREATER SANTIAGO PER 100,000[65]	
1970	102
1971	88
1972	75
1973	52
1974	66
1975	92
1976	92
1977	178
1978	205
1979	153
1980	160
1981	159
1982	178
1983	215
1984	125
1985	85
1986	78
1987	54
1988	55
1989	80 (provisional)

As the graph shows, typhoid fever dropped substantially and more or less steadily from 1971 through 1973. Dr. Ferreccio attributed this decline to improvements in personal hygiene and social conditions, thanks in part to demands people made for better housing, treated drinking water, sewer systems, etc. Then, as the graph also shows, in 1974 the rate of typhoid fever started climbing for the first time in decades, and in 1975 began to shoot up alarmingly, from a low of 52 cases per 100,000 people in 1973 to 92 cases in 1975. By 1977, the rate was up to 178 — an epidemic level not known since much earlier in the century. In 1978 the rate climbed to what would turn out to the graph's first peak, 205 cases per 100,000 people, the highest rates being among school-aged children.[66] Then it dipped only to rebound to a new and even higher peak in 1983 of 215. At this level, according to the Medical Association, Chile had 25 percent of all typhoid cases in the Western Hemisphere but less than 2 percent of the region's population.[67] Then the rate dramatically dropped in 1984 to 125 and continued to decline. Not until 1988, however, did the incidence of typhoid fever in Greater Santiago decline to near the 1973 level.

INCIDENCE OF HEPATITIS A IN CHILE PER 100,000

1975	45
1977	89
1985	105
1989	80

Graph #2 reveals a similar pattern for infectious hepatitis. The number of cases of hepatitis A shot up from 45 per 100,000 Chileans in 1975 to 89 cases in 1977, climbing steadily to a peak in 1985 of 105 cases, and was still in 1989 at the level of 80 cases per 100,000 population.

Investigations into these two epidemics concluded that the main source was infected bodily waste that contaminates water and food, especially vegetables. In Greater Santiago, a metropolis of nearly five million people, there is not a single plant for even primary treatment of raw sewage. The sewers dump all home and industrial waste water into Santiago's Mapocho and Maipú rivers, making up the bulk of the flow during the dry season. Not far downstream, these rivers are used by farmers to irrigate vegetable crops for the Santiago market such as lettuce, cabbage and parsley.

Using contaminated water on such crops has long been in violation of Chile's public health regulations, but shrinking the government and in particular reducing its regulatory role vis-à-vis private business has resulted in few and inconsequential inspections. Early on in the neo-liberal government, personnel cutbacks left only two environmental health staff available for four hours a week to check for the use of contaminated water in a 150 square kilometer area. Even when farmers were found using contaminated water, they were given 90 days to cease operation.[68] The government, ideologically bound to its "subsidiary role" and with its penchant against subsidies (at least for small operators), neither destroyed the infected crops nor offered these small farmers one-time partial financial support for switching to other crops not prone to infection. Some health policy analysts have argued that such measures would have been cost-effective, given the economic costs of such diseases.[69]

Also, as part of the government's cutback in spending for the common good, little was invested in sanitation projects. Repairs in Greater Santiago's water treatment plants were neglected. By 1982, the largest plant, supplying 80 percent of the tap water, had only 10 of its 16 filters operating properly, undoubtedly affecting the level of micro-organisms in the tap water.[70] Bottled spring water increasingly became the choice of the few who could afford it.

Two or three families crowded into small one-family houses in the *poblaciones* only compounded poor personal hygiene and sanitation. Many impoverished rural families winding up in Santiago's *poblaciones* were not used to the sanitary precautions required by close city living.

Another factor compounding a contaminated living environment for millions of Chileans is that they no longer had access to safe water in their homes. On top of policy-induced increased joblessness and reduced wages, the Chicago Boys hiked water rates with the hope that higher user fees would make the public water company "self-financing" with a view toward privatizing a profitable company. As a result, in some neighborhoods, more than 60 percent of the houses were disconnected when they could not pay their new bills. Meanwhile public investment in safe water fell to an all-time low.

Dr. Ferreccio also told us that many people took the severance pay they received when the government eliminated public sector jobs they had held for years and, unable to find employment, opened small food-vending operations. "With the government saying, 'Maximum freedom to private enterprise,' there were few if any regulations and certainly no sanitary inspections," she said. Inspections of restaurants and food-vending operations plummeted from 120,000 in 1973 to 3,000 in 1978 and thereafter. The reduction in inspections coincided with the alarming increases in typhoid fever cases.

A costly lesson here is that investing in protecting the public's health does not make "business sense" for the profit-oriented ISAPRES. The epidemic was eventually stemmed only when public outcry forced the government to overcome its ideological dogmas and intervene in the marketplace. In 1984, for instance, the government prohibited the sale of certain vegetables such as lettuce from areas thought to be irrigated with contaminated waters. That was the year the number of cases of typhoid fever dramatically fell from 215 to 125 per 100,000 persons.

Free-Market Fallout

Not surprisingly, the Pinochet government's health policies were a burning issue in the 1989 presidential election campaign.[71] Adding fuel to the fire was the fact that Pinochet's hand-picked successor Hernan Büchi first came into the public eye as the vice-minister of health who fashioned the privatization decrees and the ISAPRES in particular before moving up to become the top economic policy minister. Many Chileans, as repeatedly shown in pre-election polls, were infuriated by what they believed free-market measures had done to health services.[72] A month after Patricio Aylwin's inauguration, a resounding 57 percent of those polled ranked health policy as the number one priority facing the new government, considerably more than the 16 percent in the same poll who ranked low wages and salaries as the number one problem.[73] Obviously most Chileans had not forgotten that health care is not just another commodity on the market but a right for all.

9

Schooled in the Marketplace

Official statistics indicate that in 1986 265,000 more Chileans were enrolled in formal education than in 1973[1] and that by 1987 the average years spent by each Chilean in the classroom had risen to a little more than eight years, almost double the figure for 1973.[2] According to free-market advocates,[3] Chile has been firmly placed on the path to higher-quality education and to education more relevant to the nation's economic needs. Chileans are now free, they say, to make a range of choices: which schools to attend, public or private, and which courses of schooling make sense for them.

Higher education in particular has "opened up." We are reminded that post-secondary education had previously been offered by only eight publicly funded universities. Today more than 60 universities, public and private, compete for students. Moreover, those not opting (or apt) for a traditional five-year university track now can choose from over 70 "professional institutes" and 136 "centers for technical training."[4] Thanks to this "modernization," we are told, higher education is now accessible to more Chileans — 213,000 as compared to 145,000 in 1973 — and is grounded in the marketplace, so students are more likely to choose careers promising employment opportunities.

An Educational Legacy

For generations in Chile there had been a broad consensus that education was a public service which the government should strive to make available to all regardless of their financial means. The premise was not only that education was an individual's right but also that the entire society's social and economic well-being depended on raising the educational levels of all its members. Education, by qualifying persons from low-income backgrounds for better-paying jobs, was seen as a primary channel for reducing inequality and democratizing the society. The Constitution of 1833, that of 1925, and the constitutional reform of 1970 all affirmed the principle that the government was responsible for education.[5]

In implementing this principle, succeeding governments despite political differences expanded the national system of tuition-free public education and of government assistance for pupils and students from low-income families. By the 1950s, the government even financed the lion's share of the budgets of the Catholic University and the other five nominally private universities in addition to the public universities.[6]

Chileans were long proud of their public education system, a system that produced six presidents and two Nobel Prize winners. Teaching was a respected profession offering middle-class security and social mobility.[7] The national school of education was highly regarded. The quality of education in Chile benefited from a tradition of teachers and other educators continually striving to modernize and make improvements.

In Latin America, perhaps only Argentina had more notable achievements in education.[8] Between 1935 and 1973, the coverage of formal education in Chile grew from 23 to 53 percent of children and young people under 24 years of age;[9] four-fifths of those enrolled were served by public schools.[10] Over this period the number of Chileans in school mushroomed several times faster than the growth in the school-age population. Through the years of Frei's Christian Democratic administration, the number of university students increased by 85 percent, and in the brief three years of the Popular Unity administration, university enrollment increased a further 89 percent.[11]

Schooling had been gradually extended to children of blue-collar workers, peasants and the poorest urban families. By 1973, virtually every youngster attended grade school, which had been made into a compulsory eight-year cycle.[12] Through the 1960s to 1973, governmental programs gave access to higher education to children whose parents had little schooling.[13] By 1973, nine percent of those enrolled in universities were sons and daughters of blue-collar workers.[14]

Among other shortcomings, there were serious disparities between schools in the cities and the rural areas. In 1968, for instance, *El Mercurio* reported that the schools in one town on the southern island of Chiloe lacked "chalk, books or furniture."[15] Moreover, cobwebbed bureaucracies, frittering away public resources, no doubt cried out for a housecleaning.

Laying the Foundation for Imposing the Free Market

From the first days of the dictatorship and through (roughly) 1975, the military authorities concentrated their efforts in the educational arena on "purification." Their goal was to ferret out of every nook and cranny of the educational system, private as well as public, all the "elements" — persons, institutions, books, and ideas — that they considered leftist and subversive.

Soldiers occupied universities and any number of high schools and grade schools. Teachers, students and staff members known to have supported the overthrown government or suspected of opposing the junta were rounded up and taken off to athletic stadiums, buildings and Navy ships hastily turned into makeshift prisons and interrogation centers. Many were never seen alive again.

Those detained or suspected who survived were blacklisted. The mere fact of once having been a student or a staff member at a school branded as having been "communist" was enough to be denied every available opportunity, even years later.[16]

Military officers were appointed presidents of the universities. (Not until 1981 was a civilian appointed to head up a university.) Many teachers and students believed that their classrooms were monitored by informants of the extreme right or by military in civilian guise. As one university teacher driven into exile recalls, "The classroom was converted into a place where the informer, not the instructor, becomes the judge of performance."[17]

Curricula were also "cleaned up," most notoriously in the social sciences and education. The goal was to suppress anything that analyzed the country's social-economic reality.[18] Social sciences, which had once flourished in Chile, became something of the past.[19] Special courses on "National Security" or "The Doctrine of the Military Regime" were added to curricula and obligatory for all. In these courses, the history of the nation was presented very differently than it had been in the past. Heroes from the armed forces were spotlighted. The recent past was completely distorted or simply omitted.

Decentralizing and Privatizing the Schools

In 1980 the Chicago Boys finally launched their educational "reforms." Thanks to two decrees, number 3,063 in 1979 and number 3,476, Chilean education would never be the same.

The first decree ordered the municipalization of the kindergarten, primary and secondary schools traditionally in the hands of the national education ministry. The second directed the national government to pay a subsidy to private and municipal schools for each student enrolled. Private grade schools receiving these subsidies are prohibited from charging tuition, and the per-student subsidy to private high schools is reduced in proportion to the tuition charged. The changes resulted in the creation of two new categories of primary and secondary schools — municipal schools, and "private subsidized" schools — in addition to the traditional, but never numerically significant, private tuition-charging schools (now referred to as "private paid").

The arguments for the municipalization cited parental and local control over municipal schools and parental choice from a variety of schools. Furthermore, once government subsidies to a school based solely upon the number of students in attendance[20] replaced government funding based on a school's financial needs, municipalized public schools would have to work hard to attract and retain students and compete with privately run schools. Privately run schools, by attracting students, minimizing drop-outs and using the per-student government payment efficiently, could turn a healthy profit.

Once again, the Chicago Boys envisioned only a "subsidiary role" for the national government, that is, doing only what local government and the private sector could not. The national government should supervise education, set standards and test educational results. For the neo-liberals, however, education is no longer the responsibility of the government, but of parents and "the entities they freely choose."[21] The government should seek to guarantee the attainment of minimal educational goals especially by the poorest citizens, but achieving higher standards is a matter of the voluntary efforts of parents and their municipalities.[22]

Universities received marching orders to make themselves as "self-financing" as possible and thereby reduce their heavy reliance on government funding. Accordingly, tuition fees were significantly hiked. True to the spirit of the market model, tuition fees were differentiated to reflect the actual costs of each field of study.

Government spending on education, the Chicago Boys argued, should favor primary and secondary education, not university education (university education had cornered 47 percent of the government's education budget in 1974), since the vast majority of university students come from upper-income and middle-income families.[23]

Along with scheduling ongoing cutbacks in government spending for higher education, the Chicago Boys changed the method of government funding of the public and the traditionally government-subsidized private universities (notably the Catholic University), to phase in per-student payments and loans to students. As with the change in government funding for primary and secondary education, universities were to compete with one another for government funds on the basis of student enrollment. The assumption posited was that a larger enrollment reflected a superior educational performance attracting more students. Indeed, each university would be entitled to a per-student payment for every student recruited from among the top-scoring 20,000 students in the national university aptitude examination. (This indirect subsidy was soon limited to the traditional universities and the handful of public professional institutes carved off them.)

Implementation

Transferring primary and secondary schools to the municipalities began in 1980, municipality by municipality. The process was suspended in 1982 due to the government's severe financial constraints in the economic crisis. By that time, 86 percent of the schools had been handed over. In 1986 the process was completed.

In 1980, of the grade school pupils in metropolitan Santiago, 67 percent attended public schools, 22 percent attended private schools subsidized by per-student government payments, and 12 percent went to elite private tuition-charging schools. By 1987, the percentage of grade school students attending the now municipalized public schools had fallen to 43 percent, while the percentage in subsidized private schools had risen to 47 percent. In greater Santiago this worked out to 170,000 fewer grade-school pupils in the public system.[24]

The Chicago Boys also encouraged the founding of new private universities. Founding a private university — once a matter of a rare special act of Congress — was transformed into a breezy administrative procedure. Higher education status was granted to "professional institutes." The institutes, almost all privately operated, offer professional degrees with programs of study lasting four years or less in career fields (other than the twelve fields reserved by law for universities) such as advertising, design, public relations, public administration, and various teaching specializations.

The 1981 changes also granted private "centers for technical training" — a number of which already were operating — official status and prestige as institutions of "higher education." These centers usually offer two-year programs with a six-month practicum leading to certification as, for example, an executive secretary or hotel auditor. Neither the private professional institutes nor the centers for technical training are eligible for any sort of government funding.[25]

Government spending on higher education was sharply reduced, by 1987 to half of what it was before the policy changes.[26] Spending has even turned out to be significantly less than projected in the original decree. With the economic recession, the government cut back spending on higher education, especially per-student payments to universities once seen as central to the reform.

The government also cut funding for student loans, by 26 percent between 1983 and 1987. Students must now document family financial need, measuring up to stringent requirements, and have certain minimum grades and also come up with a co-signer vouching for the family's creditworthiness. For those students in real need this last requirement is positively catch-22. Only about a third of the students who do manage to qualify for a government loan obtain the amount they requested.

With its redefined, more limited role, the government, after an initial flurry of costs resulting from the changes (such as severance pay for teachers) reduced its outlays for education overall. In 1976 dollars, the education budget in 1973 was $448 million. The government's expenditures for education had declined by 1988 to $436 million (also calculated in 1976 dollars), yet the number of school-age Chileans significantly increased during this same period. Viewed in relation to the size of the nation's economy, the government's education budget, as a percentage of the GDP, fell from 5.72 percent in 1972, the final full year of the Popular Unity government, to 2.73 percent in 1988. The government's outlay for education on a per-capita basis fell 29 percent over the same period.

Higher education of any sort has been turned into an expensive proposition, even for families in which both parents attended university and who once took for granted that a university education would be within easy reach for their children. Registration and tuition fees have soared; by 1988, they were bringing in about half of the revenues of the public universities.[27]

"Taxi Teacher" — A Case Study

Pedro Rodriguez has been a high school philosophy teacher since 1965. "I was born here in Santiago, but I started out in the provinces. In those days a young teacher would do a stint in the boonies to get points so as to have a better shot in the competition for a good school in Santiago. That's how I got placed here."

"Here" is a public high school for girls in Santiago's fashionable Providencia municipality. "Before the Chicago Boys," he says, he was certain he was in the right profession. Now he wonders how much longer he can hang on. He looks exhausted — worn for a man in his late 40s.

Rodriguez notes that since Chile's national school system was decentralized into a municipal system the value of his paycheck (even though he works in one of Chile's wealthiest municipalities) has shrunk so much that he has had to start teaching two shifts, one in this school and one in a new subsidized private high school. "They call us taxi teachers," he says. "We have to zoom from one school to the other." With the two jobs, he teaches from 8 a.m. to 8 p.m. — 15 classes a day. (A little-known "reform" imposed by some Chicago Boy is that teachers are now paid by the "chronological hour" — sixty minutes — not the "pedagogical hour." Thus they must teach four 45-minute classes to get paid for three hours.) Rodriguez notes he also often has to correct tests until midnight or one in the morning and on weekends: "Burning midnight oil doesn't even get figured in our contract hours."

"You can't be a good teacher like this. You have no time to talk with the students. And we're giving the same classes, from the same notes, as we did twenty years ago. And we teachers have a lot of problems at home because of the long hours we work," he says.

The subsidized private school where Rodriguez teaches is no better and in many ways worse than the public one where he works. (A review of teachers' pay in March 1990 by the Ministry of Education found that the hourly rate in private schools subsidized by the government averaged 25 percent less than the pay in the municipalized schools, low as that is.[28]) "To make a profit, they squeeze the teachers. After all, it's a business," Rodriguez says. The owner of the school where he taught two years ago has eleven schools in Chile and four more in Argentina. "He owns a gold mine up north. His chain of schools are his other gold mine." That school's director nonetheless frequently complained that the amount of the government's payment to the school for each student enrolled was not adjusted for inflation for several years; therefore, he told the teachers he could not raise the hourly wage. Rodriguez was fired from this school. "The director called me into his office because he smelled a union being started. He wanted me to be his ear. I refused."

Across the Board Losses

Sociologist Eugenio Tironi quotes a teacher who thinks that the changes in the working conditions of Chile's teachers has meant "a loss in cultural enrichment, that is so necessary. Now I can't go to the theater, purchase books, play sports, nor even aspire to some possible further self-improvement because these activities have their price and I know that in the municipality where I work they will never translate into an increase in what I get paid."[29]

Another earthshaking change for primary and secondary school teachers inherent in the dramatic reduction of the national government's role in education is that they no longer belong to a nationwide system. They thus no longer have the prospect of moving up to better positions around the country as they gain experience and improve themselves. Moreover few municipalities can afford to offer teachers opportunities for further studies as the national system used to do.

Teachers in most private schools as well as the public municipalized schools are on "indefinite contracts." In effect, they can be fired at any moment without any stated reason, just like all other Chileans working under the neo-liberal Labor Code. In fact, to lower costs and better compete with the private subsidized schools, the municipalities in 1987 unceremoniously fired some 8,000 teachers, most of whom received zero severance pay as they were classified as "recent hires" since the schools where they taught had just been municipalized.[30]

The official status of a teacher has catastrophically changed, especially for older teachers. Before municipalization, teachers such as Pedro Rodriguez were national public employees. They enjoyed social prestige, job security and guarantees granted by a statute protecting all national public employees with rights to due process and defense against any accusation. Now they are not even regular municipal salaried employees (as are, for instance, school janitors) but "workers" under contract of a municipality's education corporation.

The public universities have been run down. Walking into any university building, it was plain to see. With direct and indirect government contributions slashed, total revenues in 1989 were at their lowest level since 1970, despite substantial tuition increases and other efforts at "self-financing." Adjusting to the fiscal crunch — and rather than lay off staff at a time of such high unemployment — the public universities reduced salaries and wages. Vacancies went unfilled. Still, salaries and wages accounted for almost all the expenditures; most maintenance and investment in facilities was indefinitely deferred. In 1989, 92 percent of the severely diminished budget of the University of Chile's medical school was taken up in salaries and wages, leaving precious little for maintenance of existing equipment let alone acquisition of anything vaguely up to date. "We are living off our inheritance," one white-haired professor commented. Basic research had been put on hold. Staff morale, we were often told, had understandably sunken. Students whose families can financially manage it in increasing numbers choose to go to one of the more reputable private universities.

Private universities avoid having full-time teachers; instead, to use the phrase of one of the university teachers we spoke with, they "rent a prof" by the hour. Some 7,000 university teachers were working part-time in 1990. In fact, in private universities most of the teachers are moonlighting faculty members of public universities. The private universities can get away with hiring part-time (and paying poorly to boot) because they contract teachers who have received their training and do their research and have their basic sustenance covered through full-time positions in public universities. Some educators told us that they view this as the public sector subsidizing the private; others spoke of it as exploitation of the miserable salaries of teachers in public higher education; and others as the private universities expanding the job market for poorly paid teachers at the public universities.

Widening the Gaps

Decentralizing the national school system has visibly widened the gaps between the schools in poor and rich municipalities. Inequalities among schools have been reinforced along the lines of the socioeconomic differences in neighborhoods and the families whose children attend them. Schools in the better-off municipalities are able to supplement the government per-student subsidy with contributions from other municipal revenues, parents, and businesses. Schools in low-income municipalities, on the other hand, are unable to count on resources other than the government per-student subsidy.

True to free-market principles, decentralization puts the better-off municipalities in a position to attract the better teachers with higher pay. In 1987, the well-to-do (Santiago) municipality of Las Condes paid full-time teachers between 38,000 and 80,000 pesos a month, while the low-income (Santiago) municipality of Cerro Navia paid between 30,000 and 38,000 pesos a month.[31]

Random visits to municipalized public schools in working-class and other poor neighborhoods revealed buildings that have gone years without a paint job, numerous broken windows, libraries virtually devoid of books, abbreviated school days, the elimination of entire subjects from the curriculum (financial necessity wrapped in the guise of the virtue of the "curriculum flexibility" now allowed to the municipalities) and — perhaps most tragic — exhausted, dispirited teachers and administrators. Seeing the broken windows, we couldn't help recalling Lavín and Larraín celebrating the decentralization of the schools, saying, "No more broken windows waiting for the approval or financing of the Ministry of Education to be repaired." In reality, many municipalities now find themselves with all the responsibility but few resources. In 1988, the municipalities earmarked on average only 2.6 percent of their budget for investment in their schools.[32] At one secondary school in the municipality of Santiago Centro, with over 4,000 students attending school in two shifts a day, the municipality allots the equivalent of only $140 three times a year for repairs and other "minor expenses."[33] As a vice-principal of a high school in a middle-class municipality volunteered, "We're living off the past: the good teachers who were formed under the old system, the buildings we got from the [national] government."

National Standards and Testing

In 1983, the neo-liberal government (in line with its "subsidiary" normative role) did introduce nationwide testing of fourth and eighth grade pupils. "A good idea — chalk up one point for them," longtime Chilean educator and critic of the free-market policies Ivan Nuñez told us.[34] The results, however, were far from good. Not surprisingly, they repeatedly revealed a considerable gap in test score averages between, on one hand, the municipal public and subsidized private schools and, on the other, the private tuition-charging schools.

The average results for the municipal schools barely reached 50 percent of the established norms. For the subsidized private schools, scores were only two or three points higher. More revealing was how considerably higher were the scores for richer neighborhoods' municipalized public schools and the subsidized private schools on the one hand and those for their counterparts in the poor neighborhoods.[35]

Interestingly, over the period since the changes, only in the well-off municipality of Providencia has the number of students attending the public schools increased as a portion of students in all schools in the municipality.[36]

For many young people, the national university aptitude exam is a major stumbling block to admission to a public university or to one of the reputable private universities. By far, most of those who do score satisfactorily are products of the better-funded schools — be they municipal, subsidized private or private.

Not only do the financially better-off students go to the better-off primary and secondary schools, but their families can afford to buy extra preparation for the national aptitude examination. These students during their final year of high school enroll in a "pre-university" on the side, which is far from inexpensive. And those who don't do well on the exam the first time and have the money to do so often put in an extra year of pre-university training and try again. For those who are rich but dumb — or as the head of one private university put it to us, "Chile's Dan Quayles" — the new private universities are a godsend since most require low minimum scores.

Buying In

When the schooling privatization thrust was decreed, a spate of entrepreneurs did respond to the call of the Chicago Boys to jump into the school business, often buying up dilapidated mansions and converting them into barebones schools. At the time it took only a small investment, and credit was easy. The government's per-pupil payment (based on the Ministry of Education's average expenditure for a pupil at each grade level in 1980 plus 10 percent adjusted for inflation) was generous enough that it looked like the ventures could hardly fail to make money, especially since teachers could be hired cheaply and by the hour. After the 1982 economic collapse, however, the government suspended the adjustments in the per-student payment in accordance with the consumer price index,[37] and bank credit tightened drastically. School entrepreneurs cut every corner they could, especially squeezing teachers' pay (made easier because collective bargaining was outlawed in schools that received more than 50 percent of their budget from government subsidies). A number of schools failed — one (Liceo Cervantes) had 5,000 students and failed in the middle of the school year, leaving the municipality with little choice but to take it over. By 1990, over 80 schools had fallen into the hands of creditor banks that reportedly were pressuring the new civilian government to take them over,[38] and newspapers advertised schools for sale. The principal of a private subsidized primary and secondary school, known for admitting students of parents undergoing political persecution or who themselves were expelled because of activism from municipal schools, claimed he needed to draw upon his inheritance to support the fairly shabby school. "The Chicago Boys have made education into a business. But given the size of the government subsidies plus the tuition most parents can afford, it doesn't really pay the dividends, and therefore education has become anemic. Only with rich kids can you make schooling a paying business."[39]

The fact that many have deserted the municipal schools to attend the government-subsidized private schools does not prove that they are better schools, as the free-market promoters like to claim. Some educational researchers counter that these new schools capitalize on the good name the traditional private schools have with many parents. Moreover, they argue, many school entrepreneurs advertise heavily and, through this means and others not related to quality, have been more successful at attracting students.[40]

Free-marketeers assert that if the government's presence in education is diminished the private sector will bridge the gap. Lavín and Larraín make much of this, citing a couple examples such as the (privatized) telephone company helping to fund a school in a poor neighborhood ("the Alejandro Graham Bell School"). But a 1990 survey of the schools in the municipalities in greater Santiago found only a few cases of business support. Some administrators reported that overall there was even less business support since municipalization because now business people think the schools get a lot of resources.[41]

The Results

Since the shrinking of the government's role in education, average scores on standardized tests in grade schools have declined. Also the percentage of children of grade-school age enrolled in school has notably dropped. This is new for Chile: before the "reforms" all children, with few exceptions, were enrolled in grade school. By 1986, coverage had fallen to 93 percent, and by 1987, to 85 percent.[42] The decline in coverage has been almost entirely in the poorer municipalities.[43]

Over the same period the grade school drop-out rate has increased. In 1982, as the changes were underway, it was 2.8 percent; by 1985, it was 8.6 percent. Again, the increasing problem was centered on impoverished neighborhoods like La Pintana, Cerro Navia, Pudahuel, and La Granja, where the rate had risen to over 10 percent.[44]

As for high school, there seems to be a similar pattern, especially since 1985, although high school coverage has never been as complete as that of grade school. The high school drop-out rate is no doubt lower than the grade-school rate partly because many who might be likely to drop out never start high school in the first place. Moreover, it is more difficult to define the high-school age population (some in the 15 to 19 year range, for instance, might still be in primary school and some others might well have completed high school). Nevertheless, it is estimated that by 1987 coverage had fallen to 56 percent[45] — low for Chile. Between 1982 and 1985, very tough years economically for most Chileans, the high school drop-out rate jumped 50 percent.

The percentage of young people between the ages of 18 and 24 enrolled in higher education *of any sort* declined from 10.93 percent in 1974 to 9.14 percent in 1987.[46] Over this same period, the number of university-aged youths increased by almost 400,000, but the number of students enrolled in universities, including the new private ones not receiving public funds, fell by 17,000.[47]

Sociologist Clarisa Hardy cautions that these signs of educational decline should be attributed not only to the cutbacks in public resources for primary and secondary schooling[48] but also to the overall economic policies that have hit poorer classes hard, making staying in school difficult (and irrelevant for immediate survival needs), even for young children.[49]

Several former university students told us how they had to drop out for financial reasons. Rosa, from a lower middle-class family, passed the national university aptitude exam with flying colors and so much wanted to go to the university that, in addition to going further into debt, her family sold off much of their furniture. "Our house was bare," she recalled, "but at least I was in the University of Chile." Nonetheless, after a year of struggling, she and her family just couldn't keep up with the tuition payments, and Rosa had to withdraw.

So what about those statistics cited at the beginning of this chapter on increased school enrollment and longer schooling that the Pinochet government liked to point to as indicators of success?

There has been a considerable growth in the number of children enrolled in pre-school. But the percentage of children and adolescents beyond pre-school age in school in 1973 and the percentage in 1986 is virtually identical (53 percent). Given the historic and nearly worldwide tendency for this percentage to expand, not to progress is to go backward. Enrollment has also declined, as already indicated, in primary schools and, within secondary education, in vocational schools. It is precisely primary and vocational schooling that are the most significant to low-income families.

Statistics such as the *average* number of years in school mask the real differences within a population increasingly economically polarized. The average number of years of schooling of the residents of 20 of the 34 municipalities in the Santiago region is below the regional average. Among these municipalities are the poorest — La Pintana, Huechuraba, Cerro Navia, Pudahuel, Peñalolen, Lo Espejo and San Ramon — in which number of years of schooling averages only between 5 and 7 years. By contrast, in well-to-do communities like Providencia, Vitacura, La Reina and Las Condes, the average number of years in school for residents over fifteen years old ranges from 10 to 11 years.[50]

Making education a profit-oriented business and no longer a service to the community has meant that rural areas are increasingly neglected. Rural municipalities generally lack resources, and there are few subsidized private schools in the rural areas. Educational entrepreneurs in their drive for profits need the "economies of scale" available only in cities.

Local Control?

Municipalization might hold the potential for local control and relevance in education, but that potential certainly could not be realized in Chile's authoritarian political context.

General Pinochet appointed every single mayor in the nation. Some teachers said they worked in subsidized private schools despite often even lower pay than in municipal schools because in the municipal schools they would have to join the political party supporting the dictatorship. "Participation" has been so non-existent that administrators in several municipal schools we visited complained that the mayors and their staffs are not required to give them (and apparently have not) an accounting of how the government per-student payments are spent. These same administrators did say, however, that in general there was less red tape in their lives since municipalization.

If Chile really does democratize in the future, there will be the opportunity to see how the "local control" potential in municipalization might be realized. Even then, as we have seen, local participation and control will be hollow without first addressing the inequalities in financial resources for education among the different municipalities.

Degrees for Sale

Reflecting the Chicago Boys' bent for imposing "user-fees," public universities now not only charge hefty tuition fees but the fees vary according to calculations of the cost of teaching a particular course of studies (*carreras*). Different undergraduate majors therefore come with different price tags. In 1988, for example, at the University of Chile "cheap" degrees in fields such as teaching ran a little more than the equivalent of 14 monthly minimum wages for a year's tuition. Somewhat more expensive were journalism and law which cost the equivalent of 18 monthly minimum wages and engineering the equivalent of 19 for a year's tuition. At the Catholic University, the other prestigious publicly subsidized university, tuition fees for a year in medical school in 1989 were the equivalent of 24 monthly minimum wages. For the families of an estimated 90 percent of the students in public universities, such fees (not to mention all the other costs of going to school) posed a tremendous challenge.

Private Universities

For those who can afford them, the private universities offer a new educational option. The system got off to a slow start. Only one university was founded in 1982 and only two more in 1983. More were planned but never got off the drawing boards during the free market's economic debacle in the early '80s. In line with the free-market model, per-student payments were to "follow" the best students to whatever university they chose, private as well as public. With the government's fiscal crisis, however, this indirect government financing was restricted to universities existing prior to the reform. Moreover, students at private universities were declared ineligible for government loans.

Nevertheless, starting in the late 1980s, after some recovery from the depths of the recession, private universities mushroomed. *El Mercurio*, in a gushing January 1990 article titled "Utopia on the March," reported 25 private universities.[51]

The business strategy of these first new private universities set the pattern for the industry. The age-old formula for success: charge as much as the market will bear and cut costs to the bone. Accordingly, the fees at the private universities run high, much steeper than even the increased ones at the traditional universities.[52] Many private universities, however, have had to reduce their fees because of difficulty in filling classrooms and therefore have concentrated on holding down costs. They offer only a limited number of undergraduate degrees (*carreras*)[53] for which there is considerable student demand and that are inexpensive to teach because they require only a minimal investment in facilities and equipment — "chalk-and-blackboard" majors. The private universities thus typically offer law, accounting, business economics, psychology, and journalism. No majors that are expensive to teach — for example, biology and medicine — are offered for they could hardly be profitable (in contrast each public university is required by law to offer some of these costly courses of study).

For the same reason, none of the private universities carries out any basic research, according to a 1989 study of private higher education.[54] Teaching tuition-paying students is what pays, not research. Forget about serious libraries and laboratories.

The Chicago Boys like to point out that by 1990 the private universities had 55 percent of university enrollment but spent only 42 percent of the combined budget of all universities.[55] But, as we have seen, boasting of the private sector's "efficiency" ignores the scant investment in facilities in many of the new private universities and the real ways the public universities subsidize the private universities.

The private universities cater to anyone who has or can borrow the money to pay. Academic entrance requirements are "minimal."[56] Most of them also tend to offer those majors likely to appeal to the higher-income students such as business administration since they are the ones who can pay.

Not that every private university student is rich, as we learned with the experience of Rosa. Two students we interviewed scored high enough in the national aptitude exam to enter a public university but only one located in the provincial town of Iquique. Even though the monthly tuition of 33,000 pesos was less than the 45,000 pesos at a typical private university in Santiago, Iquique wound up costing them more because the cost of food is higher there and they had no relatives there to live with (not to mention how boring they found provincial life) so they transferred to a private university back home in Santiago.

Perhaps the kindest thing one can say about the quality of the private universities is that it is mixed. The respected authority on Chilean higher education, José Brunner has estimated that out of the 43 private universities in 1990 only five have the potential to be good universities.[57] In visiting several private universities we found that the facilities varied greatly, from old houses downtown converted into basic classrooms to new buildings on something of small campuses. The facilities are, however, generally better than those of the University of Chile — except, as already noted, when it comes to the laboratories, libraries, and the like that the public universities inherited.

Professional Institutes and Centers for Technical Training

Many academics charge that the quality of all too many of Chile's universities — as well as professional institutes and centers for technical training — is scandalously low and have proposed greater government control. But proponents of the free-market model argue that, in the words of a report commissioned by the World Bank, "This issue is best left to parents and students, who would assess the value of what is offered and choose accordingly."[58] In the end, thanks to students' and their parents' market choices, the best will float to the surface. Meanwhile, *caveat emptor*.[59]

Parents and students are targets of heavy advertising campaigns, which serve as the principal source of "information" about the schools. Higher education has become almost like Coca-Cola, with ads seemingly everywhere for this or that institute or center, complete with pictures and stories of successful graduates. Victor Lorca Gallado, a former accountant and now the owner and president of ESANE, a center for technical training with 1,200 students, told us that his yearly advertising budget exceeds what he pays his entire teaching and administrative staff in three months. One professional institute regularly took out expensive full-page ads in *El Mercurio* before going bankrupt.

Tuition and other charges at the professional institutes vary greatly depending upon, among other things, the socioeconomic status of their clientele. In the more fashionable neighborhoods there are professional institutes marketing to upper-income young women certificates in, for example, public relations, that charge even more than the Catholic University for a medical degree. The least expensive are the few public ones that, as part of the changes, were spun off from the public universities. But professional institutes don't so much charge lower tuition than the universities — a month's tuition even at the less expensive ones runs somewhat more than a month's minimum wage — but their programs are one year shorter than five-year university programs and thus total tuition, and therefore, for most students, total indebtedness is somewhat less.

The centers for technical training, receiving no government financial support and spending heavily on advertising to lure students, yet seeking to turn a profit, are by no means inexpensive.

But while tuition fees vary greatly (depending on the prestige of the school, for instance) they generally do charge less than many professional institutes and, more significantly, their programs are only of two years' duration. (The bright young woman Rosa who had to drop out of university was, when we met her, unhappily enrolled at a center that is part of a small chain, and was studying to become a bilingual secretary.) In any case, a certificate from a center for technical training is a world apart from what most people mean by a higher education degree and is, as we will see, often of questionable value on the job market. As some might argue, such is the logic of the entire free-market system: you get what you (can) pay for.

The "reforms" in higher education relinquished the development of post-secondary technical education to market forces, even more thoroughly than with the universities. Sociologists Pilar Vergara and Teresa Rodriguez view the centers for technical training as "a paradigmatic expression of an educational system organized according to the laws of the competitive marketplace."[60] Their study of the centers concludes that the unregulated competitive marketplace is not good at regulating the quality of the centers.[61] They found most of the centers poorly equipped, often teaching outdated skills. According to this study, a center near the place we stayed in downtown Santiago was hardly atypical. Walking by in the evening, we'd sometimes peer into the windows of drab classrooms to see (at first with some measure of disbelief) 30 or so people, mainly young women, banging away on old Royal and Remington typewriters — and this in a country where computers in offices have become commonplace, as Joaquin Lavín revels in reporting.

Official figures exaggerate the qualifications of teachers in the centers, Vergara and Rodriguez concluded, even though those figures reveal that 28 percent lack a college degree. Teachers are poorly paid, most contracted on an hourly basis with no fringe benefits. Underpaid teachers often have to hold down jobs in offices or elsewhere, invariably resulting in high absenteeism, lots of lost class time through late arrivals, excessive rates of substitute teachers and little teacher contact with the students outside the classroom. Vergara and Rodriguez also found that most of the centers are unconnected with the productive world and therefore their programs are rarely based on any serious analysis of what is needed on the job market.[62] In the absence of any system of accreditation, the content of the curriculum is often done "in an intuitive manner."[63] Not surprisingly, the certificates reportedly are not taken very seriously on the job market. Once again, the most high-priced centers attended by students from well-off families are an exception.[64] Many students from the run-of-the-mill centers have to put up with dead-end jobs that have few formal qualifications making it hard to justify the years of efforts and sacrifices, sometimes enormous, expended by these students and their families. For these reasons and many more they detail, Vergara and Rodriguez conclude that the market is not capable in itself of fostering quality in these educational institutions.[65]

The institutes and centers nevertheless *can* be highly profitable.[66] In our interview with Victor Lorca, the owner and president of ESANE, in his ostentatious, rococo office, he frankly admitted that ESANE admits anyone who applies. "The only qualification is you have to pay." Indeed why would a center turn down any would-be paying customer? Even drop-outs still must pay through the end of the term. (The drop-out rate in the technical training centers, especially in the first semester, is notoriously high, running even as high as 50 percent in some fields such as computer studies.[67])

Vergara and Rodriguez found that the fact that the management of most of the institutes and centers is in the hands of "entrepreneur-educators" has many negative consequences which "fall directly on the students."[68] Many times they found entrepreneurs not familiar with educational problems and who, in the absence of effective procedures for accreditation and supervision, "do not hesitate to sacrifice pedagogical effectiveness to the goal of maximizing short-term profits."[69] They also found administrators who did know something about education but were poor administrators. As a consequence, widespread serious administrative and financial problems have brought on drastic cutbacks and a resulting deterioration in educational quality, even the closing down of institutions (leaving the students and their families holding the bag).

Lack of certification makes it difficult or impossible in some cases for students to transfer from one institute or center without starting all over again. In this virtually unregulated educational industry students are often trapped in an institute or center once signed up and unable to transfer if dissatisfied — captive customers. This in practice gravely undermines the supposed advantage of the free-market system, namely, that competition among sellers to attract buyers fosters excellence.[70]

The Free Market and the Job Market

Throughout the market-driven higher education system there is an absence of planning, most notably of coordinating what students major in and the likely job market. University journalism studies is but one example. By the 1990s, roughly one thousand students a year were starting to graduate with degrees in journalism. Such a high number is directly attributable to the free-market educational policies of the 1980s: to a great extent journalism has become popular because it is a "cheap" degree since most of the required courses are "chalk-and-blackboard." Yet where will the jobs come from? Of the about two thousand journalists in Chile in 1990, 400 were unemployed.[71]

The nub of neo-liberal theory is that the market freed from public intervention itself will correct such a situation: in due course enough people will find out that no one is hiring journalism graduates and therefore incoming students will choose other careers, even if the schooling costs more. But "in due course" how many lives will have been seriously harmed by learning "the hard way"?

In their study of non-university higher education, Vergara and Rodriguez found the job market already saturated for what was being offered for training for work in the commerce and service sector (as explained, those are the bulk of the careers offered).[72] They also found widespread student naiveté about future employment prospects in the field they had chosen to study. Most seemed confident that with their degree in hand and a little effort they would find a position. "It is easy to perceive in the lack of realism in the students' projections the influence of the distorted images projected by the advertising done by the institutes."[73]

The other side of the coin is that the market-driven educational system doesn't tend to stimulate the development of specialties and degree-holders in those fields that, although they are needed by the country, are not good business for the educational institutions. This is the case of most fields of study oriented toward productive activities because the large investments needed for facilities and equipment exceed what is likely to be able to be financed by private and, in many cases, for-profit institutions whose revenues come strictly from enrolled students.[74]

Free-market policies have fostered educational institutions that inculcate the values that drive the market-run society. A commercial mentality has pervaded higher education. Presidents of educational institutions are more entrepreneurs than educators, was a comment we often heard. Most students have to go heavily into debt and, therefore, they choose to study things that they believe will help them pay back their loans. A broad humanistic education, once widely accessible, now is a luxury only for the rich.

Education for Democratization

Educational fees that reflect actual costs — "real tuition fees," as the Chicago Boys sometimes call them — might not be such a bad thing, many people might think, if needy qualified students can avail themselves of scholarships. That way those who can afford to pay will not drain public resources that can be used for other social needs. But in 1980 — ironically at the height of the "Chilean miracle" — the Chicago Boys eliminated scholarships. Ivan Garcia, a teacher we met when visiting high schools, told us that in 1978, after three years of catch-as-catch-can jobs to try (unsuccessfully) to scrape together the money to enter the university, he finally won a scholarship for what he thought was his "big chance." But in 1980 when all scholarships were abruptly terminated, he had no choice but to drop out or apply for a government student loan. He got a loan which is indexed for inflation and charges interest. Repayment started two years after graduation, and now more than a third of his scant earnings as a teacher goes toward paying off his student loan.[75]

Students enrolled in professional institutes (except the few public ones) and centers for technical training find that the government offers them no assistance, even in the form of loans. Those with financial needs, therefore, might well find the lower fees at the centers even more out of reach than the higher ones at public universities offering government-financed loans.

As with primary and secondary education, the claim that thanks to free-market privatization young Chileans and their families now enjoy an array of higher educational choices proves to be a mirage visible only from certain neighborhoods. In the poor neighborhoods comprising more than half the population of Santiago, only 2 percent of those over 24 years of age have ever set foot in any sort of institution of higher education, while in the "other Santiago" the percentage is at least ten times higher and in its wealthiest neighborhoods much higher still.[76] If we look only at university enrollment, the percentage of students coming from working-class households has appreciably declined since the imposition of free-market policies.[77]

For the neo-liberals, it is not an appropriate role for government to assist citizens aspiring to higher education to obtain it. (That was made abundantly clear with the neo-liberal government's refusal to subsidize or even provide student loans for non-university higher education.) In their mind it is enough that government guarantee a minimal level of education for all and that the higher-education marketplace function freely and competitively. The rest depends on the talents and efforts of the individual.

From the viewpoint of the champions of the free-market model, the previous long-standing "socialistic" model of a society striving to enable all who desire more than a minimal education to obtain it is to put fancy notions into the heads of the poor. In the words of the Chilean government's Social Report 1984-1985: "Values that correspond to models of unattainable lives should be not be fomented among the poorer sectors of society."[78]

Indeed higher education in free-market Chile no longer reduces social and economic inequalities by incorporating ever more young people from the poorer urban and rural classes. It no longer mixes together people of different classes in their most formative years but accentuates the differences by segregating them into a hierarchy of different classes of schooling. Perhaps most fundamentally it teaches those who haven't the capacity to pay for an education that is "worth something" that they have only themselves (and their families) to blame if they fail on the job market. What has been radically undermined, just as on the primary and secondary levels, is higher education's tremendous potential to democratize a society.

10

Low-Income Housing and the Mortgage Crisis

In a 1977 presidential address, Pinochet expounded on his administration's free-market housing policies:

The basic principle that sustains the action of the government in housing policy is that a house is a right that is acquired with effort and the savings of the family.... It is no longer a gift of the government, the product of the sacrifice of many for the benefit of a few privileged.... It is not the role of the government to construct houses, assign them, or administer a loan portfolio. Only when it is proven that the established channels are not fulfilling exactly their duties — and while those distortions are corrected — should the government assume such responsibilities in a subsidiary fashion.[1]

When this principle was incorporated into the 1980 constitution, it was clarified by calling housing a "good" instead of a "right."[2] This principle was a sharp departure from the philosophy of the Christian Democrat and Popular Unity governments.

In Santiago's *poblaciones*, the sprawling shantytowns which stretch out on the western side of the city, area residents (who are called and refer to themselves as *pobladores*) are systematically excluded from the formal markets for jobs, land, credit and housing. For these Chileans as well as their counterparts in regional cities and in rural areas, the difficulty of buying or renting their own homes often overshadows all other battles in their daily struggle to survive. At the same time, the quiet facades of middle-class houses in Chile often belie problems of serious overcrowding and impossible mortgages.

The creation of enough housing for low-income citizens is problematic even in most developed nations. The private sector has little incentive to build for or lend to poor people. In much of the Third World, where people living in poverty often make up the majority, the poor have acquired housing through some combination of individual initiative and governmental assistance.

Before

The process of urbanization has gone hand in hand with industrialization in Chile since at least the 1920s. Santiago stands at the center of Chile's most temperate and fertile valleys. By 1990, after decades of rural migration, the majority of Chileans lived in urban areas — forty percent of all Chileans in the metropolitan area of Santiago.

To accommodate growing urban housing needs in the 1950s, the government created tax exemptions on the construction of houses below a certain value. A system of savings and loan associations helped provide credit and stimulate construction for the emerging middle classes, and workers' pension funds were used as sources of low-interest, long-term loans for the formally employed working class. Many of the country's poorest were still left out.

During the course of the reformist project of the Christian Democratic administration of Eduardo Frei (1964-70) and the radical program of Salvador Allende (1971-73), housing for the poor became a priority as lower income groups, through their organizations and the electoral process, had pressured the government to incorporate them into housing projects. As with social spending in general, public resources devoted to housing increased significantly.

In the face of an estimated deficit of 420,000 houses, the Frei administration designed an ambitious program to build 360,000 houses over six years, the majority for low-income citizens. Construction and credit lines were managed directly by government agencies.[3] This ambitious goal proved overly so and was modified over the course of the Frei administration. The size of the government-built houses was reduced, and through a controversial emergency program some poor families were given vacant lots. Such modifications assumed that poor people would gradually increase the size of their houses with their own labor and a willingness by future governments to continue to provide credit and construction materials.[4] During the six-year Frei administration, an average of 40,000 units were built each year (over half by the government) and a total of 100,000 lots assigned.[5]

In much of Latin America poor people excluded by poverty and inequalities from access to housing have taken matters into their own hands by organizing land occupations. Governments across the political spectrum in Chile and elsewhere in the third world have been forced to come to terms with such initiatives by accepting their existence. They have provided support and services that have helped to normalize the precarious situation of squatters and provided alternative housing. Often invasions have taken place on government land or land that the government purchases after the occupation.

In Chile such land occupations became common occurrences as early as 1957 and accelerated rapidly in the late 1960s as many urban poor living in inner-city tenements and shanties became frustrated by the pace and middle-class bias of government housing programs. Their attempts were encouraged by leftist political parties and church-based groups. In the months of political leniency before the election of 1970, land invasions reached a crescendo. Over 300,000 squatters lived on these sites, called *campamentos*, when Allende took office.[6]

The Popular Unity coalition saw its housing program as a fundamental part of a broader transformation of society; they rejected minimal solutions such as providing lots and assigned government agencies primary responsibility for constructing houses for the poor and providing loans with which to buy them.[7] During the emergency program of 1971 over 89,000 houses were constructed, 85 percent by the public sector.[8] Over the three years of the Allende administration an average of 52,000 houses were constructed annually.

A Divided City: The Deregulation of Santiago

The September coup of 1973 ended almost a decade of sustained government efforts aimed at eliminating historical housing deficits. Repression abruptly halted land occupations, closing off what had become a tacitly accepted outlet for urgent housing demands. Repression of neighborhood organizations in the *campamentos* and other poor areas, even those concerned simply with feeding children, was brutal and systematic.

As the Chicago Boys consolidated power within the military regime, they implemented a series of decrees which put private property at the center of urban and housing policy. They argued that land was not a scarce resource, but that "scarcity" was created artificially by restrictions on land sales and use. As a result, taxes on unimproved lots and real estate sales were lowered or abolished, taxes on capital gains eliminated, restrictions on land use were greatly reduced, public land was sold off and the area of greater Santiago zoned for urbanization was greatly expanded.

Free-marketeers, backed by real estate moguls, argued that such expansion and deregulation would lower the costs of land and housing. This coincided with the period of easy international credit, which, as discussed earlier, rewarded speculative investment in real estate and commerce rather than encouraging productive enterprise. Taxes on the sale of urban property were reduced and property assessments that were made at abysmally low levels during the 1975 recession were never reassessed during the entire Pinochet period.[9]

Instead of lowering housing costs, the result of these reforms was that land prices and therefore costs rose much faster than they had when land use had been regulated. In some upper-class areas they rose as much as 100 percent annually in real terms during the period 1976-1981.[10] One United Nations official in Santiago, for example, purchased a housing lot in the late 1970s for $2 a square meter in what became the exclusive neighborhood of Dehesa. In 1990 the plot was valued at $70 a square meter. Land prices in less desirable areas rose less dramatically but enough to raise the price of even the most basic housing.

At the same time that these market criteria were implemented in real estate, a series of interventions by the government in Santiago entrenched a geographical separation of classes unparalleled in Latin American metropolises.[11]

During the deregulation of real estate markets and the municipalization of most services, the military government divided greater Santiago into thirty-two municipalities (from the previous sixteen). Richer communities were separated from their poorer neighbors. By redrawing the city to create units of "social homogeneity," the government argued it would be able to better "focus" public services where they were most needed, since otherwise the poor became hidden among wealthier groups.[12] The Santiago community of Nuñoa, for example, was divided up into three separate municipalities of low, middle and upper income groups.

The results were quite different from the stated intention. Most public services became the responsibility of each municipality, which had to rely primarily on its own tax base for resources. In effect, the newly independent city governments of the poorest areas of Santiago were allowed to administer their own poverty.

The discrepancies between public spending for rich and poor became even more pronounced. The wealthiest municipality of Providencia spent 27 times more per capita between 1980 and 1984 on public services and investment than the municipality of La Pintana, one of the poorest.[13] Even national public investment, which has greater redistributive possibilities, was concentrated in wealthier municipalities. The three wealthiest municipalities in Santiago (Las Condes, Providencia, and La Reina) received over 58 percent of the total outlays by the Ministry of Public Works between 1982-1984, even though they contained only 10 percent of the population of Santiago.[14]

Eradicating the Poor

A final step that further segregated Santiago's rich and poor was the program of "eradications," or forced relocations, implemented in Santiago from 1979 to 1984. The *campamentos* that had formed under the Frei and Allende governments had created pockets of squatter settlements even in the midst of wealthy eastern municipalities. Starting in 1979 the Pinochet government improved the housing situation and legal status of some of these *campamentos* and relocated others. The primary criterion for deciding which "black spots" should be improved and which "eradicated" was land value: *campamentos* near the city center or well-to-do municipalities to the east were relocated. Over 30,000 families, or 150,000 people were moved from *campamentos* to minimal housing units (less than 50 square meters in size) on the distant southwest edge of greater Santiago.

When *campamentos* were eradicated, the residents were divided up into several groups and dispatched to live in different municipalities of the city, destroying important informal networks of extended families and friends that had made survival easier. Perhaps more importantly, through forced relocations the government managed to fragment the very vital popular organizations that had taken root in the *campamentos*. Ties of community and solidarity that had been forged with the land invasions, consolidated during the mobilizations of the Popular Unity coalition, and revived with the protests of the early 1980s, were severed. The new neighborhoods of relocated families were founded on distrust of one's neighbor as well as of the government.

Twenty-two percent of eradicated families were sent to the municipality of La Pintana, ten miles from the center of Santiago and at least an hour and a half by a combination of buses. Created in the municipal reorganization of 1979, La Pintana saw its population increase by 77 percent from 1982 to 1986 (to 136,000).[15] Many residents were promised their new neighborhoods would have swimming pools and tennis courts. When they arrived, they found themselves with very basic houses, but little else.

La Pintana, as an undeniably poor community, supposedly was to benefit from the neo-liberal "focusing" of social services. By the late 1980s, this "planned" community had a total of 6 telephones (only three of which were public) for a population over 130,000, no post office, no library or public utilities office, no movie theater, no parks or green areas, and only one paved road.[16] When we visited La Pintana in 1990, one woman told us, "Forget about the pools and tennis courts — I'd be happy if my children could see a few trees!"

A 1987 university survey shows that eradicated families do value the houses they received (and for which they must make payments), but found their new communities to be lacking in jobs, schools, health care, and basic commercial needs.[17] The burden of providing public services for these groups passed from the wealthy municipalities where they had lived before, to already over-burdened municipalities that had no say in whether or not to accept the eradicated families. While land on the periphery was cheaper, studies show that providing basic services like electricity, water and sewage at such a distance can be 17 times more expensive than providing it in the central areas of Santiago.[18]

According to the same 1987 survey, only 26 percent of heads of households had regular work, and 35 percent were unemployed or on the government minimum employment program.[19] Those who had previously earned their livelihood by cleaning houses or providing services to higher-income groups near their *campamentos* now found themselves a long way from their sources of employment and hampered by unreliable and expensive transport (in 1988 daily transportation from La Pintana took up 26 percent of the minimum wage[20]). The residents of La Pintana cannot afford to employ each other or sell to each other. (In our walks around these neighborhoods, there was no sign of a corner store or a workshop, common enough sights in the more central *poblaciones*; the most sophisticated entrepreneurial project we saw made and sold popsicles.)

Many women live alone or with young children in La Pintana . Soon after arriving their husbands returned to areas where they knew they could count on relatives and find work. Many of their older children have also left to find work on the other side of the city. Young people who have stayed in La Pintana face all the dangers of their marginalization: unemployment, gang violence, drugs (primarily glue) and the despair reflected in a rising suicide rate. According to a respected survey, by 1987 over 12 percent of the families eradicated had left the houses they were assigned. Among those removed from *campamentos* in wealthy communities, the figure was 20 percent.[21]

Many La Pintana residents we met were relocated in 1979 from a *campamento* in the wealthy municipality of Las Condes. The eradicated *campamento* is now the site of Santiago's ritziest shopping mall and the first McDonald's.

Sociologist Ernesto Tironi likens the social structure of Santiago to that of South African apartheid, with municipalities like La Pintana constituting *de facto* townships. Indeed the spatial segregation of classes is such that Chileans of the "two Santiagos," rich and poor, modern and marginalized, rarely encounter each other.[22]

The Free Market in Housing

Since 1974 the reliance on the private sector to fill housing needs — in the face of continuous urbanization, deregulation of real estate, two deep recessions and widespread impoverishment — has resulted in severe crowding and shortages. Housing starts have not kept pace with population growth, much less shrunk the 400,000-plus housing deficit that existed when the armed forces seized power.[23]

The simple houses of the *poblaciones* often are home to two to four extra families. These *allegado* ("drop-in") families, often adult children of the owners of the house, live with their spouses and children one family to a bedroom, often three children to a bed. Within four walls they try to create nuclear family life, each family usually with its own TV and separate paraffin or gas stove, but the costs of such crowding in demoralization, promiscuity, violence and family disintegration are high. Of course, such conditions have a psychological effect not only on the "*allegado*" families, but their host families as well.

In 1990 approximately 180,000 families in Santiago were forced to live as *allegados*, and over 60 percent of these families were among the poorest 40 percent of Chileans.[24] A 1985 survey of 28 poor neighborhoods in Santiago found that 53 percent of households shared space with additional families or individuals, and 41 percent had 3 or more people per bedroom.[25] In the past such pressures led families to take on the risks involved in land seizures; under military repression and free-market policies, such pressures simply led to despair.

Under the tutelage of the Chicago Boys, Pinochet's government shut down most agencies that were directly involved in constructing housing. Government programs produced only 30,000 housing units during the period from 1976 to 1980.[26] With construction left to the private sector, the total number of houses built in the mid-1970s plummeted, dropping in 1975 to a level not seen since the 1950s. According to the economist José Pablo Arellano, the acute shortage of housing today has its origins in the dismal pace of construction in the mid-1970s.[27] By 1980, housing construction partially recovered, fueled by easy foreign credit, an over-valued peso and a national spending binge. Even so, the private sector built houses that assured profits, that is, homes for the well-off. In 1979 over 58 percent of houses built in Santiago were located in the upscale eastern municipalities, where only 12 percent of the metropolitan population lived.[28]

By 1990, over 60 percent of Chilean families were unable to satisfy their housing needs on the market. They had little recourse but to turn to the government for some type of aid.[29] But the Chicago Boys had done away with the public and non-profit financial institutions that once helped poor working and middle class Chileans to aspire to become home-owners. The System of Savings and Loan Institutions (SINAP) collapsed in 1977 in the wake of banking deregulation, and in 1980 the pension system, which had once offered low-interest long-term loans to workers, was privatized. As we've said already, private lending went more to speculative investments than to affordable housing. Moreover, mortgage rates skyrocketed so that many of Chile's newly impoverished middle classes, as well as the poor, were unable to enter the housing market without government aid.[30]

As a result, a greater number of Chileans have had to compete for diminished public funding. Public spending in housing and urban development fell 42 percent in 1975 from the previous year and only in 1988 did it recover to the levels of the early 1970s.[31]

A Reluctant Subsidiary Role

Neo-liberal officials argued that the key to good housing policies, as with other social programs, was to spend less but target assistance at the poorest families. They argued that in the past too much of public spending on housing had gone to support middle-class needs.[32]

The core of the Pinochet government's housing program was the provision of a limited number of one-time housing vouchers granted at the time of purchase, as opposed to the ongoing indirect subsidies that previous governments had provided through subsidized low interest rates. Two types of voucher programs were set up: the first, a subsidy of 75 percent of the cost of a "basic" house, aimed at poorer families; the second, a subsidy aimed at the lower middle classes to cover from 25 to 75 percent of the initial cost of a house, the percentage decreasing the higher the value of the home. Free-market advocates argued that vouchers would allow recipients to buy a home on the regular housing market, giving them a greater choice than previous programs of direct government construction had, and strengthen the private construction industry.

Poor families applying for a basic government voucher are judged according to three criteria: social situation (a combination of a number of poverty indicators), family size, and a certain minimum amount of savings. This last criterion is a catch-22 whereby the poorest are disqualified from programs supposedly designed for them. Numerous families living as drop-ins have, over the course of years, been unable to save the required minimum to qualify, with emergencies often wiping out what they had been able to put aside. Most of those who do meet the savings criterion are not the poorest.[33]

During the first years of the program of vouchers for basic housing (1979-81), the poorest third of the population received less than 24 percent of the assigned public resources, while the middle third of income earners captured 64 percent of public housing resources.[34] From 1980 to 1982 over 90 percent of the variable vouchers went to the 40 percent of the population with the highest incomes.[35] Many middle-class Chileans were unable to get loans on the private market, and so were forced to apply for subsidies aimed at poorer families. Middle-class families maneuvered around limits on the housing value by purchasing an unfinished house that they would immediately expand.[36]

In 1983 the government granted a 13 percent subsidy on the sale of 14,000 high-priced homes (with an average value of $35,000) that the private sector could not sell on its own in the aftermath of the economic crash.[37] Chileans in the highest 10 percent income bracket captured 67 percent of the total housing subsidies granted in Santiago in that year.[38]

Targeting later improved, partly due to a lowering of the savings requirement. Even so, there remained some "seepage" of resources beyond the targeted groups. In 1985, of the spending targeted for housing for the poor, the poorest 30 percent of the population received 43 percent of resources, while the middle 40 percent captured 49 percent.[39]

The Reluctant Private Sector

Even when vouchers ended up in the hands of poorer families, there was no guarantee that they could take their certificates to the private sector and find affordable housing. On average, over 60 percent of recipients were unable to find housing within a year of receipt of the subsidy. Many of them had to wait several years, forcing the government to repeatedly grant extensions on vouchers.[40] The basic government program assumed a subsidy of 75 percent of the cost of a house with a maximum value of $4000, a type of house that private construction companies have no interest in building on their own. After 1982 the government had to organize the construction of these basic units by contracting directly with construction companies. Only with such contracts has the private sector been willing to build thousands of identical basic units to which families are assigned. This effectively eliminated the element of recipients' choice.

In addition, the size of the basic house these companies built declined from an average of 54 square meters in 1978 (which compares favorably to houses built by previous governments), to only 31 square meters in 1983.[41] Many construction companies reduced costs by shrinking lot-size and building units as small as 28 square meters in two-story apartment buildings that are impossible for owners to expand. Moreover, those who received individual houses could not count on additional technical or financial support to facilitate later expansion.[42]

To make matters worse, these houses have been built without related investments in parks, schools and other basic infrastructure. "Before there were integral housing solutions. Health clinics, social centers and market areas were all planned. Part of the Ministry of Housing was in charge of this aspect,"[43] notes Chilean architect Joan McDonald.

While private companies might compete to lower the price of construction, much of the benefit was lost by their tendency to bid up the price of land, a situation that would not occur if the government were purchasing land for low-income housing directly, or had not sold off most public land in the first place. In the aftermath of a sweeping deregulation of land prices and use, a portion of housing subsidies simply went to enrich land speculators.[44]

Much of the basic low-income housing is on the cheapest land on the outskirts of the metropolitan area. For many, such exile is not necessarily preferable to having no house at all: of 100 *allegado* families in the municipality of La Florida who were offered subsidized housing in 1990 in the far-away and notorious municipality of La Pintana, only two families accepted.[45]

An official who has been in the housing ministry since the 1960s (who insisted on anonymity) told us that private construction companies were proving more and more reluctant to build basic housing because of price ceilings, levels which he was sure would be adequate if the government were to build basic housing itself. Unfortunately, he said, such an alternative could not even be broached in the neo-liberal ideological climate.

The private financial sector did not respond as the Chicago Boys had predicted to provide the loans necessary to complement the cost of housing not covered by the government vouchers and personal savings. Long-term loans for the small amounts necessary to complement the subsidies, often around $1000, are rare on the private credit market, particularly given the risks of lending to low-income groups. After 1982 the government began to bridge the gap by providing complementary loans in almost all of its subsidy programs, a role it had initially rejected. But poor families who qualify for vouchers have not always been able to count on complementary government loans, since they lack a steady income, or because the informal nature of their employment makes it difficult to document their income.[46]

This shift towards greater government responsibility resulted from the mounting housing deficit and the economic crash in 1982. Another factor was stepped-up opposition to the military regime that had its base in the protests in the *poblaciones*. In 1983 two large land invasions in which 8000 homeless families occupied land on the periphery of Santiago were the only successful land invasions during the Pinochet years.

The Numbers War

From 1980-1986, which covers the more interventionist phase of the free-market government, housing subsidized by the public sector averaged 35,000 units a year, which is indeed an improvement over the total of 30,000 units built under government programs over the period 1976-1980. With housing built in the nonsubsidized private sector, the average rises to 49,000 a year. But this was not sufficient even to freeze the housing deficit, which was growing by 80,000 houses a year.[47]

The Pinochet government presented Chile's housing situation to the world using a free-market measure, equating the number in need of housing with the number who could afford to buy. To reduce the housing deficit on paper, the Chicago Boys began to claim that it was equal to the number of people who applied for government subsidy programs (plus a margin of 10 percent), a formula which calculated the deficit at 420,000 houses in 1986 and kept it constant through 1989. In reality, many families cannot accumulate the required savings and handle the paperwork to apply for these programs, and so do not appear in these numbers.[48] In 1990 the Ministry of Housing of the newly elected Aylwin government acknowledged a quantitative deficit of 800,000 houses, and an additional qualitative deficit (substandard housing that needs to be replaced) of 300,000 houses. This means that 1.1 million families, or an unprecedented 39 percent of all Chilean families, lacked adequate housing.[49]

The Fear of Foreclosure

In the Chile of the Chicago Boys, one must struggle not only to obtain a house, but to hang on to it. Throughout the 1980s thousands of middle-class homeowners have slipped into default and risked or undergone evictions. In 1990 one of every three home mortgage holders in Chile was in default on payments.

In the wave of deregulation and privatization of banks that occurred after 1975, home mortgages held by the non-profit savings and loan associations and by pension funds were sold to private commercial banks. At that same time the banks sought to rewrite the mortgage loans so that they were denominated not in pesos but in Development Units (UFs), a banking unit whose value in pesos fluctuates daily according to inflation, which in an open economy is closely tied to the peso's exchange rate. Most Chileans favorably associated the UF with a system to protect savings from inflation implemented during the Frei administration, and had the added incentive of a one-time reduction in the remaining principal owed, so most willingly converted their mortgages to the UF type, while new borrowers were given no choice but to contract debts in UFs. Owing in UFs was not a problem so long as wage adjustments kept pace with inflation, as was much the case from 1977 to 1981.

During the boom years of 1979 to 1981, many middle and upper class Chileans had easy access to loans, although the private banks and financial institutions, controlled by a small group of domestic conglomerates with access to foreign loans, charged interest rates as high as 18 percent (plus an additional origination fee that often reached as high as 20 to 30 percent of the amount of the loan).[50] It was not uncommon for middle-class families to commit over 30 percent of their income to loan payments, and the banks, swimming in inexpensive dollars, were more than willing to allow them to take on such burdens. In effect, as the Chilean economist Jorge Scherman writes, "Debtors as well as lenders 'bet' on the success of the neo-liberal economic model, with hopes of future growth, bigger salaries, more and better jobs."[51]

In December of 1981 the peso began its slide from 39 to the dollar. By 1984 the peso had sunk to a 100 to the dollar, and by 1989 hovered around 320. Major financial conglomerates failed, bringing down with them two-thirds of the banks and the overdrawn elite with their imported luxury cars.

As we've seen, at the urging of the international financial institutions, the government (contradicting its professed free-market doctrines) intervened massively to prop up the private banks and a variety of corporate and wealthy individual debtors. But such relief was not forthcoming for small mortgage holders. To the contrary, in 1982 the government reduced the real value of the minimum wage and eliminated the right of organized workers to wage increases equal to inflation. In other words, after 1982 home mortgages in UFs were adjusted dramatically upward, reflecting steep peso devaluations and high inflation, yet family incomes were not. José Aylwin of the Chilean Commission of Human Rights in 1988 summarized the plight of many middle-class Chileans: "Debts contracted in UFs worked until the economic crisis of 1982. Then the cost of living continued rising, but wages were frozen or kept low and today debtors are in danger of losing their houses."[52]

Between 1981 and 1985, wages in general lost 15 percent of their real value, and by 1987 the purchasing power of the minimum wage had fallen to half that of 1981. The value of the UF rose 259 percent between 1981 and 1987.[53] As dentist Carlos Aguilar, president of the Chilean Federation of Home Mortgage Holders, explained to us, "This country has two currencies. We receive our paychecks in pesos, which keep losing their value, and we pay our debts in UFs, which by definition are inflation-proof."[54]

The differential between the rise of the value of debt payments and the drop in income levels since 1982 means that for many poor and middle-class households in Santiago, monthly mortgage payments now ran between 40 percent and more than a 100 percent of family income. A survey by the Chilean Federation of Home Mortgage Holders showed that most of its constituents were paying an average of 60 percent of their income for food alone.[55] The level of default among low-income families in debt to the government was very high (almost 50 percent). The level of default among those who borrowed from private banks was still a considerable 15 percent. As the size of the mortgage decreases, the level of defaults increase, indicating that those most affected were from the poor and middle classes.[56]

Resuscitated private banks proved less lenient with their debtors than the government had been with the banks themselves. Often, particularly with houses bought during the boom years, mortgage balances now exceed house values. Dr. Aguilar of the Federation of Home Mortgage Holders offered his situation as representative of many middle-class families: his own house, purchased in 1981, after nine years of mortgage payments had a balance of UFs valued at 9 million pesos, but the house was valued at only 5 million pesos.[57] Indeed, sometimes the debts reach three times the market value of the house.[58] And if a house is foreclosed by the banks, the debtor remains liable for the difference between the value of the house and that of the debt. During the 1980s, over 50,000 families lost their houses to the banks.

Only a stopgap government-sponsored refinancing program begun in 1983 kept many homeowners from being evicted. This relief program reduced the monthly payments of mortgage holders by extending the term of the loan, but this ultimately raised the total payments over the life of the loan. Effectively, they were enabled to meet their mortgage payments by borrowing more money. We were given the example of a family in the Santiago municipality of La Florida (known for its distinctly middle class make-up) that bought a house in 1982 with a loan of 1060 UFs. After four years of regular payments and the government-sponsored refinancing, the family owed 1067 UFs.[59] According to economist Jorge Scherman, this policy of debt relief by the Pinochet government was "the internal counterpart of what has been done with the Chilean foreign debt: postpone and burden future generations with commitments that are not payable."[60]

The tragedy of the middle-class debtor's plight came home to us one evening on the subway during rush hour after interviewing Jorge Aguilar, a small businessman and president of another mortgage holders' association affiliated with the Socialist Party.[61] After we heard him talk for hours in general terms about the causes of the mortgage crisis, we rode home on the subway with him, affording the opportunity to talk more informally. We asked why this issue meant so much to him. Aguilar lives in a modest house in La Florida, but the arrears on his mortgage became impossible for him to pay. Five days before the 1989 elections the police came in his absence and tried to dislodge him. As his neighbors organized to defend his house, Aguilar got the local candidate for congress to intervene with the police and his bank to delay the eviction. When pro-Pinochet candidates did badly in the election, the bank, Aguilar said, took it as a sign that it was time to renegotiate his loan on favorable terms. Even as he told us his story, the woman sitting across the aisle in the subway began to tell us of her own eviction less than a year before.

In the 1989 presidential election an independent conservative candidate, Francisco Errázuriz, a wealthy businessman and self-proclaimed "populist" from the "center-center," made the middle class rallying call for the elimination of the UF the crux of his campaign. Errázuriz managed to take 15 percent of the vote. This gives a sense of the importance of the issue of housing debt, as well as the traditional swing power of the Chilean middle class, which after a decade and a half of a free-market dictatorship, is strapped and struggling to hang on.

Conclusion

President Allende's minister of housing Juan Hamilton summarized the housing program implemented by the Chicago Boys: leaving construction to the private sector, the government wound up having to intervene and "built smaller houses, of lower quality and in fewer numbers."[62] Even so, in the campaign leading up to the 1988 plebiscite, the Pinochet government began to televise the slogan, "Today in this country there are more families with a house of their own." The president and his minister of housing stepped up public appearances at government-funded housing projects; in May, General Pinochet appeared in the *población* La Pintana to proclaim, "I must continue (in office) so that everyone might have a house."[63] Such media-propagated illusions proved ineffective against the reality of the housing situation in Chile. In the plebiscite the *poblaciones* overwhelmingly voted against the Pinochet government.[64]

After eight years of leaving virtually all housing and urban development to market forces, government housing programs became much more effective after 1982, when the government finally intervened to assure the construction and credits that the private sector alone proved unwilling to provide. Unwilling to admit any failure of free-market policies, some Chicago Boys argued that such government actions were temporary responses to the economic crisis of that year rather than to the disastrous housing situation that grew out of the previous eight years. In fact, the crash of 1982 only put the inadequacies of free-market programs in greater relief.

What is apparent from the free-market housing experiment in Chile are the serious limitations to relying on market forces to respond to everyone's need for housing. The private sector built low-income housing only when given clear guarantees by the government in the form of a ready buyer with a government voucher and a complementary government loan in hand. Even then such efforts did little more than slow the growing deficit in housing. The private sector freed from government controls speculated on urban land and drove up housing prices even for poor people. At the same time, the other private sector, namely the grassroots efforts and organizations of poor people, were given very little room for participation.

11

The Privatization of Social Security

One of the last and perhaps the crowning achievement of the seven "modernizations" announced in 1980 by the Chicago Boys was the privatization of the national social security system. The government-backed system of industry-wide programs through which employee withholdings were combined with employer contributions was replaced by a system of private financial institutions competing to invest an individual worker's retirement account. This market-based system, the Chicago Boys claim, gives a Chilean worker the freedom to provide for retirement according to his or her choice, with the knowledge that salary withholdings will be invested and accumulate individually in the transparent and shrewdly efficient hands of a private fund manager rather than be lumped together with withholdings of other employees. Also with the new system, employers are "freed" from mandatory contributions for their employees and thus are more competitive in national and international markets.

Social Security Before

In his history of social security in Latin America, Carmelo Mesa Lago calls Chile "the pioneering country in the western hemisphere," which by 1970 had developed one of the most advanced and progressive systems in Latin America. Social security had its origins in Chile in the 1920s when the Congress, pressured by increasing labor organization among industrial and mining workers and under siege by a reform-minded military, established three government-backed mandatory programs called *Cajas de Prevision* ("Foresight Chests"), one for industrial workers, one for public employees and another for office employees.[1]

These *cajas* were designed to enroll only workers who made below a certain income on the assumption that the risk of disabilities and unprotected old-age was greater among those with low income. Over the ensuing fifty years, middle-class workers, professionals and their families, mostly as a result of their organizational efforts and the political parties representing them, were incorporated into the social security system through *cajas* that catered to the various occupations (doctors, school teachers, plumbers, and so forth). By 1973, over 75 percent of working Chileans were in the various social security systems.

Many blue and white collar workers of different political views with whom we spoke felt strongly about the principle of solidarity that had been implicit in the *cajas*. Obligations were shared by workers, employers and the government, and each group had its representatives among the directors of a *caja*. Although benefits were linked to salary levels, redistribution occurred from higher to lower paid employees, since low-income workers often received more in pensions than they had paid in, and from one generation to the next, since withholdings from active workers helped pay for the pensions of retirees. Workers received small wage supplements according to the number of their children, and women could retire with fewer years of payments into the system, an acknowledgment of the value to society of the unremunerated work of raising children.[2] The *cajas* had hospitals and recreational centers serving all employees equally, and accumulated pension funds were invested in low-interest housing loans for affiliates.

As early as 1970, however, most Chileans agreed that the system needed to be modernized. Almost 90 percent of those in the system belonged to one of the three main *cajas* (those of industrial workers, public employees, and office employees), but a total of 35 *cajas* catered to smaller groups as diverse as the armed forces and railway workers, each with its own separate set of rules passed by Congress. The uncoordinated manner in which benefits were expanded to new groups had generated various problems. While all the *cajas* covered the same contingencies (primarily retirement, health care, and disability), the level of benefits from one *caja* to the next could vary considerably. One of the most blatant inequalities was that white-collar workers could retire with benefits equal to their full salaries after as few as thirty years of service, while factory and most other blue-collar workers qualified only at the legal retirement age (sixty-five for men and sixty for women) and received benefits much less than their earnings when working. Top executives and military officers even retired with the right to maintain in retirement the same salary levels and raises of the people who replaced them. Also employers and workers could collude to evade proper assessments since only the last five years of employment were used to calculate benefits.

Critics also pointed to the growing cost of the social security system, made worse by the spiraling inflation of the 1960s and early 1970s. In 1973 the total costs shared by the worker and the employer for contributions to social security and health benefits programs could amount to as much as 66 percent on top of the base salary. Often when not enough had been paid in to cover current benefits, especially in the *cajas* of public employees, the government picked up the difference.[3]

Starting as early as 1955, presidential administrations of the right, center and left tried to implement a series of reforms to eliminate inequalities and reduce overlapping bureaucracies among the *cajas*. Changes for the most part aimed at eventual unification of the *cajas* into a single government institution. This has been the course of the social security systems of many countries that made the transition from the nineteenth century German model based on specific groups of workers to one of more unified government administration.[4] Only countries late to introduce social security, notably the United States, started off with a system of unified government administration. Even so, the failure of any president to enjoy a majority in Congress meant reform proposals were repeatedly blocked, and legislation to reform social security was stalled in Congress in the months before the military coup in 1973.

Reforming the *Cajas*, 1975-1980

Many of the long-needed reforms to the social security system were finally implemented under the authoritarian rule of General

Pinochet. Some reforms implemented were those proposed under earlier governments. The most important instituted a universal retirement age of sixty-five for men and sixty for women, regardless of occupation. Pension levels and other benefits such as allotments for dependents were also made more uniform. These changes immediately eased the fiscal situation of the *cajas*, since those who had been allowed to retire early now would pay into the *cajas* for more years and accordingly received benefits for fewer years. Other changes were typical of the regime's free-market social policies. The employer contribution to social security was first reduced, then completely eliminated by 1980. The real value of pensions was allowed to drop 26 percent by 1982 from its 1970 level.[5]

The New Pension Fund Administrators

When the Chicago Boys unveiled their plan to privatize the government-operated social security system in 1980, they made a series of long familiar criticisms against the existing social security system. According to them, the *cajas* needed to be replaced with privately owned investment companies because the *cajas* discriminated through their diversity of benefits and retirement requirements; because many *cajas* suffered deficits and considerable payment evasions; and because they were administratively inefficient. In fact, by 1980 many of these problems had already been eliminated and the remaining ones in the system, while certainly significant, could have been remedied.[6] An official of the agency overseeing the private social security system (who insisted on anonymity) told us, "As a scholar of social security systems, I would have to say that every remaining problem in the old system was correctable; however, as a government official, this would not be my position."

With the new system, the private Pension Fund Administrators (AFPs) compete for employee retirement withholdings. AFPs are formed solely for the business of managing retirement funds, which are held in individual accounts invested in stocks and bonds approved by a government commission. When an employee retires, he or she can choose either the programmed withdrawal of accumulated funds or the exchange of the balance of accumulated funds for an annuity from an insurance company.

In the United States perhaps the closest equivalent would be an individual retirement account (IRA or Keough) invested in a mutual fund. An important difference is that within a generation the private AFP system will be the single mandatory form of providing for the retirement of the Chilean work force, while in the United States the government-run social security administration will assist the majority of the population. Another difference is that in Chile employers are no longer obligated to contribute to their employees' retirement security, as most are in the United States.

According to Pinochet's decree on social security, all persons entering the labor force after 1982 were required to join an AFP; those in the old *cajas* were given the choice of remaining or transferring to the new private and individual system. In 1981 the government undertook an intensive public campaign aided by intensive advertising campaigns by the AFPs to encourage Chileans not yet retired to switch from *cajas* to AFPs.

Over and above the promised future bounties of the AFPs themselves, two immediate material incentives were offered to those who would switch. The first was a "recognition bond" the government promised to those who switched systems, a bond that would collect interest and be added to their AFP funds upon retirement. The amount of the bond varied according to the number of years an employee had contributed in the old *caja* system. The second incentive was a significant drop in the percentage withheld for retirement from one's paycheck. Employees who switched to the AFPs immediately saw total withholdings from their paychecks reduced from between 26 and 31 percent to 21 percent.[7] This meant a significant increase in take-home pay — the equivalent of as much as an additional month's pay every year. (The government claimed that this was because AFPs were more efficient, but the difference in withholding levels was an arbitrary decision by the government that could just as easily have been extended to those in the *cajas*.[8]) These incentives helped spur a massive exodus of active workers from the *cajas*, whose affiliates dropped from 1.7 million in 1980 to only 490,000 two years later.[9]

The exodus left the *cajas* top heavy with retirees (who, of course, could not switch). Now the number of employees receiving retirement benefits from a *caja* far exceeds that of those still working and paying into it (and with the decree no new workers join a *caja*), a sure formula for a slow death for the defunded *cajas*. The resulting deficit, picked up by the public treasury, gave the government a strong incentive to keep a lid on cost of living allowances in benefits paid to those retirees in the old system. Those remaining in the *cajas* have been punished not only by higher contributions, but once retired their benefits will not have kept up with inflation. In 1985 the Pinochet government suspended the inflation adjustment of pensions of those in the *cajas* for one year, with the result that over one million pensioners lost 10 percent of the real value of their benefits.[10]

The privatized social security system does not include the armed forces and the national police. When the AFPs were formed in 1981, the government declared that it was forming a special committee that would announce within six months how the military and the police would fit into the new system. No announcement was ever made, and the military and police *cajas* are still going strong. Apparently the junta listened to the Chicago Boys except when it came to its own retirement funds.

The members of the armed forces and the national police have retained virtually all of their special retirement privileges. They have maintained not only very high retirement benefits but also early retirement and such institutions as adjustments in line with successors' salary increases. Information on the financing of the "uniformed" *cajas* is difficult to come by (as are financial data on the armed forces and the police in general). In 1987, however, the average level of retirement benefits from these *cajas* was three and a half times greater than the average from the civilian *cajas*.[11]

It can be misleading to evaluate any social security system in its first "easy" years. AFPs have been receiving many contributions from active employees, and paying out few benefits. In 1988, the AFPs were paying out to less than 13,000 retirees, a fraction of their more than two million account holders.[12] Almost all pensions presently being paid in Chile are still covered by the *caja* system. In addition to all those who retired before 1982, the *cajas* must carry the burden of those employees who were near retirement age in 1982, since anyone switching with the "recognition bond" had to make at least five years of uninterrupted payments to an AFP before retiring.

Even so, the results of the first decade of the transition to the new market-led social security system tell us a good deal about its implications for the economy and what lies ahead for Chileans when they retire.

Free-market critics of the old system of *cajas* complained that it granted special privileges to better-off employees and resulted in a net transfer of income away from those who most needed it. In fact, just the opposite was true. A study by economists at the policy studies institute CIEPLAN concluded that in spite of inefficiencies and privileges (many of which had been eliminated by 1980), the old system of *cajas* progressively redistributed income. In the year 1969, the poorest 40 percent of the population paid less than 10 percent into the social security system, yet received 15 percent of the benefits. A similar redistribution occurred which was favorable to the next 30 percent of beneficiaries, who paid in 22 percent of the contributions and received 26 percent of benefits.[13] By contrast the AFP system, with its strict tie between an individual worker's contributions and benefits is at best neutral, or, as we shall see, even regressive when the flat commissions collected on all accounts by the AFPs are figured in.

Women who spend half of their employable years raising families instead of earning wages will accumulate less in their AFP accounts and are likely to have to live out their last years with much smaller retirement benefits than their male colleagues. Even if a working woman accumulates the same amount in her AFP account during her working life as a male counterpart, her monthly benefits will be smaller, since the AFP (or insurance company) calculates a lower monthly payment that factors in her earlier retirement age and longer life expectancy.

Government officials and the financial conglomerates that own the AFPs have argued that the new system would instill the values of savings and investment in employees as they watch their savings accumulate and increasingly identify their own future with that of the AFP investments and the economy in general. It was also seen as a guarantee against payment evasion, since evasion would reduce the retirement benefits of the individual in question.

We found (and by all reports) unskilled and service workers show very little interest in the AFPs at all. When one bright young waiter showed us his pay stub, we had to explain to him what the AFP deduction was all about. Another told us that his AFP account didn't mean a whole lot to him, since with his low pay he would be lucky simply to qualify even for the minimum pension guaranteed by the government for those who make 20 years of regular payments.

Lack of interest is most likely compounded by the fact that employers now contribute nothing to the old-age security or health care of their employees. The only contributions employers make are unemployment and liability insurance premiums that together equal less than three percent of the total wage bill. Such minimal obligations make Chilean employers firm believers in the privatization of retirement and the envy of their counterparts elsewhere. The theory of the free marketeers is that in national economic terms this savings allows employers to hire more workers and, as the demand for workers increases, wages will be pushed up.

The switch to the AFPs has reversed 50 years of a steady increase in the percentage of Chileans covered by a social security program. In 1991, the proportion of the labor force not covered by a pension scheme was 35 percent, compared to 75 percent of the labor force covered under the *cajas* in the early 1970s.[14] Because employment is often irregular, almost half of the two million affiliates of the AFPs were not up to date in their payments and therefore ineligible for most benefits.[15] This drop in coverage is partly related to the changing structure of work in Chile; now a greater portion of the work force is engaged in informal work or seasonal labor or is self-employed, activities that easily fall through the cracks of protective coverage. Those with an AFP must have at least 20 years of regular payments to the social security system to qualify for the minimum retirement pension, a requirement that will exclude large numbers of workers, particularly women who make up much of the informal and seasonal labor force. Unfortunately, the workers left out are often those most in need of protection against old-age impoverishment. The government does provide a public assistance pension to retirees who do not qualify for the minimum pension, but in 1992, public assistance was less than half the amount of the minimum pension, and by law could be given to only 300,000 people a year.[16]

According to a study published by the conservative Chilean policy institute Centro de Estudios Publicos, one of the principal characteristics of the new social security system is "the greater degree of freedom given to the individual, manifested during his working life in the possibility to save more than the legal requirements, greater freedom to postpone or advance retirement relative to the legal age, and to choose the AFP. At the end of his working life the individual decides which type of pension and administrator suits him best." The same report tell us, "The AFPs compete for affiliates through the level and structure of the commissions they collect, the profit they obtain for funds, and the quality of service they deliver, allowing the worker to incorporate himself in the AFP of his choice."[17] If an affiliate is unhappy with an AFP, after six months he can transfer his funds to another one.

In fact, few Chileans make their choices about AFPs based on informed decisions. Surveys show that affiliates rarely make decisions about which AFP to join based on where costs are lowest or where they will get the highest return. Instead the most important factors are the total number of assets managed and the image that an AFP is able to project through advertising. We spoke with one employee who complained of having no choice at all, since his boss imposed one AFP on all employees in order to reduce payroll paperwork.

In order to retire before the legal age, employees in the AFP system must have accumulated sufficient funds in their accounts to sustain a level of benefits equivalent to half of their average salaries over the last ten years worked. Given the salaries and wages of most in the system, this option is likely to be available to only a few well-paid Chileans. Labor economist Jaime Ruiz-Tagle estimates that only 22 percent of the Chilean work force in 1987 made a salary that might allow them to retire with more than minimum benefits.[18]

While the old *cajas* often discriminated unfairly between those classes of employees who could and could not retire early, they could also make accommodations for types of work that were particularly risky or physically exhausting, such as those in mining, one of Chile's most important industries. Now employees in such occupations must work until they are 65 if they cannot accumulate enough in their AFP accounts to retire early, almost certainly the case of those in such occupations.

Free marketeers argued that the private AFPs would manage retirement funds more efficiently than the *cajas* had since they would compete for clients by offering higher profits on funds and lower administrative costs. Competition, in practice, has been through advertising and sales campaigns rather than in decreasing costs and higher benefits. In 1983, Chile spent twice as much to run both the old and the new social security systems as it had to run the system of *cajas* in 1980 before the change. Administrative costs per affiliate in the AFPs have remained higher than in the *cajas*, with marketing and sales commissions making up over thirty percent of the AFPs operating costs.[19]

The new system has a built-in inefficiency: employers who once had to deal with a single *caja* now by law must deduct and make payments to multiple AFPs as well as to the *caja* for those remaining in it, creating considerable additional paperwork and delays in transferring funds.

AFPs make their profits as private corporations in two ways. One is from the difference between what they pay to insurance companies for disability insurance and the 3.5 percent they charge affiliates for that service. The other is a flat service fee or commission taken from the 10 percent deducted from employee earnings for their retirement accounts. In spite of claims that AFPs' operations would be completely "transparent," the amount of the fee or commission has been less than clearly disclosed. Soon after the introduction of the new system, the government suppressed its rule that required AFPs to factor the commission into publicized rates of return. The flat fee can vary among AFPs, but within each AFP the fee deducted will be the same whether the affiliate's monthly income is $20 or $2000.[20]

A 1982 survey of those Chileans in AFPs revealed that 75 percent did not know what fees they were paying and 23 percent thought they knew but were wrong.[21] Pedro Corona, the president of Cuprum, one of the few AFPs that has eliminated the flat commission, spoke out publicly in a newspaper interview:

> The claims made by some AFPs in advertisements in the metro of high returns is simply deceitful. It just isn't so for those (affiliates) who have low incomes or irregular work, and therefore suffer a proportionately large reduction of their contribution through the flat commission.[22]

Corona gave an example. One AFP advertises a profit rate of 8.65 percent. A worker earning only 26,000 pesos might well think that's terrific and sign up. But the advertised profit rate refers to the fund in general, and not the real profit level of an individual account. In reality, an affiliate with such an income has a negative profit of -12.38 percent. "The reason is very simple," Corona explains. "If your income is low, the weight of the flat commission is proportionately much greater, so much so that the AFP would have to have a fabulous profit level to compensate. More than 67 percent of Chileans in the new system earn less than 40,000 pesos (1990)."[23] Many Chileans will be lucky if their accumulated deductions simply don't shrink.

With the decree establishing the system of AFPs, the labor minister claimed, "The cost of the reform to the public treasury is zero."[24] In fact, the huge and ongoing costs of the social security privatization are being borne by the public treasury.

These costs derive from three principal areas. As we've already said, the public treasury will cover the gap between what the *cajas* take in and pay out. This deficit in retirement funds grew from 1.7 percent of Chile's gross domestic product in 1981 to 5.4 percent in 1987.[25] During the 1990s this will increase yet further as most of those now paying into the *cajas* retire and begin receiving benefits.[26]

The second "transitional" obligation paid out of public funds is the "recognition bonds." Since few have retired so far under the AFPs, hardly any of these bonds have yet been paid. During the course of the 1990s they will increasingly come due, reaching a peak in the second decade of the twenty-first century.

Thirdly, the government guarantees minimum benefits to retiring workers who after 20 full years of payments to an AFP have not accumulated funds sufficient to provide themselves with the minimum level of benefits. What percentage of the work force this may prove to be remains unknown and depends on the future capacity of the Chilean economy to provide stable jobs and rising wages. As we have already discussed, work on the free market has been characterized by temporary jobs and falling or stagnant wages. Even World Bank consultant Tarsicio Casteñeda, while praising the system, acknowledges that in contrast to much lower original estimates made by the government planning office, as many as 34 percent of men and 45 percent of women who pay into the AFPs won't accumulate sufficient funds to give them the minimum benefits.[27] Another estimate suggests that if real rates of return on AFP funds drop to a modest 3 percent, and the rate of regular payment compliance continues at around 60 percent, than the government would have to supplement the pensions of about 65 percent of workers.[28]

The cost of assuring lower-income workers the modest minimum pension (which equaled only $38 per month in 1988 — 85 percent of the minimum wage) falls to the government, even though the AFPs benefit from a lifetime of commissions and fees on the withholdings of all workers. Some Chilean policy makers we interviewed suggested it might become inevitable for the government to form a publicly owned AFP for the lowest income workers. Such a two-tiered system would not restore the capacity to redistribute income of the old *cajas*, but it would at least allow the government the fiscal benefit of collecting fees, since a significant part of the minimum retirement benefits will come from public funds.

If future earnings of Chilean workers do not increase substantially, the cost to the public treasury of providing minimum benefits to a large portion of the retired population will be significant. And unlike the costs of covering the shortfalls of the remaining *caja* pensions or the one-time recognition bonds, this fiscal burden would continue indefinitely.

Free marketeers might argue that picking up the costs of the transition *is* the proper purview of the government, just as guaranteeing minimum benefits is an appropriate "focusing" of government spending. But, while eliminating a system with the potential to progressively redistribute payroll withholdings across classes, the government has taken on new medium-term burdens without having a clear new source of revenue to finance it.

A quick look at the figures published by the Chilean Central Bank for the Pinochet years shows a moderate rise in social spending (though not adjusted for population growth). This may seem surprising given what we have seen of free-market policies. But a closer look shows that the lion's share of social spending now goes to prop up the old and new social security system. At the time AFP system was implemented in 1981, social security absorbed 30 percent of total social spending. By 1988 it had risen to 49 percent of total social spending, a tendency that will certainly increase long before it declines, thereby almost certainly crowding out severely needed increases in other areas such as health and education.[29] In 1990 social security spending by the government surpassed 7 percent of GDP, and absorbed 40 percent of tax revenues.[30]

Finally, the government implicitly guarantees the solvency of the AFPs. When four of the largest AFPs went under in 1982 along with the financial conglomerates that owned them, they passed briefly into government control before they were sold again. If an insurance company fails, the government is liable to pay between 75 and 100 percent of any annuity payments the company owes. Despite the free-market rules of the game, it seems the government is expected to bail out the private sector.

New Concentration of Wealth

Free-market advocates refer to the AFPs as the "indirect" arm of the "people's capitalism," propelling privatizations and leading to a democratization of ownership in industry.[31] Reality is quite otherwise.

The AFPs invest funds in a variety of financial instruments approved by a government commission. After 1985 the AFPs were allowed to invest in stocks of those companies in the process of privatization. By 1989 they had acquired a 32 percent share of the companies privatized. Defenders of the AFPs and of the privatizations claim that some 2.9 million Chileans who pay into the AFPs are now owners of the privatized corporations.

With the debt-related crisis of the early '80s, which abruptly cut off all foreign credit, AFPs became the most important source of internal savings. The new social security system provided fresh financing in an economy strapped for credit. Accumulated retirement funds reached $5.75 billion by mid-1990, equivalent to 18 percent of GDP. In this context, control over where such funds were invested became paramount.

But Chileans who pay into their retirement accounts have no say as to how their funds are spent. They have no more say in the decisions of the AFPs than someone with a savings account in a bank would have in its investment decisions. With the exception of one small AFP (catering to copper workers), affiliates do not own a significant portion of the stock of the AFP itself and so have no say in how the AFP is run, much less in the companies the AFP has stock in.

Who does control the AFPs? In 1980 they were set up and

owned primarily by the same traditional financial conglomerates that controlled the major banks. As already mentioned, with the severe recession of 1982-1984 four of the largest AFPs failed and passed into government control. When they were resold over the following years, controlling shares of many of the AFPs were purchased by U.S. financial consortia. A Bankers' Trust holding group (which includes three other international banks that are important holders of the Chilean debt) owns a controlling interest (40 percent) of the biggest AFP, Provida. The U.S. company Aetna controls 51 percent of the next largest AFP, Santa Maria, and the American International Group controls 99.96 percent of the AFP Union. The three foreign companies together control 65 percent of all AFP stock and 55 percent of the retirement funds of Chileans. The remaining AFPs are for the most part controlled by local Chilean financial groups.

There are many interlocking interests. For example, Bankers' Trust also owns 98.5 percent of the huge National Insurance Consortium, which sells workers' compensation insurance to its own AFP as well as to several other AFPs. This allows Bankers' Trust to capture a larger share of the insurance and administrative costs deducted from workers' pay. At the same time, Bankers' Trust effectively determines investment decisions for the Provida funds, which can be funneled to the 13 privatized corporations in which Bankers' Trust has a stake, whether they are the most prudent investment or not. Other economic groups have woven similarly complex webs. Aurelio Becerra, a supervisor of a smaller Chilean-owned AFP, Cuprum, complained to us about such unfair advantages and the lack of government restrictions on such obvious conflicts of interest.[32]

Finally, as the lucrative investment opportunities provided by privatizations come to an end, the international companies that control the AFPs have been pushing for government permission to invest AFP funds in foreign stock markets, arguing that this will provide Chilean workers with the highest rate of return on their pension funds. Although the lure of individual return rates on retirement funds is a powerful one, many Chileans consider this possibility to be outrageous given the need for productive investment within Chile and in social areas such as housing.

Future Insecurity

The creation of a privatized social security system has been fundamental to the larger economic project of the Chicago Boys. The system of individual capitalization eliminates all potential within the social security system for redistribution and solidarity. At the same time it frees employers from their previous contribution while financially shoring up the national and multinational conglomerates that control the AFPs and much of the Chilean economy. The AFPs funneled a tremendous amount of capital to revive the failing economy in the early 1980s and to help carry through the Chicago Boys' final round of privatizations beginning in 1985. The apparent wide distribution of ownership of property in fact turns out to be just so many tentacles all connected to a small number of foreign and national conglomerates.

The substantial and growing costs of the transition to a privatized system will continue to fall heavily on the public coffers at least until the second decade of the next century, to the detriment of other social programs such as those in health, housing and education.

The private system undoubtedly benefits the higher-income Chileans who under the old *cajas* paid in more than they received, and for whom security in retirement was less of an issue anyway. For many middle class and professional Chileans, the AFPs may prove beneficial and undoubtedly have a certain appeal. But there is a very strong possibility that a very large percentage of Chileans (especially women, and temporary or seasonal workers) will either be excluded completely from the benefits of the private system or condemned to receive the government-subsidized minimum (and minimal) retirement benefits. These are, of course, the groups who most need social security. The full impact of the privatization of the social security system will not be fully manifest for another thirty years, when the "easy dividends" of the early years are over.

PART FOUR:

LAND AND THE ENVIRONMENT

12

Fruit Boom: By and For Whom?

Traveling south from Santiago, down the Pan-American Highway, it is hard not to be struck by the countless large and high-tech fruit-packing and cold-storage plants. We thought we were back home driving through one of California's major agricultural valleys.

Under Pinochet Chilean fruit exports undeniably "boomed." Shipments overseas of grapes, nectarines, plums, peaches, pears, and apples grew at a compound rate of nearly 20 percent annually over 18 years, from about $40 million in 1974 to nearly $1 billion in 1991.[1] While Chile has been expanding its exports of many fruits, table grape exports have led the boom. Chile has become the world's number one exporter of table grapes. From 1980 to 1988, grape exports jumped fivefold.[2] In the 1989-90 season, boxes of grapes accounted for three-quarters of the 58 million boxes of fresh fruits exported. Of the nearly half million tons of table grapes entering world trade in 1990, an astounding 90 percent were grown in Chile.[3] More than 95 percent of grape imports to the U.S. are from Chile.[4] And, although Chile has been slowly diversifying its markets, about half of all of Chile's fruit exports go to the U.S.[5]

Chilean fruit producers and exporters have achieved success to a degree beyond that of any rival Southern Hemisphere nation. Productivity on some Chilean fruit farms, especially in grapes, now stands on par with that of California, from which much of the technology was borrowed. "Nothing remains for us to learn from California," a young agronomist-turned-grape-grower told a seminar we attended on the future of the Chilean fruit industry.

Computers monitor temperatures and track pallets from packing shed to market. Electronic equipment selects fruit by color and size. Chile's fruit producers even are getting fruits to faraway northern hemisphere markets in better condition than some of those countries' own producers. In the newest producing zone, the northern region outside Copiapó, Israeli-style computerized drip irrigation is transforming the fringes of the world's driest desert into vineyards. The world's largest artificially cooled packing plant is in Curicó, south of Santiago. Sophisticated freshness-preserving technologies keep apples, pears and kiwis up to twelve months in the condition in which they were harvested. These technologies allow growers to sit out post-harvest periods of glut on the international market and quietly wait for higher prices.

A booming fruit export industry has generated notable "upstream" effects. The mushrooming demand for crates, cartons, and other paper products has been a boon to the forestry industry. Highly perishable exports prompted Cardoen Industries, better known for its weapons and explosives, to produce refrigerated containers for sea and air shipments.[6]

The Chicago Boys triumphantly point to Chile's fruit boom as a "miracle" that justifies faith in the free market, demonstrating what can be achieved only through opening up an economy to the international winds of competition and freeing private enterprise from government meddling. But the roots of the boom are many and diverse, and some of them hardly can be claimed by the Chicago Boys and indeed run counter to their doctrine of at most a subsidiary role for the government in economic development. And by the 1990s much tougher times confront the industry which are likely to highlight the need for a strong public sector role.

Naturally Advantaged

Most fundamental to Chile's success is its extraordinary geography. Chile unquestionably enjoys a comparative advantage in marketing fresh temperate fruits. The fact that the seasons of the northern and southern hemispheres are opposite of each other — it's summer in Chile when it's winter in North America and Europe — has been pivotal for Chile's success. Chile harvests fruits from October to April, the months when northern hemisphere countries produce so little fresh fruit that they have no call to protect domestic growers (except perhaps in the few transitional weeks between seasons). Chile's southern hemisphere competitors — countries that traditionally held substantially greater shares of the world market than Chile — have suffered from a host of difficulties and disadvantages. South Africa, for instance, during the years of Chile's fruit boom found the doors to its exports in many northern countries shut because of anti-apartheid boycotts. Argentina has been plagued by the Mediterranean fruit fly and protracted economic crises. New Zealand and Australia are farther than Chile from the prime markets (except notably the Japanese market), an additional distance that can be critical for highly perishable goods.

Because of Chile's extraordinary length, grapes at different latitudes mature at different times: in late spring (early December) grapes are ripe for harvest in the northern area around Copiapó, then in La Serena, next in San Felipe and Los Andes, finishing yet farther south in March, April and even May with Talca and Chillan. This special situation makes Chile the only country capable of supplying a steady stream of grapes to North American and European consumers in their winter and spring months for an uninterrupted period of six months.

Because of its "string-bean" shape, Chile's fruit orchards are almost all less than a hundred miles from a seaport for loading into the refrigerated holds of waiting ships. With a reasonably adequate road network (largely built by an "interventionist" public sector before the Chicago Boys came into power) and (now) well-functioning ports, internal transport costs are low. By contrast, in rival Argentina, for example, orchards are as far as one thousand miles to a seaport.

Chile, moreover, is blessed with a considerable area for cultivating temperate-zone fruit. In its central valleys, as in California, there are good soils, and the considerable temperature differences between night and day enhance the size, color and taste of fruit. Also, as in California, lack of rain during harvest months and the many hours of sun and low humidity are ideal for fruit cultivation. Pests and diseases are relatively absent, thanks to Chile's isolation (extraordinarily inhospitable deserts lie to the north and a towering mountain range seals off the long eastern land border).

The fruit industry has also been able to count on a supply of abundant water whenever needed, thanks to good sources of water and an extensive network of irrigation canals built through public and private collaboration long before the fruit boom.

Crucial Early Government Investment

The vision of a major fruit-export industry, and investments toward that end, stretch back decades before the free-market regime. By the 1930s, Chilean fruits had already gained a reputation for quality in northern hemisphere winter markets.[7]

A qualitative leap forward occurred in the 1960s through an investment partnership between government and the private sector. The governmental National Development Corporation (CORFO) drew up and carried out through the decade of the '60s a national "Fruit Plan." CORFO recruited a number of the country's brightest young agronomists and fruit experts to elaborate the plan, which was designed from 1962 to 1965, and implemented beginning in 1966. Orchards were surveyed and catalogued according to variety, age, condition, and their future output estimated. Potential demand from foreign markets was analyzed, and production goals set accordingly. The Plan called for boosting fresh fruit exports by 12 percent per year between 1965 and 1980. To achieve such an ambitious goal, the government proposed major public expenditures for agricultural research, technical assistance, credit for planting orchards, and modern infrastructure. These efforts included the introduction of new plant varieties (mainly from California), the construction of processing, storage, packing and refrigeration facilities, a government-operated nursery to ensure the propagation of disease-free plants, national fruit research and plant inspection programs, and pre-shipment credits designed to subsidize fruit exports.

Many of these efforts were facilitated by a special collaboration between the Chilean government and the state of California mounted during the same period, with the stimulus of the U.S. government's Alliance for Progress. In 1965 a 10-year program of technical collaboration with an emphasis on fruit production was launched between the University of California and the University of Chile financed largely by the Ford Foundation. Numerous

Chilean students and faculty members received graduate training at the University of California's Davis campus, center for some of the most advanced agricultural research in the world, while University of California faculty gave courses and seminars and carried out fruit research in Chile. The program, according to U.C. Davis's Lovell Jarvis, "enabled the University of Chile to establish a first-rate faculty in the fruit-related sciences, update the curricula of its teaching programs, and begin modern fruit research. Spillover effects strengthened government agencies and other universities. The ties established between academics in Chile and California also greatly facilitated technological transfer thereafter."[8]

Through the 1960s, the area planted, fruit yields and quality began to rise. Exports grew by 9 percent annually from 1962 to 1970. Indeed volumes increased sufficiently in order to charter special fruit cargo ships rather than place the fruit on all-purpose liners. As a consequence, fruit handling improved, allowing it to reach foreign consumers in better condition.[9] We should keep in mind that much of the area planted during this period matured and began to produce only after 1974. Indeed one of the causes of the rapid growth in fruit output from the late 1970s and onward is the significant amount of vineyards planted before the time of the free-market regime.

Increased Foreign Demand

Another key contributor to Chile's fruit boom lay outside Chile: the significant rise in foreign demand for fresh fruits. In the '70s and '80s, notions of healthy eating and the "yuppification" of tastes (backed by rising incomes) stimulated a growing preference for fresh produce over canned or frozen and a widening market for exotic species. At the beginning of the '80s in the United States the per capita consumption of fresh fruit in the winter was a little more than 3 pounds; by the end of the decade it was almost 9.[10]

Of course, some promotional efforts were behind the increased demand for fresh fruit year around. The Association of Chilean Fruit Exporters took out some radio advertisements in the U.S. and tried marketing seedless grapes in Europe as a snack food.[11] Counterpart associations in California boosted Chilean efforts in the U.S., reasoning that the more people are turned into grape consumers in the winter months the more they will eat grapes during the rest of the year (based on the "banana theory," namely, that people get more easily into the habit of buying something when it's available year-round).[12]

Land reform

Sergio Gomez, a leading analyst of Chile's agriculture, has concluded, "The development of the country's fruit industry would be unthinkable if the large estates [*latifundios*] had remained the dominant feature in the countryside."[13]

Chile needed a thoroughgoing land reform in order for the fruit business to take off — it also needed to have it over with. Before the mid-1960s, the Chilean countryside consisted primarily of several thousand gigantic *latifundios* and a scattered multitude of "parcels." Although some 10,000 estates accounted for only 7 percent of the total *number* of farms, they monopolized 81 percent of the Chile's agricultural land (and many belonged to the same extended families).[14] Many rural Chileans, much as medieval peons, played out their lives on the same estate from cradle to grave surviving as laborers paid in part by the right to work a small plot for themselves.

Questions of justice apart, such a concentrated control over resources lay at the root of Chile's agricultural backwardness. In a countryside dominated by ostentatious private wealth, farming and entrepreneurism seldom, if ever, met. Most estates showed little interest in productive use of the land. For many elite Chilean families, the reward of estate ownership was the prestige of quasi-nobility based on the size and grandeur of a rural estate, not in increased output and financial gain. By the 1960s, the threat of land reform further inhibited investment. For their part, most small landowners, by definition, possessed few, if any, resources to invest or invest in. Thus there was little investment in agriculture, and yields remained low. The agricultural economy seemed permanently stagnant: far from producing for export, more and more basic food had to be imported into such an obviously well-endowed agricultural country. Chilean agriculture was anything but booming.

Land reforms under the Frei and the Allende administrations, between 1965 and 1973, expropriated 43 percent of all agricultural land (measured in terms of its productive value).[15] Gone were the *latifundios*. By August 1972, there were no longer any privately owned farms larger than 80 "basic" hectares (that is, equivalent to 80 hectares — 200 acres — of prime irrigated central valley land).

Such sweeping land reforms and some four-fifths of rural workers organized in militant unions created a climate of extreme uncertainty that made any private investments in the fruit industry seem foolhardy. The Pinochet regime put an end to uncertainty. Owners of private property quickly felt safe from further land reform.

Pinochet's "regularizing of land holdings" by and large did not — to the surprise of some — restore the *latifundios*. Twenty-eight percent of expropriated land was restored partially or fully to former owners, but 52 percent of the expropriated land was divided into parcels and sold to 45,000 of the beneficiaries of the Frei and Allende land reforms. The remaining 20 percent of all expropriated land was auctioned off to the highest bidders, thus enabling a large number of non-peasants to purchase land.[16]

The government-instituted agrarian reforms also left a lasting legacy of taxation based on assessment of the most productive use of the land. This government intervention helped spur the investor dynamism now found in the countryside. And, according to the U.S. agricultural attaché in Chile, once the days of the Pinochet regime appeared numbered, any fear of the return of land reform further motivated owners to more productive use of agricultural land.[17]

By the mid-1970s, Chile had a market in farm land, something that had hardly existed before the progressive land reforms and the Chicago Boys' "counter reform."[18] The land reform process wiped out low-productivity big estates and under Pinochet ended up creating many smaller parcels of high quality, irrigated land in the Central Valley. Thus major government economic interventions that transformed the structures in the countryside laid the groundwork for private entrepreneurism.

The Pinochet government boasted that it granted "real" titles to some 45,000 land reform beneficiaries — meaning titles that could be freely sold or used as collateral, unlike titles more typical of land reforms that beneficiaries may not sell. These 45,000 Chileans — in many cases selected on the basis of political criteria — were "liberated," according to official parlance, from government-established cooperatives and transformed into yeoman capitalists.

Consistent with the military government's overall "non-intervention" economic policies, the public agencies for assisting small farmers were dismantled. The government offered small producers no support — technical assistance, subsidized inputs, farm production credit (at the same time interest rates, "freed" from government controls, skyrocketed[19]). Furthermore, the government lifted the ceiling on how much land anyone could own and allowed for corporate ownership of farm land.[20]

Thrown to the winds of the free market, over 40 percent of the new parcel owners by 1981 had sold their land.[21] Most had never before managed a farm. Many of the irrigated parcels in the central valley were bought from the new owners cheaply. Notes Chilean land reform expert Lovell Jarvis, ". . . the land reform beneficiaries had little idea of the value of such land for fruit production."[22] Who was buying on the new marketplace for land? In the words of the U.S. Embassy's agricultural attaché, "farmers better situated to tap the land's productive capabilities."[23] In addition to those who sought to reconstitute farms that they had lost to the land reforms, there were many city-based professionals — engineers, lawyers, and doctors as well as agronomists, financiers, merchants, and truckers — seeking to make money in farming. These investors were looking for new ideas. "These entrepreneurs hired administrators or even a skilled laborer to manage their farms, but sought regular advice from consulting agronomists and fruit exporters."[24]

Behind the Vines

Chile's fruit industry's technology may be forward-looking, but its working conditions constitute a leap backwards.

The Chicago Boys' "free market" in labor has been another key ingredient in the extraordinary profitability and therefore spectacular rise of Chile's export fruit industry.[25] In 1974, tens of thousands who had once been agricultural workers living on the large estates found themselves expelled. They squatted on "no-man's land" — along the edge of the railroad tracks, on the banks of rivers, or on the sides of steep hills. Or they crowded into the slum belts of the provincial towns and cities. Most did not migrate to the cities for they knew no work was there to be found. In fact, unemployed men and women in the cities would look for farm work (especially in the Central Valley so near to Santiago), even though they had no prior experience. Sociologist Eugenio Tironi comments: "In the Chilean countryside reappeared a character who had been thought to have disappeared — "*el afuerino*" (the outsider), the landless laborer (most often an unmarried man), who just as in the 19th century went from hacienda to hacienda doing whatever job, accustomed to only occasional work, poorly paid."[26]

This abundance of economically desperate workers has made it possible to pay low wages which in turn have been key in making Chilean fruit affordable to many in the northern hemisphere in spite of long-distance transportation costs. This "unnatural advantage" over, say, New Zealand and Australia where wages are at least four times as high,[27] constitutes what has been called "the other face of the fruit boom."[28]

Most employment in the fruit industry is temporary and without stability from year to year. The largest fruit-growing operation has a year-round work force of 500; its payrolls reach 5,000 at the peak harvest season and include 13,000 different individuals at one point or another over the course of the year. In Santa Maria, the area immediately north of Santiago, a study of seven area growers showed that of more than 3,000 workers, only 98 were employed on a year-round basis.[29] At least 80 percent of fruit industry workers are hired for short periods and then laid off.[30] As many as 200,000 people work as temporaries.[31] Many temporary fruit workers migrate from north to south, following the peak moments in the harvest.

This temporary nature of their employment, this insecurity for the vast majority of the rural work force is the biggest — and most defining — change in Chile's countryside. More and more of the rural workforce has been transformed in less than a generation from being workers steadily employed — and living — on one of the large estates to being workers living outside a farm and getting employed only whenever and wherever there is work.

One problem with the temporary nature of so much of the employment in the export fruit industry is, in the words of sociologist Sergio Gomez, that people work three, four, or five months but eat twelve months a year. But what is problematic for the workers is only logical for the owners. Since the demand for work has very big peaks and valleys, fruit growers hire ever fewer permanent workers.[32] Most workers now are hired only for the times when they are needed, and there are peaks and valleys even during the "season."[33] Typically the peak labor season lasts no more than three months, with perhaps four additional months of moderate demand for labor; for a couple of months during the year there is virtually no demand at all. In agriculture overall, the number of permanent workers has fallen so sharply over the years of the free-market model that by 1987 the number of employers surpassed the number of permanent-contract employees.[34]

The on-again, off-again nature of so much of the work in the fruit industry is not likely to change. More investment in fruit processing, some might think, could generate more months of employment. Yet should Chile ever try to move strongly into processed fruits production it will encounter direct competition from northern hemisphere producers (there's no season in grape jellies), and most markets for processed fruits are already saturated. Moreover, the processed industry is machine-intensive and Chile would have to import the machinery. Thus the Chilean industry's one remaining advantage would be very low wages, which alone would not be enough and by definition would mean perpetuating the workers' poverty.

Many of the workers in the fruit industry are women. Female workers are in the majority especially in the packing sheds, with men usually doing such "male" jobs as operating a forklift or the tractor bringing in the fruit. The majority of temporary workers are under 29, with young female workers (14 to 19) dominating during the peak months (January through March). Most of the few permanent jobs go to men, as do most of the jobs available during slack periods. "Nimble-fingered" women are more in demand than men and can earn more money than men during the peak months. Reportedly many women feel quite good about that and view the work as giving them some status and independence.[35]

Economist Sarah Bradshaw notes that, "Neo-liberalism in the

Chilean countryside has both forced, through economic hardship, and allowed women to participate in the traditionally 'male area' of waged labor."[36] Women working in the fruit industry often face a "double day." Their long hours in the packing shed are added on to their "domestic" responsibilities, where the traditional gender division of labor stays rigid.[37]

Many workers in the fruit industry are unemployed people from the slum belts of Santiago and provincial cities and towns who travel to the fruit areas in search of seasonal jobs. They are short on farm experience and long on formal education (it is not uncommon for post-secondary students to work in the harvests). When there is no longer any work in fruit they return home, attempting to survive on whatever odd jobs they can find.

The phenomenon of people migrating from urban areas to look for work in agriculture is with little precedent in Chile and in Latin America, where the flow has been significantly in the other direction. It speaks not to the attractiveness of the work in the fruit industry but to the high levels of urban unemployment throughout the years of the fruit boom. So much for the gloss of the U.S. Embassy: "The fruit boom has helped provide Chilean workers with a wider range of choices for employment than at any [other] time in the country's history."[38]

Fruit industry wages vary widely, although they are uniformly *much* lower than in competing exporting countries. GIA, a Chilean non-governmental institute that has carried out numerous agrarian studies, reported that permanent workers in the 1989-1990 season were paid between $1.93 a day (the legal minimum wage) and a maximum of $4 per day. Calculating the earnings of temporary workers is particularly difficult because, among other things, much of the work of the temporary workers is paid on a piece basis. No doubt, most temporary workers in the packing plants earn more than the minimum.[39] The catch (aside from the fact of the work being temporary) is that they have to work fast, with few breaks (a big complaint of the workers, according to researchers) and for as many hours as the boss orders, which in the peak season is generally 12 to 16 hours. Men working in the field are generally not paid on a piece-work basis because that could result in damage to the plants, etc. But many are forced to work longer than legal days without extra pay.

Perhaps the wages in the export fruit industry should be viewed from the perspective of the type of profits anticipated in the industry. In the late 1980s in the major fruit-growing valley of Aconcagua temporary workers were employed about three months of the year. Their wages ranged between $2 and $4 per day. One hectare (2.5 acres) of grape production typically earned the owner just under $5,000.[40]

Because the fruit industry does not offer the majority of workers year-around work and other jobs are hard to find, many families, according to another GIA study, survive in part from small government allotments [*subsidios*]. Government welfare payments thus subsidize the fruit industry.[41]

Another form of offsetting the low and unstable earnings from laboring in the export fruit industry is for a family to put to work as many members, including children, as possible. Families whose children are too little to work suffer from the most serious nutrition and health problems; their annual incomes are woefully low just when their youngsters are of an age that makes good regular nutrition most crucial.[42]

Many temporary workers find about 20 percent of their pay docked for social security. "What do I get from the 50 thousand pesos they deduct on me if they're going to give me only three or four months of work in the whole year?" asked one woman. Because of the short period of employment each year what the temporary workers would get after, say, 20 years (it's improbable that they would be hired beyond that) would amount to only the meager minimum social security benefits. In fact, most fruit workers apparently would rather have all the money they can right now. Two studies of the most modern fruit operations in the Central Valley found that 53 percent of the workers had succeeded in getting their employers not to make the deductions so they would have more take-home pay.[43] This means, of course, that a very large number of workers — in what the proponents of the neo-liberal model depict as one of Chile's most modern industries — are unprotected by any social security.

By the 1980s, with the market price of land in the fruit valleys easily at $8,000 per hectare, growers found it only logical to use as much of it as possible for fruit cultivation and not for better conditions for the workers. Workers complain of crowded, squalid barracks and especially about bathroom facilities. One researcher found only two toilets available to four hundred workers.[44] Even rudimentary child care facilities are not to be found on most of the fruit estates. Adequate wash facilities are critical for workers who come into contact with pesticides on the trees or fruit. Fruit workers also often lack a reasonably comfortable place to eat lunch without the intense sunlight and heat that can spoil their food. Most fruit workers, as poor urban dwellers, live in small houses without patios and the extra margin for survival coming from producing some of their own food.

Not surprisingly, health is a major concern of workers in the fruit industry. In one survey, 80 percent of workers surveyed said the problem of health was either "very serious" or "serious."[45] Many health problems, of course, are likely to be related to low and irregular incomes and especially to poor nutrition during the long periods without work.

Exposure to pesticides also poses a health hazard. Between 1976 and 1986, pesticide imports increased more than eightfold.[46] Since 1983 their use, consistent with free-market ideology, has gone unregulated. Not surprisingly, many of the pesticides figure on the World Health Organization's "dirty dozen" list of pesticides which have been linked to sterility (in men and women), spontaneous abortions, deformities, cancer, nerve damage and other diseases.[47] According to GIA researchers, workers on most farms are not provided with any protection (masks, gloves, plastic). Many workers complain of having to enter fields shortly after they were doused with pesticides. Many workers suffer from rashes, itching eyes, breathing problems and faintness. The poisons deployed present a problem for other Chileans too because the fruit farms are in the midst of the most heavily populated area of the country.

Worker organization in the fruit industry seems unforeseeable. By the late 1980s, only one percent of all fruit industry workers were organized — strikingly minuscule even in the context of neoliberal Chile in which 10 percent of the entire labor force is organized.[48] As elsewhere in Chile, fruit workers may have their jobs only so long as they "behave." In the words of one worker, "I had to try out to work as a pruner; six men applied for the job, and they needed only three. The slightest mistake and they'll fire you because there are lots of other men waiting to take your place." [49]

Most of the workers in the industry are not around long enough at the same place to lay the groundwork — socially or legally — for labor organizing. The heterogeneity of the workers in the industry — men, women, young people, old people, city people, rural people — similarly works against communication and unity.

Moreover, as we have seen, many people working in the fruit industry would rather work in the city. Solving social problems in the industry is not of interest to them since they like to think they are only passing through on their way to what — at least they think — is a better job in the city. Most likely, many will never get out of the industry, but as long as they think this way they shun any organizing efforts in the countryside.

Another factor, according to Chilean sociologist Gonzalo Falabella (who for years has researched the plight of the fruit workers and once worked incognito as a migrant worker) is that workers feel pitted against one another. The very structuring of so much of the work as piecework fosters an individualistic mentality — "I can make more than you if I work faster than you." (Reportedly, however, many workers think that the piecework system itself is fair even if the rates are too low.[50])

The neo-liberal Labor Code does not permit the formation of a union on a farm, however economically significant it is, where the permanent labor force numbers under eight workers. It also permits employers to maintain workers on a "temporary" status, even if they are employed throughout nearly all the year, thus they can avoid providing the few benefits mandated for permanent workers, including vacations.

In a Chile in which there were more freedom to organize, these factors could be offset by the fact that any labor actions during peak periods could be very costly to the industry. But the Aylwin government did not remove the legal impediments to the unionization of temporary workers and strikes by organized workers in the economically important fruit industry. The legislative prospects were not good: a majority of senators in the first congress since the long dictatorship had significant agricultural interests.

Coming Up Short

Free marketeers like to say that from 1973 onward the public sector played no role in the fruit boom. Indeed, the neo-liberal government went so far as to prohibit the national agricultural research system (INIA) from carrying out research on major export fruits.[51] With a strong, pervasive ideological bias against governmental economic intervention, the government went about decimating the research capacity of agricultural institutions in the public sector. Salaries and agricultural research budgets were slashed. The skilled expertise built up over decades in the public institutions was lured away by the offer of higher salaries and consultancy fees in the private sector. The neo-liberal government also permitted public employees to engage in substantial private consulting. Furthering the private domination of research, private fruit-exporting and agricultural chemical companies have seen to it that what research is carried out within public universities and research centers directly serves their immediate concerns by contracting the research.

So what's wrong with all this? A booming state-of-the-art industry that's not at the public trough. Professor Lovell Jarvis, who has looked long and hard at this question, thinks it is not nearly so desirable as the Chicago Boys would have us believe. And he is not alone.[52]

The Chilean fruit industry has done well at borrowing technologies. Most, as we have already pointed out, were brought in from California, and given the great natural similarities (except for distance to major markets), the technologies were readily transferable. The research needed to adapt and refine them was therefore relatively simple and inexpensive. But there's not much more that can be borrowed, and new fruit cultivation problems are surfacing. "Chile currently has the research expertise to borrow and adapt technologies where highly applied research is adequate, but has limited capacity to undertake more basic research needed for the solution of more complex problems which will be of long-run importance."[53] Coping with many of tomorrow's practical problems is likely to depend on today's theoretical research.[54] University professors in Chile have focused what little research they have carried out "toward highly applied issues of short-run importance, often carried out on a contract basis for the private sector."[55]

In the late 1980s, most of the professor-scientists who remained in the universities and were capable of theoretical work were professionally formed before 1974. During the late 1970s and 1980s, few Chileans began graduate training in the fruit-related sciences. "The best students," observes Jarvis, "went directly to the private sector which offered rapid advancement, responsibility, and high pay."[56] Industry support for research was not for theoretical research but for research of immediate commercial value. However, this industry support gave, as Jarvis comments, "a growing part of shrinking public research a largely private character since the results of such research were usually kept confidential or were published with a considerable lag."[57]

The rapid growth of the fruit industry has not been all that efficient. Jarvis gathered a great deal of anecdotal evidence suggesting that the "learning process" has been costly in terms of investment and management error. Of course, many errors are to be expected in any learning process especially one that is galloping along at a high speed. But, according to Jarvis, some of the errors were systemic and "the investment of additional resources in public sector research and extension could have profitably reduced such errors."[58] The highly individualized learning by the trial and error approach yielded results at a high cost (affordable only because of the high profits at the time). Research was often ill-designed, ill-evaluated, and frequently duplicated.[59]

Truncating public sector involvement in the fruit industry ensured that participating in its expansion has been limited largely to the better educated and economically more sophisticated growers. As part of the free-market model, technical assistance to farmers is not considered a proper function of the government.[60] Chile's smaller farmers, including the remnant of land-reform beneficiaries were "largely precluded from the fruit boom, mainly because they were insufficiently large and lacking the resources to gain access to the credit, technology and technical assistance offered by the fruit exporters, banks, and consulting agronomists."[61] Domination of research by private interests inevitably slants it toward the needs of large, well-financed growers as opposed to smaller farmers with much fewer resources.

The extreme bias against governmental involvement also has meant that there is no coordination in marketing (reportedly in Rotterdam and other foreign ports several ships loaded with Chilean fruit arrive notoriously often at the same time). Some growers cite a need for quality control to ensure that no operator's pushing volume even at the risk of putting inferior products on the market that well could undermine the prestige — and price — for all.

By the early 1990s, the years of easy growth are quite likely over.[62] Markets are fast saturating. Efforts to further expand by producing grapes earlier as well as later in the season puts Chilean grapes into competitive conflict with growers in the importing countries of the north. New pest and soil problems are emerging. By the end of the 1980s, export volumes were up, but profits were down. In the 1989-90 season the export volume grew 20 percent, yet revenue was down 10 percent from the year before. And while market prices have tended downward, production costs have climbed steadily, more than doubling between 1985 and 1990.[63]

As profitability erodes (or worse), more and more of the research needed by Chile's fruit industry will not be worth the investment to the *individual* exporter or grower. Jarvis concluded from his conversations with exporters and growers that private investment in research was already declining. And the capacity of the public sector for research has been seriously weakened by years of ideological fixation that shifted so many resources out of the public sector. It will not be easy to build the needed capacity, and by the early 1990's the problem was only beginning to be recognized. What is called for is more of a balanced collaboration between private and public sectors, as well as public extension and other efforts to broaden who participates in Chile's fruit boom.

In sum, Chile's boom in fruit exports has generated very skewed benefits, is unlikely to be replicable by other nations due to its extraordinary circumstances, and, as more difficult conditions emerge, will likely prove more flawed precisely because of the lack of adequate public sector involvement. Government economic actions are needed to make Chile's fruit industry both equitable and sustainable.

13

Forestry: Mother Nature on the Block

Celebrator of the free market Joaquín Lavín tells us, "Wood is Chile's new copper." Indeed one of the areas of dramatic growth during the Pinochet years was forestry, with exports increasing from $39 million in 1973 to $760 million in 1990.[1] Lavín's mining metaphor, however, is more appropriate than he would choose to admit.

Background

The geography of Southern Chile resembles the Pacific Northwest of the United States in many ways. The temperate fertile valleys and coastal ranges have been rich in forests for millennia. The diversity of animal and plant life and unique species astounded Darwin. Tree species particular to Chile such as the alerce rival the ancient redwood and sequoia in size and longevity. Since the arrival of the Spaniards in the sixteen century, land owners (and later lumber companies) cleared trees indiscriminately for agriculture, lumber and firewood. But, as in most industrialized countries, Chile developed regulatory legislation to protect and ensure the sustainability of native forests.

Undoubtedly a milestone in the history of Chilean forestry was the introduction of the Monterey pine (*pinus radiata*) to the region in the early twentieth century. Today, along the Panamerican highway, about four hours south from Santiago, rich farmlands give way to mile after mile of monotonous rows of pine. One forestry expert suggested to us that the introduction of this non-native species was the salvation of the native forests, since it grew rapidly, could be planted in already deforested areas and provided an alternative source of wood that took pressure off native forests.[2] In 1940, 70 percent of trees cut for commercial processing came from native forests; by 1988, 90 percent came from plantations, virtually all Monterey pine.[3]

The modern forestry industry in Chile dates from attempts by the Frei and Allende administrations to stimulate and coordinate diverse aspects of forestry. In Chile from 1965-73, as with the forestry industry in much of the developed world, activist government policies got trees planted and financed and even built the industrial structure that is the basis of the forestry boom in the 1980s. During these years the forestry industry grew at an average annual pace of 10 percent. By comparison, from 1974 through 1986 the industry growth averaged 9 percent, with the notable difference that after 1974 exports accounted for almost all of the growth.[4]

In addition to programs in research, training and technical assistance, government action beginning in the 1960s was in two areas. Yields from plantings of Monterey pine were beginning to outstrip the country's limited processing capacity, long dominated by the powerful Matte conglomerate. In the 1960s and early 1970s, Chile's three principal forestry industry complexes were built, all completely or partially financed by the government agency CORFO.[5] This industrial infrastructure ended the monopoly power of the Matte conglomerate and became the basis for forestry expansion over the next two decades.

The Allende administration signed five-year "pacts" to plant trees and share caretaking responsibilities on the vacant lands of small and medium-sized landholders. The government and the landholders were to share eventual profits from harvesting the trees. The government used the pacts to guide rural development in some of Chile's poorest regions and in areas denuded of native forest. They brought small and medium-sized farmers and landowners into tree plantings, raised employment and improved the level of technical forest management. Links were made to other government policies, such as the agrarian reform and housing programs. According to José Leyton, a forestry engineer who worked in the government forestry corporation (CONAF) under both Allende and Pinochet, these pacts are "the most significant attempt at the development of Chilean forestry to date." [6]

Over 625,000 acres were planted under these pacts. Almost all of it was Monterey pine, a species which requires 16 to 20 years to mature.[7] Pinochet's free marketeers reaped the harvest of years of governmental investments.

Tree Market Policies

Those who applaud Chile's free market model point to the success of forestry exports as evidence that the model works. In fact, the forestry sector is where free market policies were least important in stimulating growth. The neo-liberals' stated goals were to sharply curtail the direct role of government in forestry and to let market mechanisms determine prices and direct the use of resources, yet government intervention and subsidies were central to reorienting the benefits of forestry production away from the general rural population and toward a handful of national and foreign companies.

Pinochet's neo-liberal economic advisors gave priority to the forestry industry not only because of Chile's natural comparative advantage, the great demand for forestry products on the world market, and because they knew that the groundwork had already been laid.[8] Politics also played a big role: forestry companies (particularly the Matte conglomerate) had actively opposed the Allende government; in addition, Ponce Lerou, Pinochet's son-in-law, headed the government forestry corporation (CONAF) during the late 1970s when new forestry policies were set.

New policies directly or indirectly translated into government interventions on behalf of the country's largest economic conglomerates, some of whom already had significant investments in forestry (Matte) and others who used government concessions to create new forestry empires (Vial and Angelini). All restrictions on size and ownership of land holdings were lifted. Part of the forestry land expropriated under the agrarian reform law (around 7.5 million acres) was handed back to the original owners and the rest sold or auctioned off to interested buyers. In addition the government sold off its own considerable forestry land holdings as well as its share of the trees planted under the earlier pacts, often to third parties instead of to the original partner.

In these privatizations, completed by 1979, there was no pretense of "people's capitalism," the deceptive hoopla employed by the Chicago Boys to market the privatizations of the late 1980s. The large conglomerates picked up valuable assets for scandalously low sums. Ordinary farmers were ineligible to purchase lands they were living on if they had any outstanding debts to the government and, given Allende's pro-small holder policy of generous loans and the deep post-coup recession, most were ineligible. At the same time, new small holder beneficiaries of the agrarian reform, often indebted and without access to further credit or inputs, were soon forced to sell their plots.[9]

Similarly, the government sold off its interests in the principal forestry processing plants in the country. As with privatizations in other areas of the economy, these companies were sold at a discount, according to one estimate at least 20 percent below their value.[10] All the industrial complexes, as did much of the privatized forestry land, ended up in the hands of a few large conglomerates.

A series of tax credits favored forestry exports. Exports of forestry products were permitted to be in any form: trees could be cut and shipped out as logs, with no processing into higher-value products such as lumber, pulp, paper, furniture, etc. In 1988, the volume of tree trunks exported from Chile was three times that of lumber, although a cubic meter of trunks fetches barely a third as much as that of lumber. Similarly, the boom product of the late 1980s was wood chips (grist for paper mills) which have an export value per ton less than one-thirteenth that of processed paper pulp, which in turn has a value far below paper.[11] Having been left to concentrate on short-term profits, the Chilean forestry industry squanders the potential for capturing more of the value of the end product and thereby generating more skilled jobs, and escaping from Chile's centuries-old syndrome of exporting low-value raw materials.

Subsidizing Big Business

Without doubt the most significant move of the Pinochet government in forestry was Decree 701. After the coup, no new pacts were made with landholders for the government to plant trees directly; and CONAF only reluctantly fulfilled obligations contracted before the coup. To encourage new plantings CONAF reimbursed 75 percent (later changed to 90 percent) of the estimated costs of planting after one year, with additional reimbursements for the costs of pruning and maintaining plantations. Over the period 1974 and 1986, of the more than 2.5 million acres of trees planted and in private hands, 73 percent were planted either with these generous CONAF subsidies or by CONAF directly (through the pacts dating before the military regime and the government minimum employment programs). Between 1974 and 1990, total subsidies for planting exceeded $88 million.[12]

No other agricultural sector, not even the table grape industry, receives such regular subsidies. Not surprisingly, forestry, in part because of the heavy subsidies, has been extremely successful at attracting national and foreign investment.

With the Popular Unity program of pacts with landholders, the government could encourage planting in particular regions and select certain types of landholders (for example, poor farmers) at roughly the same cost as the Pinochet government's program of subsidized planting. And a share of the profits from the plantations eventually returned to the public coffer.[13]

With the Chicago Boys' reimbursement system, the government also intervened (contrary to the neo-liberal rhetoric) to promote tree planting with subsidies, but the market is the mechanism for distribution of the subsidies. Virtually all plans that meet certification and professional standards for planting are approved, regardless of the planter's nationality of the number of trees planted. The reimbursement, when the planting is carried out on a large scale and using temporary laborers, is enough to cover the costs and, in some cases, provide a profit to the owner. Reimbursement is given only if a certain percentage of trees survive after the first year. The very nature of the policies inherently excluded small and medium holders, who do not have access to the technical assistance needed to submit and carry out complex plans, who cannot achieve the economies of scale of the large companies, and who have little access to the credit necessary to plant and wait for eventual reimbursement, let alone to wait 16 years for the land planted to become productive.

Using the market to distribute subsidies has accentuated existing marketplace inequalities. The majority of the reimbursements are captured by large conglomerates. In 1988 almost half (48 percent) of the area reimbursed for plantings was owned by the ten largest forestry companies in Chile. A single company, Arauco-Constitución (part of the Angelini conglomerate), owned 18 percent of the land planted with government subsidies.[14]

The Forestry Giants

In March 1982, a forestry specialist told the conservative newspaper *El Mercurio*, "It is indispensable that the forested properties be in the possession of the smallest possible number of individuals so as to guarantee permanent supplies for the industry."[15] Since 1974, ownership has become ever more concentrated into the hands of a few large corporations.

To assure a constant supply of quality trees, the companies in the pulp and lumber business have progressively acquired the land and plantations near their industrial complexes and thus do not depend on purchasing trees from small landowners. Empires have been carved out of once public lands and by buying out smaller owners. The Matte and the Angelini conglomerates (the latter in alliance with the New Zealand multinational Carter Holt Harvey) together own over 40 percent of the area in tree plantations. Another seven foreign-based conglomerates (including investments by Shell, the Saudi Arabian group Bin Mahfouz, and Marubeni of Japan) own another 9 percent of the area in plantations. In wood processing Matte and Angelini together control 63 percent of the industry; the top 10 companies combined control a total of 80 percent. In the leading forestry region of Concepción, Matte and Angelini control more than 70 percent of all forestry-related activities.[16] Since the wood chip boom began in 1987, Japanese companies have entered the field aggressively by purchasing large tracts of native forests and planning wood chip factories.

The process of forestation has expelled countless people from rural areas. Small parcels have increasingly been absorbed by large plantations belonging to conglomerates. With no access to credit and often greater planting costs, small property owners have found it difficult to combine forestry with farming and other activities.

Moreover, many cannot maintain their farms, since the surrounding plantations often diminish groundwater supplies and spray pesticides that can poison nearby livestock. Those who run the forestry companies both covet neighboring land and fear any human activity on that land that might lead to forest fires. They have been known to pressure small landholders to sell by closing access roads.[17]

Contracting Labor

Forestry companies argue that they have provided jobs in depressed areas. But the forestry boom has brought limited jobs and benefits to local populations. All aspects of forestry production employ at the annual peak 60,000 workers, which is no more than 20 years ago.[18] The stagnant number of jobs in what is an expanding industry is due in part to newly incorporated technology in industrial processing. Another factor is a marked increase in how much labor is squeezed out of forestry workers.

During the Popular Unity years forestry workers achieved significant gains in pay and working conditions, as over half organized into labor unions. Industry-wide pay rates were negotiated and job security and safety were improved. The military government dismantled forestry unions with particular fervor. Besides direct repression of activist workers, a series of decrees restricted the negotiating position of forestry workers. The most significant decree changed from six months to two years the length of time at the same job for a worker to be considered permanent rather than temporary, with temporary workers forbidden to join unions. By 1983 the percentage of organized forestry workers had dropped from 50 to 5 percent.[19]

By the late 1970s, most forestry companies had reduced their permanent labor force drastically, by replacing them with temporary workers, or, more commonly, by contracting out specific tasks to middlemen who in turn contracted temporary workers. By 1983, of 2,000 employees in the forest management and harvesting company CRECEX, only 2.3 percent were permanent. This pattern is also found, though to a lesser extent, in wood-processing industries; the pulp plant Celulosa Arauco cut its permanent workforce from 2,500 workers in 1973 to 500 in 1981.[20]

Contractors, by hiring temporary workers and bidding to do specific services for specific fees, drove down costs and payroll significantly. Often contractors are entreprenuerial types or former military men who know nothing about forestry. In Concepción, fly-by-night contractors are referred to as "mushroom contractors" — since they appear from one day to the next and often abandon worksites, leaving workers unpaid if it seems that they cannot fulfill their obligations to a company on time.[21]

Temporary workers are sometimes several times removed from their true employer — most often one of the ten big companies. In some cases they are not even sure who their employer is, making legal action impossible, and health and pension coverage highly unlikely. At the same time the big companies are relieved of legal responsibility for pay, working and living conditions, and fringe benefits. The high level of unemployment and underemployment in rural areas allows contractors and processing plants to hire inexperienced workers at substandard wages and for long hours, although often at the cost of low productivity and an increase in on-the-job accidents. Lax and unenforced safety rules have caused frequent loss of limbs and the highest accident rate of any economic sector in the country.[22] According to a study by the Catholic Church in Concepción, such working conditions have not existed in Chile since the nineteenth century nitrate mines.[23] One worker described the hiring process in his plant:

> The company where I worked needed to contract more workers about six years ago. The locals began to demand better conditions so the foreman went South and brought back two truckloads of workers...Word got around. The company didn't have to go looking again because there were always eight to 10 people in the street waiting to be hired...every time at a lower salary.[24]

Even though the required skills in many forestry jobs are low, jobs often go to people contracted from outside the area rather than to locals. When we visited the town of Corral, locals told us that they had welcomed the forestry companies because they had promised to bring jobs to a depressed economy. In fact, they complained, the companies preferred to bring in contract crews from 200 miles away rather than train locals to do forestry tasks.

Just outside of Corral we visited a logging site on land owned by the Army. The right to log had been sold to a French-owned company which in turn contracted a work crew from Valdivia. The foreman told us that these crews were always sent back before two years passed because they became homesick and therefore useless. But two years, of course, is the legal limit for contracting a temporary worker, an employer advantage that would be harder to maintain with local hires.

Despite the celebrated forestry boom, even the lot of permanent workers in the industry has deteriorated. With the new Labor Code, many were fired and then re-hired at lower salaries. Some of these permanent workers have benefited from the introduction of modern safety procedures (protective clothing, etc.) and higher wages, particularly in foreign-owned companies such as Shell; but these plants continued to contract out the majority of their work. The plant itself is showcased and effectively preempts unionization, but for the majority of workers employed through subcontracts, the pattern remains temporary jobs, long hours, low wages and frequent accidents.

Destroying Mother Nature

"When I studied forestry, the text books were foreign and the species were foreign," Claudio Donoso, a professor forestry at Austral University in southern Chile explained to us. "Monterey pine was everything. Chileans got stuck in a Monterey pine mentality and lost interest in learning about the native woods."[25]

If the Monterey pine began as the savior of Chile's native forests by shifting logging from forests to plantations, under Pinochet's new order it has turned to their nemesis. The government reimbursement program worked well until there was no more good cleared land to plant. According to Donoso, the conglomerates were unwilling to plant on poorer land and assume the costs of fertilizing. Instead, "the big companies began clear cutting native forests in order to access rich and fertile soils for planting, often nevertheless receiving the lucrative planting reimbursment from the government!"[26]

Chilean law prohibits clear cutting of native forests. Forestry companies regularly get around this ban by declaring a property to be brush or "severely degraded" forest. Then they clear cut or even burn in order to replant pine. The severe reduction in staff at

CONAF has made enforcement in the expanding forestry industry almost impossible. In 1985 the non-governmental conservation organization CODEFF denounced a case in which a landowner burned down a large stretch of native forest and later collected the reimbursement for planting. The offender was fined an amount far less than his profits, proving to many that CONAF lacked both the means and the will to reinforce such laws. Donoso puts the area of native forest lost to plantations since the mid-70s at one million acres, almost a third of the total area planted.[27]

The destruction of native forests of great ecological diversity has left various plant species bordering on extinction. Burning and clearcutting the forests destroy the habitat of a variety of indigenous animals and birds and give rise to deep erosion. The replacement of native forests by continuous stretches of single-species plantations has caused further ecological damage only now becoming evident — including a pronounced drying up of waterways and ground moisture, undermining the well-being of nearby farmers and the local population.

Monocultural plantations are particularly vulnerable to plant diseases and rodents whose natural predators have disappeared. Plantation owners live in a constant fear of exotic diseases, and of rabbits and moths that could wipe out their pine trees. In their battle against diseases and pests, they resort to importing pesticides and chemicals that are prohibited in their country of manufacture, such as agent orange and 1080 poison. Through the food chain the chemicals are passed on to other animals including humans. Paper pulp plants dump untreated chemical wastes directly into rivers and bays. Air pollution in mill towns like Constitución often reaches dangerous levels. In free-market Chile there are virtually no penalties for such environmental destruction. To be sure, the costs are paid for by society at large.[28]

Managing the Forests

Over and over we heard Chileans boast that Monterey pine grows faster in Chile than in its native California. But some wonder how long Chile can produce Monterey pine competitively, particularly as vast areas in Brazil, Siberia and elsewhere are opened up to pine plantations and the Japanese invest in pine planting in places such as New Guinea, and as demand in paper production shifts toward eucalyptus, whose short-fibers are used in higher quality computer paper. If this happens, Chile will nevertheless have three million acres of pine to sell in the early years of the 21st century at whatever price the market will bear.

The planting of Monterey pine on a massive scale is a recent phenomenon. Only now is the first full cycle being harvested, and the technical question remains: Are Chile's single-species pine plantations really renewable? Since first plantings were on rich soil where previous natural forests existed and monocultures quickly exhaust the soil and groundwater, second plantings will, at the least, require high levels of fertilization at costs that growers up to now have been reluctant to pay.

Donoso insists that there is an alternative. "Chile's real comparative advantage is in hard woods. They grow here faster than almost anywhere, and are native to Chile." Native trees such as Chilean oak, *rauli* and *coigue* take at least thirty years to mature. That is about the same growing span as that of pine plantations in the United States and Europe, but the value of the hard woods is far greater than that of pine. But without sufficient research, incentives or market development supported by industry or the government, and without any enforced regulations against destroying native forests, individual and corporate landowners never took an interest in the sustained commercial management of native forests. Dependent on financial support by forestry companies, university forestry departments have focused on pine plantations. An exception are experiments in Valdivia that have shown that native forests can be managed profitably to produce hard woods. Some ecologically minded planters and forestry engineers have pushed for government planting reimbursements to be extended for replanting and managing native species. But CONAF has long delayed making a decision. In the meantime, a newcomer threatens Chilean forests.

High-tech Termites

The harbor of the southern city Puerto Montt is dominated by a towering mountain of wood shavings. These "chips" resemble what falls on the floor of any carpentry shop, only here they are the product rather than waste. The wood chips industry arrived in Chile in 1987 and within three years accounted for over twelve percent of the value of Chilean forestry exports. Wood chip factories — dubbed by the media "high-tech termites" — require minimal industrial infrastructure to turn trees into chips. The chips make for a high-volume, low-value export that is eventually converted in Japan and Europe into paper products, particularly computer paper. By 1990, there were nine of these plants in Chile, most owned by foreign companies.

These companies originally claimed that raw material for wood chips would be drawn from properly managed native forests. The Association of Wood Producers claims its member companies help preserve native forests by culling rotting native trees and converting them to woodchips.[29] Indeed over 60 percent of the logs made into wood chips does comes from native forests. But while government-approved management plans do allow for the culling of crowded, diseased, or over-aged trees, in practice many native forests of high-quality hard woods have been leveled and turned into chips. Since up to now most of the wood chip companies buy logs from forests owned by other companies they have little interest in guaranteeing the sustainability of native forests.

Application for "management" of native forests have soared by a factor of fifteen since the wood chip boom began in 1987, far beyond the capacity of the staff-depleted CONAF to monitor. According to one estimate, over 30 percent of the cuttings in native forests under management plans are illegal, amounting to thinly disguised clear cutting.[30]

Under the neo-liberal mandate for government agencies to be self-financing, CONAF in 1990 voluntarily entered an agreement with the wood chip companies by which they pay CONAF one dollar per ton of chips exported. This creates a dynamic whereby any significant curtailment by CONAF of the felling of native forests would reduce its own revenues (if not provoke the companies to end the agreement all together). One forestry consultant we talked with complained that such a policy was tantamount to having someone accused of a crime pay the judge's salary.

We visited the wood chip project known as Terranova, owned jointly by the privatized Chilean-Swiss company CAP (Pacific Steel) and the Japanese paper company Marubeni. In the mid-

1980s CAP-Marubeni purchased and applied to exploit an area of 150,000 acres of native forest south of Valdivia. CAP-Marubeni, however, insisted that it would be profitable only if Terranova were allowed to clear cut 60,000 acres of native forest (much of it on erosion-prone slopes of up to 45 degrees) and replant them with eucalyptus trees. The proposal aroused strong opposition from Chile's fledgling ecology movement and forced the newly elected civilian government to turn the problem over to a special commission for evaluation.

The Japanese forestry products industry and the Marubeni corporation in particular have a long history of one-shot extractive forestry in other countries. In the Malaysian state of Sabah, wood chip exports were banned after Marubeni failed to replant large tracts of land they had clear cut. A similar project by Marubeni on the Chilean island of Chiloe was withdrawn in the early 1980s when it came up against unexpected protests from the local church and people.[31]

Conclusion

A 1989 issue of a glossy Chilean government magazine aimed at foreign investors celebrates the country's forestry industry. "What has happened since 1974 to create this tremendous boom?" the editors ask. "Freedom is the key" — in this case the freedom to own, cut, plant and export trees and tree products, virtually without government interference as to the number and size of trees or the degree of processing. Once again, it's the free marketeers' credo applied.

Several realities, however, should shake even a true believer. It was government investments in tree plantings and industrial infrastructure made during the administrations of Frei and Allende that provided a solid foundation for growth in Chile's modern forestry industry. Moreover, these public investments were designed to promote equitable rural development. By contrast, the free-market policies of the Pinochet government sold off public lands and infrastructure on the cheap, and in such ways that further concentrated control among a few huge conglomerates. Free-market rhetoric notwithstanding, lucrative government subsidies were employed to promote tree plantings. Passing out these public monies on the open marketplace ensured that the strong and well-connected conglomerates, and not the rural disadvantaged in need of economic opportunity, would grab the lion's share. "Free-market planning," while good for big business, has meant only short-term gain for Chile. Lax and non-existent regulation has led to the destruction of native forests. Once again we have the over-exploitation of non-renewable natural resources and labor — epitomized in the wood chip boom — that we have repeatedly seen to be the foundation of Chile's economic growth starting in the late 1980s. Moreover, private business interests looking only at the bottom line in the short-term are selling off Chile's forest resources with only minimal processing, exacerbating a classic third-world pattern: over 90 percent of Chilean exports intensively exploit natural resources (mostly nonrenewable) and add little value (or employment) through processing.[32]

To free-market proponents and their allies in the big forestry companies, cutting the native forest equals growth, jobs and progress, while any limits on this freedom will result only in economic stagnation and unemployment. But this freedom provides short-term gains at the cost of losing potentially much greater longer-term gains and national development. The depletion of natural resources represents a permanent loss of key national assets that will undermine longer term development plans. Sustainable use, in which natural resources and the environment are considered economic capital that must be renewed, makes sense for the nation as a whole — but also for future economic actors. But such responsible accounting can never be expected from individual actors or corporations motivated solely by short-term profit.

Even when natural resources are factored in as assets to be sustained and renewed, one must still consider other values that are not quantifiable. How to place a value on the beauty of an ancient forest? Certainly not by how much people might be willing to pay to walk through it. Obviously, then, the market cannot determine the value of such natural resources to society at large. This was explicitly acknowledged by the initial statement (January 1991) of the government commission formed by President Aylwin on the controversial Terranova project: "Even when the transformation [of native woods to plantations] makes sense in economic terms, there are other interests expressed by a great part of society that make the maintenance and management of that resource recommendable."

Rhetoric of the "free market" disguises interventionist government policies that subsidize a handful of large national and foreign conglomerates that benefited most from expansion of the forestry industry. Chile's forest resources are being exploited by these conglomerates for short-term gain in ways that endanger their longer-term capacity for renewal. This is bad policy and bad economics. The mining metaphor of which free-marketers are fond is tragically apt.

14

Mining the Seas

"The sea is a desert, not a garden. Chile's coastal waters are an oasis in the desert of the Pacific. If you exhaust this oasis, if you fish it out, all you have left is desert," warns Luis Morales, a marine biologist who has spent much of his life working with small fishermen.

Chile's long coastline is one of the most richly endowed with marine resources in the world. The captains of the fishing industry and free marketeers boast that they have taken underutilized marine resources and opened them up to development by both small fishermen and large national and foreign companies willing to invest in modern technology. The statistics are impressive. In 1971 the total catch in Chile was 1.5 million tons; by 1989 it had risen spectacularly to almost 6.5 million tons, ranking Chile fourth in the world. Fishing exports rose from $48 million in 1973 to over $934 million in 1987, rivaling earnings from agro-exports and forest products for second-place honors after copper. Moreover, employment in fishing has quadrupled since the early 1970s to around 60,000 in 1990.[1]

Spectacular growth in fish exports and free-market policies have pushed many marine resources to the brink of irreversible depletion. Of the top five fishing countries (by total volume of catch), only Chile's fleet fishes exclusively national waters, an indication of the intensity of exploitation of its coastal waters.[2] Policies of unregulated access to marine resources have produced short-term gains in output but have precluded economically rational and ecologically sustainable long-term use. Marine fishing rights are ill-defined, and competition for resources is brutally cut-throat. In

219

the absence of clear and enforced regulation of the exploitation of marine resources by the government, later generations of Chileans will certainly be left to pay the costs.

Background

Significant growth in the fishing industry began well before 1974. Beginning in the 1940s the government development corporation CORFO encouraged fishing and in the 1950s provided credits to the fledgling fishmeal industry. Both the Frei and Allende administrations were particularly optimistic about the potential expansion of fishing and began implementation of a series of integrated policies that included studies of marine resources, favorable credit, tax breaks, and customs reductions for industry-related imports. Early development efforts focused on boosting employment, fostering cooperatives, and promoting internal consumption of fish products as well as exports. Neither administration was particularly conservation-minded; this is clear from the near collapse of the anchovy supply from over-fishing in the mid-1960s and again in 1972.

The Fishing Code, passed in the 1930s, allowed for free and unlimited access to marine resources and remained mostly intact under the Pinochet regime. The telling differences made under the free-market model were the opening of fishing to foreign investors on very favorable terms, the dramatic introduction of new fishing and processing technology, and the revision of labor laws to allow for a greater exploitation of all workers, including in the fishing industry.

Fishmeal

Although fourth in terms of the volume of catch, Chile ranks only twentieth when ranked by the commercial value of its fish product, suggesting in part only a minimal level of processing.[3] The great majority of Chile's catch — 90 percent in 1987 — goes into the production of fishmeal and fish oil.[4] The northern-based fishmeal industry, fueled by global demand for animal feed, is by far the largest fishing sector. The industry since the 1960s has undergone repeated boom and bust cycles of unregulated access to and abuse of resources.[5] The pattern has become almost institutionalized: heavy investment leads to over-capacity and over-fishing; greatly reduced fish stocks in turn become particularly vulnerable to changes in ocean currents, primarily the infamous *El Niño* that sweeps cold Antarctic waters up the Pacific coast of South America. Each cycle of collapse has been followed by a further concentration of ownership of industry and a shift to over-fishing of another species.

After the anchovy collapse of 1972-73, in which the catch fell by more than half, the Allende government took over ownership of the troubled industry to preserve employment. Under Pinochet, numerous mid-sized fishmeal companies that had been taken over by the Allende government were reorganized and sold off to the private sector. Most of them became concentrated in the hands of seven companies, four of which came to be controlled by Chilean businessman Anecleto Angelini, who now controls about 80 percent of the fishmeal industry in alliance with the Carter Holt Harvey company of New Zealand. Using his base in fishing, Angelini has emerged as head of Chile's largest economic empire, with large holdings in forestry and ownership of the country's main oil company COPEC.

The newly concentrated companies made the industry viable again through a considerable modernization of existing industrial infrastructure and fishing technology, by taking advantage of new labor laws that allowed them to impose longer hours and night fishing, and by shifting to new fishing stocks. Within four years of the 1972-73 collapse, the Chilean fishmeal industry recovered to historic catch levels, with 92 percent of the catch composed of sardine and saurel instead of anchovy. By 1986, the total fish-meal related catch was five times its pre-collapse peak in 1971.[6]

With recovery of the industry came a repetition of patterns of over-capacity and over-exploitation, creating great inefficiencies and undue pressure on limited resources. For example, in 1986 the holding capacity of boats in the fishmeal sector was 9 million tons and factory capacity was 6.8 million tons. Yet total actual catch was far less at 4 million, an all-time high.

Failed Quotas

In 1983 the undersecretary of fishing, concerned with indisputable evidence of a rapidly dwindling stock of sardines, imposed a quota of 1.3 million tons on annual sardine catches, in a break with the free-market model. Sardines were the basis of the fishmeal boom of the previous ten years, just as the anchovies had fueled an earlier cycle. The fishmeal industrialists reacted strongly against the quota, as did fishmeal workers who faced layoffs in the midst of a deep recession. Responding to pressure, the undersecretary first upped the ceiling and finally eliminated it altogether. After a peak sardine catch in 1985 of 2.6 million tons, the government still refused to once again impose a quota.[7] Since that year the sardine catch declined precipitously to 1.8 million tons in 1988 and 1.4 million tons by 1989. By 1988 biologists of the government's National Fisheries Development Institute estimated that for the annual catch to be sustainable, it should not exceed 0.4 million tons, far below the level at that time. By 1990, they estimated that the stock of the sardine had dropped by 66 percent over the course of the 1980s, putting it on the verge of depletion. As the industry shifts once again to another resource (saurel), the stock of that species has begun a rapid descent and could collapse in the next few years.[8]

Factory trawlers, land plants and small fishermen

Although fishmeal and fish oil constituted 90 percent of the total volume of production, other fish products, particularly frozen and canned fish, seaweed and aqua cultures — all for human consumption — provided around 43 percent of the value of production in 1987.[9]

By far the most important commercial fish is hake, which is fished primarily by 35 self-contained and mostly foreign-owned "factory trawlers." In addition 15,000 fishermen in small boats sell their catch to land-based freezing plants. This has created a competitive dynamic for scarce resources between the factory trawlers and the small fishermen, and among the individual fishing units themselves.

The factory trawlers dramatize the model's policy of free access to natural resources. All are owned in their entirety by Japanese, Korean and Spanish companies, yet they fish national waters just like Chilean ships by paying a nominal fee and hiring a Chilean national as captain. A fee of $20 per ton of catch is, in theory, paid to the Chilean government (2 percent of the commercial value). These large ships (up to 325 feet in length) are equipped to both catch and process fish internally, processing between 12 and 39 tons in 8 hours and entering a Chilean port every two months to transfer their product to transport ships.[10] Trawlers operate on the continental shelf along the Chilean coast at a time when most countries have prohibited them because of their devastating impact on fish resources.[11]

When the factory trawlers were incorporated as Chilean-flag vessels in the late 1970s, the Pinochet government argued that they were an important investment and would bring advances in research and technology and take advantage of underutilized resources. The reality is otherwise. Existing factory trawlers were on average 15 years old in 1987 and virtually no Chileans held any of the skilled jobs where they might learn new technology. The entire fleet of factory trawlers employs a total of 800 people, compared to the competing land-based processing plants, that generate a total of 10,000 jobs and have links to 15,000 small fishermen.[12]

According to one researcher's findings, the majority of the factory trawlers paid no taxes for the years examined. In 1982, the undersecretary of fishing complained publicly that "the operation of the factory trawlers hasn't meant greater economic benefits to the country, since these companies of foreign capital have shown insignificant profits on the books, presumably because they are hiding taxable profits behind the under-reporting of catches and over-estimating investments and depreciation."[13]

Even so, the government has not seriously regulated the trawlers. The drag-net fishing practiced by the factory trawlers is not selective: fish of low value or size or that are protected are thrown dead back into the sea. And even with catches frequently under-reported, quotas are still openly exceeded.[14] By law factory trawlers were required to host an onboard permanent inspector from the national fishing ministry, SERNAP; these inspectors were easily bought off or simply treated with contempt.

In 1980 SERNAP inspector Hector Vera ordered a Japanese factory ship that had exceeded its quota and used illegal fishing techniques to return to port. The ship was confined to port for sixty days and the local governor, a general, announced that this exemplary punishment demonstrated that "the government was protecting the national interest with an adequate system of control." Two weeks later Vera was removed from his job by orders from higher up.[15] By 1985, such conflicts were ended altogether by eliminating the requirement that each factory ship carry an inspector.

Even if many SERNAP employees are well disposed towards keeping closer tabs on the factory trawlers, staffing is woefully inadequate and the neo-liberal climate precludes any crack-down that might discourage foreign investment. By 1990, SERNAP was down to only 167 employees to monitor the world's fourth largest fish catch. The southern region of Magallanes, where by law most of the factory trawlers are concentrated, is monitored by only four inspectors.[16]

Unlike small fishermen or land-based factories, factory trawlers have virtually no links to the rest of the Chilean economy. If fish stocks are exhausted, there is nothing to keep them from moving on. The trend toward a steady decline of the hake stock is clear. Although the total catch doubled from 1985 to 1988, the average return by weight on every cast of the net has dropped by almost two thirds since the beginning of the decade, and the average size of each fish is also declining. Even though the capacity of existing factory trawlers far exceeded the government quota, in the last two years of Pinochet's rule an additional 25 more factory trawlers were approved, all of them foreign-owned.[17] With these additional vessels, there is a high risk of collapse of the hake stock. If quotas are enforced, these ships will surely undergo long interruptions of fishing and possible bankruptcies.

The risks of collapse of the hake stock are much greater for small fishermen, who cannot move to different international waters. Many entered fishing after the crash of 1982-83 shut down jobs in other areas. Their numbers and participation in the total hake catch increased dramatically, until by 1988 the hake catch of 15,000 small fishermen (of a total of 48,000 small fishermen throughout the country) almost equaled the catch of the factory trawlers. Small fishermen sell their catch to medium-sized land-based factories that generate significant employment and turn out a product of higher value and quality than the factory trawlers. Since small fishermen operate by and large in different areas from the factory trawlers, it is not clear whether they depend on the same stock of hake as the ships, or whether each is depleting its own stock. Although small fishermen and the land-based factories see their interests threatened by the factory trawlers, until recently they have been reluctant to accept limits on their own extraction from the sea.[18]

Using Up the Golden Eggs

The Chilean economist Andrés Gomez-Lobo has attempted to quantify the fishing industry's consumption of its "natural capital," using government estimates of decreases in the stocks of sardine and saurel. His findings are striking. Gross growth in the fishing industry averaged 8.8 percent over the 1980s, but, when the loss of natural capital is factored in, that figure is almost halved to 4.6 percent. In other words, during the decade of the 1980s, almost half of the growth in the fishing industry was due to the consumption of capital. In the last half of the decade the "capital" was being consumed so rapidly that Gomez-Lobo calculated an annual growth rate of *negative* 2.2 percent.[19]

The Loco Rush

In the mid-1980s, hundreds of Chileans headed south with all the enthusiasm of a gold rush to dive for locos, a shellfish resembling abalone that is coveted by the Japanese. The high prices fetched abroad drew fishermen, adventurers and unemployed to areas around Valdivia, Puerto Montt and Chiloe, all hoping to make good money diving for locos. Entrepreneurs, often investing as little as $40,000 to set up a cannery, could make their money back in less than a year.

Soon the banks of locos began to dry up, and conflicts emerged between local fishermen and outsiders over dwindling supplies of the precious shellfish. Only when locos were on the verge of depletion did the government impose limits on quantity and duration of the loco season. This drove up prices, and many fishermen began clandestine diving for locos. Illegally caught locos were sold at even higher prices to intermediaries, who stored them away only to report them when the season opened. When the loco season opened in 1988, those hidden away were presented and the quota was filled in a record five days. Many divers had borrowed to buy expensive boats and diving equipment in preparation and were ruined when the season was cut short and even the locos they had couldn't be sold. Since seasonal bans only increased the speculative nature of loco fishing, the government was reluctantly forced to place a permanent ban on loco diving from 1988 to 1992, coming full circle from free access to no access.

Cultivating the Seas

Members of the fishermen's cooperative in Valparaiso, many of whom were idled by the depletion of locos and other shellfish, spoke to us of their hopes of turning to the farming of fish as an alternative to diving for natural beds of shellfish. Cultivated shellfish fetch a good price, and the beds are renewable and are potentially ecologically sound. But aquaculture is expensive, and therefore entry is limited and the profit margins can be slim. These small fishermen expressed frustration that the government had not provided them either financial or technical assistance in establishing fish farms, passed laws to facilitate the creation of cooperatives, or given preference for aquaculture concessions to local fishermen over entrepreneurs from Santiago (including ranking members of the armed forces) or abroad.

In southern Chile salmon cultivation has been one of the most impressive areas of growth in the fish industry during the 1980s. Salmon are raised in floating cages in several of the pristine fresh water lakes before being taken out, cages and all, to sea. By 1990, over 120 operations had been established, with the value of the salmon produced nearing $100 million.[20] Problems inherent to the model of implementation, however, have marred an otherwise promising enterprise.

The private non-profit Fundación Chile pioneered the salmon culture industry. When the venture proved highly profitable, multinational companies such as the Saudi-owned Bin Mahfouz and Unilever jumped in. The latter entered the field using debt-swaps and by 1990 owned over a fifth of the salmon installations.[21] In addition to foreign capital, many professionals and engineers from Santiago installed salmon operations in the clear blue lakes and inlets of southern Chile.

Concessions for salmon installations were handed out haphazardly, with little thought to aesthetics or alternative uses of the lakes, and with little involvement of the lakeside communities. In the last year of the Pinochet government, 205 new installations were approved, bringing the total to 480, of which 120 were already operating.[22] In the face of such a proliferation, the tourist industry in some areas have protested against what they see as a visual and ecological menace.

In the lakeside resort town of Ranco, residents recounted to us that one morning they woke up to discover their picturesque lake dotted with white circles where salmon cages were to be installed by the Saudi company Eicosal. Eicosal, which together with several other companies had received from the government concessions equaling virtually the total surface of the lake, installed the first floating cages in the wee hours of the night to pre-empt local protest. When a coalition of local hotel owners, retired foreigners and poor farmers who earn much of their income during the short summer tourist season organized a series of actions including a blockade of the road leading to the lake, Eicosal was forced to back down and cut back its plans.[23]

Most entrepreneurs have installed salmon farms without the sanitation devices required by law and used in salmon culture in Scotland and Norway — most importantly vessels to collect salmon waste and excess fish feed. Producing one ton of salmon causes three quarters of a ton of waste and uneaten feed to settle to lake bottom. In the short term, a high concentration of cages without expensive anti-contamination devices boosts the investors' profits. But in the medium term the viability of the salmon farms could be undermined, since high-quality salmon can be produced only in extremely clean water. Moreover, the impact of such unchecked contamination on the entire ecosystem of the lakes is still unclear, but it could be great. While salmon cultivation is potentially renewable and ecologically sound, inadequate government regulation and the "gold rush" mentality of investors have made it a very mixed success.

Conclusions

The Chilean fishing boom has been characterized by the depletion of one species through over-exploitation before moving on to another. Certain species like the loco, oyster and the sea urchin have already dwindled well below commercially exploitable levels, and others such as the sardine and hake are on the verge of collapse. By 1990, over 60 percent of the resource base of the fishing industry was in a state of serious deterioration.[24] Marine resources have been mined as a one-time bonanza rather than fished as a renewable resource. The intensity of exploitation of Chile's seas is simply not sustainable over the long term.

In virtually every type and area of fishing, poorly regulated access had led to a level of investment in fishing capacities far exceeding what Chile's marine resources can sustain. This pattern has generated economic inefficiencies and cycles of boom and bust. In spite of the number of small fishermen, the fishing industry is characterized by high concentration: in the largest sector of the industry, fishmeal, a single conglomerate accounts for over 70 percent of production; a handful of foreign companies control all the factory trawlers and bring in around half of the total hake catch, the second most important fish export.

Investment in fishing has almost always favored increasing the size of the catch rather than the level of processing. By contrast, Canada, where investments have increased the level of processing, generates five times more foreign earnings with one fifth the catch.[25]

While in 15 years the total Chilean catch has grown fivefold, yearly national fish consumption, never very significant, has dropped from 17.6 pounds to 9 pounds per person.[26] This reflects the export orientation of government policies as well as the low incomes of the majority of Chileans. Only 3 percent of the national catch is consumed by Chileans.

The logic of free-market access to marine resources is that it is in the immediate interest of each individual participant, whether a small fisher or an owner of a factory ship, to extract as much as possible before someone else does. To restrain oneself unilaterally in hopes of helping to sustain supplies of fish over the long-term would be economic suicide.[27]

Pinochet's free-market government resorted to emergency regulations that restricted access only when the regenerative capacity of a particular marine resource was already in serious jeopardy. In many cases it was too late. Nor were free-market policy makers willing to tax those who benefited most from free access to marine resources significantly enough to aid the government to enforce regulations, invest in a rational system of resource management, and assure that local communities and small operators would be freed from boom-and-bust cycles.

Since marine and fish resources belong to nobody, access to them cannot be relegated to market forces alone. Government must actively regulate the fishing industry in order to insure a more rational exploitation, a painfully learned lesson in the fishing industries of most of the developed world. Otherwise, Chile's fishing boom will bring on a permanent bust.

15

Buses, The Free Market, and Pollution

> Santiago has become a model for urban renaissance for planners in Latin America.
> Jonathan Kendall,
> *The New York Times Magazine,*
> July 7, 1991

> Santiago, Chile — On a clear day during the Southern Hemisphere winter, the towering Andes mountains glisten with a blanket of snow. But from here they are for the most part invisible, hidden behind a thick brown layer of smog that fills this city of more than four million people, making Santiago among the most polluted cities in the world.
> This is the time of year when most Chileans would like to avoid the capital. Eyes sting. Bronchial illness surges. And, according to doctors, the march of cancer in the population increases.
> Nathaniel C. Nash,
> *The New York Times,* July 6, 1992

In few other arenas has the free-marketeers' penchant for deregulation been so single-mindedly put into practice as in that of Santiago's bus transport. Santiago's world-class pollution, as we will see, is but one of the consequences.

A 1990 United Nations study of the effects of free-market policies applied to urban transport in Chile bluntly notes that the sweeping policy changes were implemented with only "superficial" studies of the likely effects. "The prime motive for urban bus deregulation was the general belief that deregulation in general was good,"[1] the study comments.

Buses Before

At the end of 1977, on the eve of the decrees ordering sweeping changes, there were 5,435 buses of various types registered in Santiago.[2] Although the majority were privately owned, for decades government regulation was thoroughgoing in all the ways commonplace in countries around the world. The oversight powers of the Ministry of Transport and Telecommunications included route authorization, the setting of fares and frequency of services, route assignment, bus inspection, and licensing the importation of buses. Government and the industry worked jointly to establish new routes which were advertised and subjected to review by competing operators and the general public. Fares were periodically increased, often following fuel price hikes.[3]

The New Order

The withdrawal early in the free-market regime of subsidies to most public sector companies threatened the existence of the public bus company. Attempts were made to boost its efficiency, but, as United Nations transport expert Ian Thomson told us, "The overriding economic doctrine of the government having only a subsidiary role would have implied the public bus company being privatized no matter how efficient it had become."[4] Some argued that even in a neo-liberal world of privatizations there would be an ongoing need for government intervention to guarantee provision of services "unattractive" (that is, unprofitable) to the private sector; but they were told not to worry, private companies would efficiently serve the needs of all the riding public. In any case, during the late 1970s the public bus company was wound down and early in 1981 wound up. The buses were sold off cheaply; in 1990, many were still being operated by private owners, mainly in provincial cities.

At the same time, various decrees sweepingly deregulated the urban bus sector, creating a free-market heaven. Permission to operate a bus became nearly automatic. Requests to run on a route not already operated were seldom, if ever, turned down. In the jargon of the free marketeers, "All the streets were liberated."[5] Schedules, if any, were up to the private owners. "Fare freedom" was decreed (with the exception of government-set student fares — even the Pinochet dictatorship feared student protests). Owners were free to import as many and whatever buses they pleased — including used buses from elsewhere in Latin America so old and polluting they were banned there.[6] Up until the mid-1980s, emissions inspections were hardly ever carried out.

Finally in late 1987 mounting alarm at Santiago's increased air pollution attributed principally to buses led the Ministry of Transport and Telecommunications to impose significant restrictions on the quality (as determined by age of the vehicle) and the number of buses authorized to use certain heavily traveled thoroughfares. Only months later (March 1988), however, the junta decreed a law which in effect abolished all such restrictions. The previously cited United Nations report comments: "The fact that this Law was requested by the Finance Ministry seems to reflect that the deregulation of the urban bus sector was ordained on general economic policy grounds rather than being the product of any evaluation of the situation of the sector itself." Similarly an earlier restriction (in 1984) on growth in the size of total bus fleet and on bus traffic in the heavily congested city center was "not heeded and no serious attempt was made to apply it."[7]

Environmental Impact

Free-market policies set off an explosion in the number of buses. By the mid-1980s, some 13,500 buses were plying the streets of Santiago. (That's as many buses as serve Buenos Aires, which has a population three times that of Santiago. Sao Paulo, Brazil, with almost four times the population of Santiago, has only 7,000 buses.) The number of buses mushroomed because with fare deregulation (more on this later) bus owners initially made big profits, often netting over 100 percent annually in the first years after deregulation.[8]

Most bus owners opted to run on the same (or similar) routes because there they thought were the most potential customers who could afford to pay. With the free market there is no integration of routes, no "feeding" of trunk routes, so virtually every bus connects some far-flung zone to the same most common destinations. Not surprisingly, not only are there a lot of buses in Santiago but certain streets most desired by the bus owners are jammed with bumper-to-bumper yet half-empty buses. During the rush hours of the day and evening more than one thousand buses an hour, two to three lanes abreast, crawl along the Alameda, the once-grand downtown boulevard.[9] It is a stunning sight we've never seen anywhere else in the world. A gas mask is recommended, however, a point we will come back to later.

Free-market theory holds that removing the government as regulator will unleash the forces of competition, and push fares downward. Owners will seek to garner a profit by operating ever more efficiently rather than by jacking up fares or petitioning the government to boost fares (as was the case in pre-deregulation Chile). Nevertheless, with deregulation in real-life conditions, Santiago bus owners have raised fares again and again, far outpacing inflation. The basic daytime bus fare was raised by 44 percent *in real terms* between 1978 and 1982. By 1990, the fare was twice what it had been ten years earlier.[10] This is a far greater increase than the rise in the costs of buses, fuel, maintenance and certainly drivers' earnings.[11] Santiago bus fares, according to the United Nations, are the highest in Latin America.[12]

Remarkably, allowing each bus owner to set whatever fare he or she chooses has not generated the fare competition the free-market advocates predicted. Buses post their fares in their front windows, but somehow they all seem to charge the same. Moreover, not only did the fare charged by the small taxi buses draw closer and then merge with that charged by regular buses, but the difference between the daytime fare and the fare for nighttime/Sunday/holiday vanished.

Many Chileans are unable to afford the high fares. They have little choice but to walk and often walk long distances in what is a spread-out metropolis. The same U.N. study found that 31 percent of the people who live in Santiago walk because they can't afford the bus, compared to 17 percent before deregulation. Predictably, the figure is higher for the poorest neighborhoods where residents depend even more on public transport. Most of those who walk are not consumers who "choose" to walk. In the lingo of the free marketeers, it's just that no producer is willing to sell at the prices these consumers are willing to pay.

Many poor families spend at least 20 percent of their meager resources on bus transportation. Before deregulation the cost of 50 bus rides a month added up to less than 9 percent of the monthly minimum wage; since 1984 it has been 20 percent or more. Part of the high average cost is that anyone needing to take two buses to get to work has to pay double since in the privatized, deregulated "system" there are no transfers.[13]

Fares tend to go higher and higher in large part because deregulation set off a vicious circle. The explosion in the number of buses has resulted in few, and ever fewer, passengers per bus and hence higher per-passenger costs. Fares are set (unofficially) by the associations of bus owners. The associations are voluntary but, as one owner confided to us, an owner doesn't have to join an association if he doesn't mind having his tires slashed. Fares are set in such a way that the least efficient operators at least cover their costs (which implies that the more efficient operators make good profits). As a result, the prospect of guaranteed profits tends to encourage fleet expansion and thus further reduce ridership per bus, which raises per-passenger costs and, in turn, adds to the pressure to hike fares yet more. Excess capacity, in the absence of government subsidies, can be financed only through higher fares; higher fares in turn mean ever fewer riders.

Free marketeers might say that truly free-market forces (in contrast to the price-fixing associations) would drive out of the picture inefficient operators and thus reduce total fleet size. But the proven reality is that owners prefer to ensure profits for all. Enough owners are of roughly equal size and they recognize the suicide it would be for many if they engage in fare competition.[14]

Santiago's buses have the lowest average ridership, by far, of any Latin American capital. In off-peak hours lots of buses run around largely empty because the owners hope to take in at least enough money to cover direct costs. This strategy can work for the owners in part because in Chile's free-market environment their direct costs are lower than one might think: they don't pay their drivers salaries but simply a commission on each ticket sold.

Indeed Santiago's bus drivers have been turned into free-market jungle fighters. Without salaries or a union (they are not employees but "independent contractors"), drivers are under tremendous pressure to treat each other not as colleagues but as competitors. Each driver must try to beat out the other drivers to pick up a passenger before they do.

We were fascinated to observe some of the ways drivers seek to cope. Many drivers pay "pointers" (*punteros*) who stand on the corners of popular routes to flash to them the number of minutes elapsed since the last competing bus passed that point so that they can speed up or slow down so as to maximize the chance of getting passengers. Some drivers have passengers who apparently out of sympathy for their plight hand them back their tickets as they get off so that the drivers can re-sell them and pocket the fare. (Owners, of course, have taken various measures to try to eliminate this practice.)

From the viewpoint of someone like ourselves, who needed to get about by bus a lot and who could afford the fare, free-market policies could be perceived as having improved service. After all, how many times elsewhere in the world have we been just about to catch a bus and it speeds up leaving us in its exhaust? Or how many times, especially in third world countries, has the bus been so overcrowded that we can't possibly board? In free-market Santiago a slight lift of the arm often results in a bus screeching to a halt. No matter that the bus is in the center lane and that we're not standing at a bus stop. We've seen buses back up to get passengers. And only at very peak hours on certain routes has a bus been too crowded.

Of course, Santiago's bus service has hardly improved for anyone who can't afford the fare. Or for anyone living deep inside a very poor neighborhood where there are not enough people who can afford the bus to make up a market. And passengers and pedestrians alike are in danger of being run over by a bus racing to beat out another bus or by some other vehicle as they sprint out to the middle lane to board a bus that has halted for them. In Santiago before deregulation, under 20 percent of fatalities in traffic accidents involved a bus. By the late 1980s the percentage, having risen every year since deregulation, stood at 75 percent. In 1987 (the most recent year for which we could find a figure) an astounding 401 people died in bus-related accidents in Santiago and 4,037 were injured severely enough to require medical attention.

Nor in downtown Santiago is it easy to avoid the noise of so many buses. Experts report that in downtown Santiago the noise, to which buses are by far the biggest contributor, ranges from 70 to 80 decibels, right on the threshold of hearing damage. Doctors say such levels can induce nervousness, irritability, insomnia, even aggressive behavior.[15]

"At Street Level... 'Rat-Colored Haze'"[16]

But perhaps the most talked about consequence of the of free-market dogmas on Santiago's bus transport is the horrific air pollution.

Santiago has mushroomed into a sprawling metropolis of almost five million people, at least 40 percent of the population of the entire country.[17] The metropolis sits in a basin ringed by hills and mountain walls. Rains are infrequent, and solar radiation abundant. Breezes are scarce — the Spaniards dubbed Santiago's latitude "the latitude of horses" because the region's characteristic doldrums often forced them on to horseback. The basin is prone to thermal inversions, in which a layer of warm air traps cooler air close to the ground, and blocks its normal upward drift. Thus thermal inversions impede the dispersal of the sour, noxious smog into the atmosphere. And, while there are five million people, there are fewer than 200,000 trees. All of which strongly points to how especially insane it is to pump toxic gases into Santiago's air.

Gas chambers and chemical warfare metaphors are hardly over-drawn. (Visiting Chile shortly after Iraq's invasion of Kuwait, we spotted a newspaper cartoon with the caption: "Iraq's very interested in buying Chile's buses for its chemical warfare.") Carbon monoxide, nitrous oxides, ozone and sulfurous anhydride now help give Santiago the dubious distinction of being the world's third most-polluted city, after Mexico City and Sao Paulo, Brazil. Carbon monoxide levels, especially during the winter months, permanently top maximum acceptable levels and at certain hours are poisonous beyond belief. (The government gives out information in terms of the *average* levels of the day, even though the smog varies significantly during the day. Sulfurous anhydride, for instance, at peak hours is at very dangerous levels.)

By the late 1980s, 800 tons of gases and particulates were being thrown into Santiago's air daily. On a winter day without rain breathing Santiago air is equivalent to smoking between seven to 20 cigarettes in terms of the gases or an incredible 200 cigarettes a day, in terms of the particulates in the air inhaled.

Particulates are mainly hydrocarbons from incompletely burned fuels, especially the fuel burned in diesel buses.[18] (The price signals from the fuels market in the 1950s and 1960s encouraged bus operators to convert from gasoline to cheaper diesel fuel.) Suspended in the air, they are loaded with a great variety of toxic substances and carcinogens. Particulates are so tiny that they are "breathable" and therefore penetrate the smallest pores of the lungs.

By 1990 buses were held responsible for 70 to 80 percent of the particulates suspended in Santiago's atmosphere.[19] Many scientists, according to The New York Times, now think these particles of soot may be "the most deadly form of air pollution."[20]

Lionel Gil, a professor of biochemistry at the University of Chile, ran laboratory analyses of the particulate pollution in Santiago and found seven known cancer-causing substances, among them benzopyrene, thought to cause genetic mutations. "The problem we could have in Santiago," he pointed out, "is that these genetic mutations can 'sleep' for twenty years and then transform into tumors in the body. So, we may not see the worst impact of the pollution now but in 10 or 20 years."[21]

On the worst days, the levels of particulates exceed 500 micrograms per cubic meter. At some stations, levels have reached almost 900 micrograms. The Chilean government considers that 300 micrograms constitutes a state of emergency. The U.S. Environmental Protection Agency standards dictate that more than 150 micrograms per cubic meter is unacceptable. By way of comparison, the highest reading ever at a Los Angeles area testing station was 289. In fact, Santiago typically has three times more particulates in its air than Los Angeles and Denver combined, and they are the two most particulate-contaminated cities in the U.S. Japanese scientists at the Fukuoka Environmental Research Center, noting that Santiago's particulate levels run 20 times higher than in other industrial countries, rank Santiago No. 1 in the world in pollution in qualitative terms.[22]

Especially in the winter months when thermal inversions compound the seasonally rainy, raw weather, Santiago hospitals and clinics are packed with patients with respiratory ailments linked to the valley's polluted air. Visiting a public pediatric hospital for Santiago, James Smith of the Los Angeles Times in 1989 found dozens of mothers filling the emergency waiting room with their wheezing, gasping infants and toddlers. Inside, doctors administered oxygen to most of the children for a couple of hours, then placed them in purified plastic enclosures and gave them injections to reduce lung inflammation. One of the anguished mothers, María Quintero, told Smith, "They gave us this oxygen spray can and a tube to give him clean air when he fights to breathe, but it doesn't help much. He quiets down and can sleep a few hours, but he wakes up and starts crying and suffering again."

The acting director of the hospital commented to Smith, "We can solve the medical problems easily, but the child then goes back into the same environment and he needs to come back here three or four days later."

Acute respiratory illnesses, greater susceptibility to infections, conjunctivitis and other eye ailments, increased cases of asthma and increased severity of asthma cases figure high on the list of immediate health disorders caused by Santiago's staggering air pollution, according to medical specialists.[23] Especially hard-hit by polluted air are young children and the elderly, in addition to those with pre-existing respiratory problems.

Our own experience of Chile's air pollution includes running three or four blocks down the Alameda through the gritty exhaust of hundreds of barely moving buses — late to a non-governmental conference on the environment — and almost passing out. As always, when we remarked about the horrible pollution, the locals told us that if we thought this was bad we should come back in the winter to see real pollution. No, thanks.

The bus congestion and the resulting pollution grew so intolerable — literally! — that, no matter how ideologically committed the regime was to a laissez-faire world, some restrictions were decreed at long last in 1987 on almost all vehicles, including buses. But, as already indicated, bus owners and drivers have generally been successful in their efforts to weaken enforcement and to water down any measures which imposed greater restrictions on diesel buses than on other vehicles.[24]

Conclusion

Free-marketeers will surely retort that the negative consequences (high fares, inefficiencies, uneven service, congestion, pollution, etc.) are due to the *absence* of genuine free-market conditions because of the highly imperfect competition among the bus owners. But in the real world shouldn't we expect that owners sooner or later will collude to, among other things, in effect fix fares? Prohibiting such behavior would require government intervention, an anathema to the free-marketeers.

While this chapter focuses on the effects of the free-market model on Santiago's bus transport, the central valley's severe air pollution is hardly Chile's only grave environmental problem. In our look at public health in Chile we discussed the heavy contamination of rivers with industrial and human waste, and in two previous chapters we analyzed the destruction of the country's once-rich fisheries and southern forests. The same *New York Times* article quoted at the beginning of this chapter reports that "Chile has some of the world's dirtiest factories, belching sulfur dioxide, arsenic and heavy metals into the atmosphere."[25] Free-market Chile has no regulations regarding toxic waste.[26] The environmental case against "free-market fever" is so dramatic that even the *New York Times*, whose praise for Chile's free-market policies has almost always been unstinting, lays the blame for Chile's environmental nightmare with "the free-market model of the University of Chicago economist Milton Friedman" [which] "was pushed at all costs, creating a political atmosphere in which concern for the environment did not exist."[27]

PART FIVE:

CONCLUSION

16

A Second Look

What is Chile really like? We have tried to look beyond a critique of some highly touted macroeconomic indicators to document the actual working of free-market policies on the Chilean economy and society. It's time to briefly review what we have found and draw some lessons.

Economic Growth and Poverty

Only by 1989 — 14 years into the free-market policies — did per capita output climb back up to the level of 1970. Indeed the "miracles" refer to recoveries from depression-like collapses in 1975 and 1982 that resulted in tremendous dislocations in people's lives, and that can be attributed in large part to the free-market model.

With free-market policies, the rich got richer. They did so mainly at the expense of many middle-class Chileans: between 1978 and 1988 the richest 10 percent increased their share of national income from 37 to 47 percent, while the next 30 percent saw their share shrink from 23 to 18 percent. Poverty widened dramatically: from 17 percent of Chileans in 1973 to 45 percent in 1990. Among the impoverished, the percentage forced to live in extreme poverty more than doubled.

Privatizations

According to free-market advocates, selling off publicly owned enterprises was supposed to do away with an inefficient public sec-

243

tor, cut government spending and financial obligations, and throw open the doors for ordinary Chileans to join the ranks of property owners. In reality, matters have been stunningly different. First of all, many of the largest companies privatized in the 1980s had been generating significant revenues, not deficits, for the public purse. Nevertheless, they were sold off in non-competitive circumstances at scandalously low prices (tantamount to heavy government subsidization) to a handful of Pinochet insiders and national and foreign conglomerates — a far cry from "people's capitalism." Receipts from privatizations did provide one-time cash infusions handy in the short run for covering over government budget deficits and meeting payments to foreign creditors, but at the cost of diminished public revenues ever thereafter.

Many of the publicly held companies affected by the first wave of privatizations, most notably banks, a few years later failed in large part due to their financial mismanagement in private hands. Contrary to the repeated avowals of the free marketeers, the government bailed out these private firms. Once restored to profitability (at enormous public expense), they were again sold off to private investors.

One huge public company and the only major one not privatized is CODELCO, the giant copper corporation nationalized by Congress during the Allende administration. Ironically, it was the government's dividends from CODELCO that enabled it to resuscitate the many failed privatized firms during the 1982-84 period.

Public companies for decades had played a major role in planning and investing in the development of the national economy. The Chicago Boys claimed that the private sector would pick up that role; over the years, however, the private sector has shown itself more keen on short-term profit-taking and speculation than in strategic long-haul investments (with perhaps fruit cultivation the exception that proves the rule). The consequences down the road for the nation's economic well-being could be serious.

Foreign Debt

The Chicago Boys de-regulated the financial industry, opened wide the doors to foreign goods, clung dogmatically to an unrealistic monetarist policy, and allowed a private sector, led by a few financial conglomerates and an elite minority of consumers, to recklessly rack up one of the highest debts per capita in the world. When, predictably, the financial system collapsed, the government — again, despite repeated doctrinaire free-market pronouncements that it would never do so — picked up the pieces by assuming much of the bloated private debt. The nation's foreign debt soared from a little over $5 billion at the start of the free-market regime in 1975 to a peak of over $21 billion only ten years later (an amount approximately equal to that year's entire economic output). The government's willingness even in the midst of a severe recession to use public resources first and foremost to make payments on the debt privately contracted with foreign banks generated further praise of Chile in international financial circles as a model for other debtor nations.

The government's fiscal crisis resulting from its assumption of the private foreign debt supplied a rationale for aspects of the neo-liberal project such as further deep cuts in social programs.

Through over $6 billion in "debt swaps," valuable national assets were traded away in exchange for the cancellation of debt paper of dubious value. A number of multinational corporations used this mechanism to gain control cheaply of privatized public companies and natural resources such as forest lands and minerals.

Labor

Chile's neo-liberal Labor Code decreed ground rules that clearly tip the scales in the favor of business. It imposed severe constraints on labor organizing and collective bargaining and maximized employers' flexibility vis-a-vis workers. Stripped of its rhetoric of "worker freedom," the Code narrows negotiations of the terms of employment down to the smallest unit: the individual worker and the employer. Attempts by workers to organize to oppose the far-reaching economic and social policy decisions during these years were either prohibited or made extremely difficult by labor market conditions. Wages plummeted in 1982 during Chile's severe recession and remained virtually stagnant throughout most of the decade, even as economic output recovered and even after it surpassed previous levels.

Health

The neo-liberal health care "reforms" gutted Chile's pioneering national health care system. In a radical departure from the past, access to health care is now based on income. There are now two worlds of health care services: good to excellent for the elite few; grossly underfunded, rundown, over-burdened facilities for some 70 percent of Chileans. There are more funds than ever before for health services for the high-income few, while 85 percent of Chileans pay more and receive less.

The logic of the market-driven system is ever more costly expenditures (including for questionable procedures) on the health of the small minority of Chileans who are financially well-off. Among other inefficiencies, the privatized free-market system generates an excessive demand for high-amenity health care and invests little in preventive health care. For-profit private enterprise also does not invest in sanitation and other aspects of public health; with government health budgets slashed and pervasive de-regulation (including a virtual elimination of inspections of restaurants and other food handlers), incidences of typhoid fever and infectious hepatitis, after decades of steady decline, shot up to epidemic proportions. Even free-market dogmatists saw the need for public interevention.

The employer contribution to health care has been virtually eliminated. Thus, with the well-off having "escaped" into the world of private health insurances and private HMOs and given the deep cuts in social spending by the neo-liberal government, many Chileans in the middle-income range wind up subsidizing the public health care system.

On a number of occasions the neo-liberal government policy makers did intervene in the health marketplace — but in every case to shore up the for-profit health insurance companies to the detriment of the public system.

It is telling that the armed forces did not opt to join the privatized health care system but have maintained for themselves their own public health care system.

Education

Free-market policies have profoundly transformed education in Chile from a right of all (to be ever more fully realized through public investments) to a commodity available in varying quantity and quality according to one's purchasing power. Introduction of individual per-pupil vouchers and encouragement of for-profit schools in the name of providing greater choice, together with the dismantling of a national educational system in the name of decentralized control, have greatly widened the differences in educational opportunities and results. Education's democratizing potential, so strongly operative before, has fallen victim to the neoliberal "reforms"; indeed schooling now reinforces and widens social and economic polarization.

Much of what is still achieved in education, as in other social services, owes a great deal to the legacy of public investments in human resources and physical infrastructure made before the neoliberal model. Over the years of free-market policies those investments have been severely depleted. The teaching profession has been particularly victim to the neo-liberal policies.

A market-driven educational system fails to serve those with special needs (for instance, those with physical challenges) who lack abundant family financial resources. They are relegated to the now resource-scarce public sector.

Notions that the market will promote and even control for quality in education have proven unfounded. In post-secondary education, in many cases, a school's advertising budget more than its educational quality determines its reputation and therefore its marketing success.

Post-secondary education to a great extent has been narrowed down to training in particular skills. Even though the higher education system is now "market-driven," it often fails to coordinate what students study with the job market they will likely encounter since there is a strong tendency for what is taught to be what is fashionable and what costs the least to teach and therefore brings in the most profits to the school.

Housing

Acting on their free-market faith in the private sector, the Chicago Boys pulled the government out of the housing business, claiming that the private construction industry would respond to the housing needs of the lower-income majority. At the same time, their deregulation of the urban real estate industry touched off speculation, dramatically driving up land prices and consequently pushing the costs of even rudimentary housing out of reach of more and more Chileans. The nation's serious housing deficit only worsened. The percentage of Chileans without adequate housing increased from 27 percent in 1972 to 40 percent in 1988.

In 1982, after eight years of relegating housing and urban development to market forces, the government entered the marketplace with supplemental vouchers and housing credits for low-income households, and even contracted private companies to build houses. Such dilatory and half-hearted governmental marketplace interventions did little more than slow the growing deficit in housing, and middle-class families captured a significant share of the subsidies.

What is apparent from Chile's free-market housing experiment is that it is naive to expect the private sector on its own to respond to low-income citizens' need for housing. In societies with great disparities in income and therefore low-income households, government "intervention" is essential.

Deregulation of urban transport

The doctrinaire deregulation of Santiago's urban bus transport dramatically demonstrates what a hellish world an unqualified free-market world would be.

A major effect of the sweeping de-regulation has been record (and unbearable) air pollution. In addition, Santiago's numerous, often half-empty buses now charge the highest fares in Latin America, unaffordable for many who depend on bus transport. And, while some of the principal thoroughfares are severely congested with buses, the poorer neighborhoods have little or no service. Bus drivers no longer are salaried employees but earn a commission on each fare collected; they therefore must often risk the safety of everyone to try to make a living.

The problems caused by the free-market policies imposed on the urban transport sector are only one dramatic case of the grave environmental problems resulting from Chile's "free-market fever."

Social Security

Free-market policy makers set up an obligatory, private, for-profit system of individual retirement funds, Pension Fund Administrators (AFPs) that superseded the public social security system that had favored lower-paid employees. This private pension system beneifts those paid the highest salaries, while now most Chileans either have no retirement coverage at all or will receive the government's minimum (and minimal) pension. Employers benefit from the "reforms" because they no longer are obligated to contribute anything at all to their employees' retirement security.

The supposed wider distribution of ownership of assets through the investments made with retirement funds proves to be largely illusory. The real winners are the national and foreign conglomerates that own the companies that control the invested retirement funds and thereby have gained control of much of Chile's economy.

A sharp downturn in the Chilean stock market could have devastating consequences for the retirement security of millions of working people. The mounting financial burden of the transition to a privatized pension system (paying remaining pensions in the old public system and paying minimum pensions in the new private system) has fallen entirely on the public coffers now deprived of the contributions once flowing in through the public social security system.

The Fruit Boom

Exports of fresh fruits from Chile undeniably have soared, from about $40 million in 1974 to nearly $1 billion 17 years later. Once again, the free marketeers who would credit the successes to "private enterprise unfettered by government meddling" ignore some of the foundations on which the successes of the 1980s rest that are the products of governmental economic initiatives (invesments in feasibility studies and infrastructure, land reforms, transfer to Chile of publicly funded research in California, etc.) They also are wont to ignore the extraordinarily favorable foreign market conditions in the late 1970s and 1980s.

The success of the fruit industry only highlights how the rewards of that success have not been at all fairly shared with the workers, the vast majority of whom can find only seasonal work and must labor very intensively under a piece rate system. In addition to the enormous obstacles to labor organizing inherent in an industry in which the majority of workers are seasonal and must migrate from farm to farm, the neo-liberal government's labor regulations in effect prohibit organizing. Moreover, the absence of government-directed development policies has meant that few smaller farmers have benefited from the industry. Domination of research by private rather than public interest has biased it toward the needs of large, well-financed growers as opposed to smaller, poorer farmers. Increasingly, the more lucrative aspects of the industry such as overseas marketing have been taken over by multinational companies.

Touting the considerable growth in fruit industry exports tends to hide from view how much less than efficient the privatized, free-market road to success has been. The highly individualized learning by the trial-and-error approach yielded results but at high costs (tolerable when profit prospects were high). Much research has been ill-designed, ill-evaluated, and unnecessarily duplicated. Public sector involvement in research and extension might have made for greater efficiency and participation by smaller farmers.

The "easy years" of high profits for the industry are clearly over. Foreign markets are saturating, and competitors from other countries are strengthening. As profitability erodes, more and more of the research needed to overcome new challenges facing Chile's fruit industry will exceed the capacity of the individual exporter or grower, while years of neglect have eroded the public sector's capacity for the needed research and extension.

Natural Resources

Free-market Chile has plundered its rich forestry and fishery resources. Earlier public investments in these important industries, such as tree plantings and fishing cooperatives, aimed at fostering broad rural and regional development laid a solid foundation for a good part of the later growth for which free marketeers take sole credit. Sell-offs of public lands and infrastructure concentrated natural resources in the hands of wealthy national and foreign interests. Contrary to the model's rhetoric, the government handed out subsidies to encourage tree planting; but its distribution of them through the market rather than by targeting beneficiaries resulted in their going mostly to forestry conglomerates who were able to further concentrate ownership of forest lands.

In fishing, the pattern has been similar: While tens of thousands of small fishermen have seen their livelihoods threatened, a single conglomerate now accounts for over 70 percent of fishmeal production, the country's biggest fish export, and a handful of foreign-owned factory trawlers account for half of the hake catch, the second most import fish export.

The over-exploitation of non-renewable natural resources as well as human labor has been the basis of much of the growth in the fishing and forestry industries. In the fishing industry unrestricted access and boom-and-bust cycles have exhausted one fish species after another; by 1990, over 60 percent of the resource base of the fishing sector was in a state of serious deterioration. The growth of the wood chip industry and government subsidies for planting non-native pine and eucalyptus trees have led to the leveling of native forests of far greater value in the long run if managed in a more regulated fashion.

Without government measures to foster the development of high-value products, the private sector in both the fishing and the forestry industries has emphasized exports with only minimal processing. Years of free-market style "boom" in these industries have reinforced a pattern characteristic of underdeveloped economies: in 1990 more than 90 percent of Chilean exports were based on the exploitation (and in most cases over-exploitation) of natural resources with only limited generation of employment and ties to other industries. Such shallow growth generates numbers which may look good in the short term but does not lay the groundwork for more significant development in the longer term. Short-sighted profit-taking seems endemic to unregulated private operators.

Lessons

Given this experience of free-market economic and social policies in Chile, what are some of the key lessons we can draw?

Chile's free marketeers have lived off the legacy of previous generations' public investments.

Free-market ideologues fail to acknowledge the contributions to many of their "successes" made by interventions by earlier governments in Chile (fresh fruit and forest product exports, the government revenues from the national copper company, the declining infant mortality rate, among others). In social services (notably in education and health) past public investments have been steadily run down and a great deficit is being handed to future governments.

Chile's free-market policies have concentrated control over economic power and its rewards.

The "successes" of Chile's free-market policies have been enjoyed primarily (and in many areas, exclusively) by the economic and political elites. In any society shot through with enormous inequalities in wealth and income, the market (if not offset by other forces) works to further concentrate wealth and income.

Rather than increased competition, the real outcome of free-market policies has been a clear trend toward more concentrated control over economic resources (abundantly clear in forestry, fisheries, privatized firms, and the administration of individual retirement funds). Economic concentration is now greater than at any other time in Chile's history. Virtually every dynamic facet of the Chilean economy is now solidly under the influence, if not yet outright control, of multinational corporations. (Indeed multinational corporations have reaped rich rewards from Chile's free-market policies; not surprisingly, they enthusiastically applaud the model and push to implant it everywhere.)

A growing concentration of income, with the richest Chileans getting richer (the top 10 percent in 1990 captured 47 percent of the total income), has been at the expense of many in (or once in) the middle classes who have born the brunt of many of the changes (especially the privatizations of public companies and of social services and the undermining of union activities). Santiago has become sharply polarized in working, living and consumption patterns; many Chileans now speak of "two Santiagos." It is unconscionable to consider any economic and social project successful when the percentage of those impoverished has increased more than doubled.

Not only has income distribution grown more lopsided and poverty widened but also with the free-market model the level of income is now crucial in determining access to health care, schooling, retirement security, recreation, and other social services. Many such goods previously were considered to rightfully belong to all but now are commodities increasingly available only to those who can afford to buy them.

Free-market policies have made Chile's economy not less, but more, vulnerable.

Economic development worthy of the name should reduce a nation's vulnerability to external ups and down. Quite the contrary, the free-market model of export-led development has made Chile more vulnerable to economic troubles (and even market whims) in Japan, North America and Western Europe. Generations of government policies and investments, often in collaboration with the private sector, to foster the development of higher value products have been jettisoned. Even though by 1990, 57 percent of Chile's economic production was for export (compared to 33 percent in 1960), the focus was still on products with little value added. The concentration of income and the widening of poverty constricts the development of a dynamic domestic market that could serve as a counterbalance to international slumps. The extreme vulnerability of Chile's economy was dramatized in 1990 when the discovery (under suspicious circumstances) of a cynanide-laced Chilean grape in the U.S. resulted in the loss of much of that year's crop worth tens of millions of dollars.

The Chilean government, while espousing a "hands off" policy, repeatedly intervened in the marketplace; invariably it supported big local and foreign business interests.

Free-market ideologues are reluctant to acknowledge that even the Pinochet government intervened in many cases in the marketplace in last-minute attempts to offset the havoc wreaked by its free-market policies (low-income housing, air quality, public health, etc.). With the economic collapse of the early 1980s (itself a product of the model's unregulated financial sector and its excessive vulnerability to external changes) the government intervened massively; the public sector rescued a private sector that had self-destructed (and in the years that followed the public sector was stripped of much of its resources by the free marketeers). Moreover, the free-market government often intervened on behalf of private national and foreign business interests (in debt management, privatizations of public companies, natural resources, education, the changes in social security, and with the ISAPRES vis-a-vis the public health care system), invariably privatizing what was valuable and socializing the costs.

It is not a coincidence that in Chile, under free-market reign, the anti-regulatory, laissez-faire attitudes toward business fostered scandalous plunder (privatizations of valuable and revenue-generating public companies and other assets such as public forest lands at ridiculously low prices and on easy terms, reckless private sector foreign borrowing, resuscitations at public expense of failed private banks and businesses, paying big lumber companies lucrative subsidies, etc.).

Unregulated market forces are notably short-sighted, even self-destructive.

Chile's privatized banks failed in 1982 because of speculative investments and other forms of mismanagement, while the government-run banks that had not been privatized remained solvent.

Much of the basis of Chile's macroeconomic recovery since the mid-1980s is unsustainable. Natural resources are being exploited in highly unsound ways; future productive capacity (and the potential for much greater returns in the longer run) are being sacrificed. Multinational corporations have been attracted by extremely liberal laws regulating investment, the removal of profits, the workforce, and the exploitation of natural resources; once the resources have been largely extracted such investors are likely to pull up stakes. Private investment by Chileans in productive capacity in most areas of the economy has been remarkably low; by the 1990s, in many sectors of the economy production facilities were running at, or near, capacity without adequate plans for expansion. Human resources are also being depleted. (Many workers, including among the teaching and health professions, are exhausted and do not benefit from any ongoing development of skills.) Market forces without public intervention are not good at planning (as we see in higher education and natural resource industries).

Market mechanisms alone fail to meet the social needs of many.

In a society of significant inequalities in wealth and income, market forces often work against the majority. This is most striking in the area of social needs such as in health care, education, housing, social security.

Free markets do not guarantee a "modern" society

The free marketeers have packaged their agenda with ample doses of rhetoric about "modernization." In fact, much of what they have done (in labor, social services, foreign investment, natural resources, and the environment) is a clear throwback to 19th century capitalism.

A truly democratic society is essential for markets to work on behalf of everyone today and in future generations.

Every society that has tried to do away with the market has faced monumental headaches. The problem comes when a useful device gets raised to the level of dogma. Free-market dogmatists think that the market should no longer be viewed as a mechanism, useful for the allocation of goods and services, which needs to be regulated by society, but rather as a principle by which to regulate society itself.

Those who would cling with blind faith to free-market ideology lose sight of what the market cannot do. With a deep belief in the powers of the market, they fail to accept that the market is a tool which, with all its virtues, has serious shortcomings if left to its own devices. For the market responds not to human needs but to money. The market — left to its own devices — mirrors inequalities in "buying power." We should not delude ourselves into thinking that it registers the needs and choices of all people in a society characterized by inequalities in wealth and income. The market is also blind to many social and resource costs; it deeply discounts the future. In the case of Chile, market indicators report "growth" and "success" as foreign exchange earnings soar when native forests are leveled for chips for overseas paper mills; but in reality assets of enormous value are being squandered through short-sighted private profit-taking. Finally, as we have said, the market, left to its own devices, leads to ever greater concentrations of economic power. It thereby seriously compromises both economic competitiveness and political democracy. If the market alone is a society's guiding principle, those already with greater economic power will doubtlessly accumulate more. Be they local or foreign private interests, they will tighten their grip on all that is worth holding. The more concentrated economic power, the more undermined is the market's potential usefulness in meeting human needs.

There is, however, a different path — and one that avoids dogmas on the other extreme that would do away with markets and their mechanisms. This path holds that markets have to be regulated by society *and* that the society has to be meaningfully democratic. If a democratic society is defined as one striving to equitably distribute both economic and political power, then the more democratic the society, the more equitable are likely to be the results of market mechanisms — indeed the more *freely* the society can allow market mechanisms to operate without fear that the results will violate its deeply cherished democratic values.

A democratic society is likely to choose to use government to help the market serve the needs of all, present and future generations. A government can make rules and allocate resources to counteract the tendencies of the market to fail to respond to human needs, to overlook many human and natural resource costs, and to concentrate economic power.

Such a government would develop and enforce rules to keep ownership of economic resources from becoming too concentrated. It could use taxation and credit policies to benefit the smaller and weaker producers. It could deploy a whole gamut of public policies — credit, taxation, land, social services, labor regulations, job training, environmental protection, resource cost accounting, etc. — to actively disperse buying power. Such interventions are not "anti-market." Policies that disperse buying power actually help the market realize its potential to efficiently respond to the needs and preferences of all.

Nowhere are markets free. While free-market ideologues want us to view markets as the interplay of impersonal "objective" forces, in fact, markets reflect the balances and imbalances of power within every society. The challenge for Chilean society — and our own — is to distribute power democratically so that the results of market mechanisms are, not less, but more equitable and more sustainable.

Epilogue:

Continuity and Change[1] Since the Transition to Civilian Rule in Chile (1990-94)

Stephanie Rosenfeld

In the 1988 Plebiscite, the Chilean people were asked to vote "Yes" or "No" to eight more years of military rule by General Augusto Pinochet and the Chicago Boys. The Plebiscite was a referendum on the past 16 years, as well as a vote for the future. The dictatorship claimed the economic "miracle" as its greatest achievement, and warned that chaos would reign if Pinochet lost. The opposition's campaign for the "No" vote made a moral appeal against the widening poverty and inequality brought about during the dictatorship, and inspired a vision of hope and happiness in a democratic future. The Chilean people decided. General Pinochet lost the plebiscite in a 54.7% to 43.0% vote, and Chile's transition to elected civilian rule was underway.

The presidential elections that followed a year later were a second referendum on the Pinochet years and the Chicago Boys, and again the Pinochet team lost. Patricio Aylwin, a Christian Democrat supported by the Center and the Left, ran against Pinochet's hand-picked successor, Hernán Büchi. Büchi had been Minister of Finance from 1985-89, and represents the more "pragmatic" neo-liberals. Aylwin won the presidency with 55.2% of the vote, to Büchi's 29.4%, with right-wing populist supermarket baron Francisco Javier Errázuriz picking up 15.4%.

On March 11, 1990, the dictatorship finally gave way to elected civilian rule, and General Pinochet passed the presidential sash to Patricio Aylwin. The right-wing parties associated with big business and the dictatorship became the new "opposition," and the Concertación, the coalition of political parties that led the campaign for the "No" in the plebiscite, became Chile's new governing coalition. The Concertación is dominated by the centrist Christian Democrats, and includes the center-left Party for Democracy (PPD) and the Socialist Party.

With the transition a period of economic reform began, but a wholesale rollback of the neo-liberal model was *not* on the agenda. Nearly-unregulated access to natural resources and cheap, "flexible" labor remain the foundation of Chile's economic "miracle."

Once in office, the Aylwin government did not pose a fundamental challenge to the neo-liberal model for a number of reasons. The Aylwin administration was a transitional government, and successful consolidation of electoral democracy was its number one priority. Economic measures that might have threatened political consensus or economic growth were not considered. The Concertación government inherited an economy that was booming by regional standards, and hoped to better distribute the gains of that growth rather than question its basis. A combination of sustained economic growth, low inflation and growing social spending was the Concertación's formula for stability.[2]

Anti-democratic legacies of the dictatorship also blocked change. While Pinochet lost the 1988 Plebiscite, the Concertación's participation in the Plebiscite *process* was perhaps Pinochet's crowning victory. The Concertación beat Pinochet at his own game, but in the process, they accepted the rules of the game, as laid out in the 1980 Constitution and other Pinochet-era laws. Significant authoritarian enclaves within the government, such as the so-called designated senators[3] and the National Security Council[4], served as guardians against reform. General Pinochet remains Commander in Chief of the Army, and the president does not have the constitutional power to remove him. These authoritarian institutions put in place by Pinochet and the neo-liberals left the Concertación little legal leeway for change.

The social movements which had led the struggle for democracy during the darkest years of the dictatorship found they had little influence or bargaining power with the new government. Organized labor, which had been decimated by repression and neo-liberal economic restructuring, along with the women's and other movements, were marginalized from the political process by elite party politics.

Perhaps the most important reason that the neo-liberal model has gone fundamentally unchallenged since the return to civilian rule, however, is that during the 1980s the economic thinking of important sectors of the center-left opposition to the dictatorship and the neo-liberals began to converge in some fundamental aspects.[5]

While the new government did not define itself as neo-liberal, it shared some basic ideas with the neo-liberals.[6] In broad strokes, both agree that the market and the private sector should lead the development process. Both also emphasize economic growth as the key to the elimination of poverty, and reject short-run government interventions aimed at reducing inequality or that risk creating inflation. Both agree that export growth is fundamental to Chile's development, and requires maintaining an open and efficient economy. Along this line, the Concertación has aggressively sought a free trade agreement with the United States, and has already signed such agreements with Mexico and other Latin American countries.

Indeed, in economic terms, the programs proposed by Büchi and Aylwin had many similarities. Concertación leaders met with businessmen before the elections and promised that they would not seek to change the basic structure of the economy. Maintaining the stability of the economy would be a top priority.

In economic policy, the Concertación government has differed from the neo-liberals mainly in its attention to poverty and social policy. The Concertación pushed for reforms in many sectors, and increased government spending on social and poverty-alleviation programs by some 30-40% over the levels at the end of the Pinochet years.

The Concertación also rejects the neo-liberal view of the state, which reduces the state's role to the defense of national security and private property, with minimal regulation of the economy and the lowest level of welfare and social services that is politically viable. In the Concertación's view, the government has an important role in regulating business and the market, as well as insuring a minimum level of welfare. As a transitional government, however, the Aylwin administration did not seek a substantial reform of the role of government. The second Concertación government, the Frei administration (1994-2000), ranks "modernization" of the state as one of its key initiatives. Eduardo Frei Ruiz-Tagle, also a

Christian Democrat, is Aylwin's successor, and son of Eduardo Frei Montalva, who was president of Chile from 1964-70. Under Aylwin, the rush of privatizations of state-owned firms was halted, but privatizations that occurred during the dictatorship were not questioned.

The Reforms

The new government acknowledged as problems many of the areas that the dictatorship hailed as miracles. Issues glossed over or ignored by the neo-liberals were at last open for discussion, and the Concertación acknowledged the "social debt" owed to those Chileans who had yet to benefit from the economic "miracle."

Expectations were high, and nearly every government program and economic sector was on the Concertación's agenda for some sort of reform. Health, social security, housing and education all needed major reforms and more resources. Organized labor wanted to regain lost labor rights, and to address the issues of low wages and precarious employment. Constitutional and electoral reform were on the table. The fishing and forestry industries needed regulating, and the transportation sector also needed reform.

Yet while the Concertación had won a majority of elected seats in both the Chamber of Deputies and the Senate, the presence of nine institutional or "designated" senators appointed by the dictatorship gave the Right a majority in the Senate. As "democracy" resumed, nothing could pass through the legislature without agreement from the minority Right. Even the seemingly modest reforms proposed by the Concertación were difficult to get through the legislature. In the search for consensus, proposals that could not be agreed to by the Right fell by the wayside. Many areas in which more substantial reforms were sought, such as Constitutional and electoral reform, were far less successful than the Concertación had hoped. The neo-liberal political and economic model implemented during the dictatorship began to face the test of "democracy" — a democracy that had been shaped by the dictatorship to make it very difficult to undo the neo-liberal legacy.

Tax reform and reform of labor legislation are the two reforms that the Aylwin administration considers its major accomplishments. By negotiating an increase in corporate and value-added taxes, the Concertación raised money to fund social programs targeted at the poorest Chileans.

Labor Code reforms lifted many restrictions on what unions and employers can legally agree on. Modifications to the Code include restoration of the legal right of unions to form federations and confederations; elimination of the 60-day limit on strikes, and the broadening of activities in which unions can legally engage. But the reforms leave intact most of the "flexibility" on which the neo-liberal model is based. This means most employers continue to enjoy the freedom to hire and fire at will, without real sanctions or restrictions. Organized labor's principal demand, obligatory collective negotiations at the industry level, rather than at the firm level, was denied, and legal obstacles continue to be an effective barrier to rebuilding the union movement. José Piñera, author of the 1979 Labor Code, called it a building that could not be burned down,[7] and indeed it remains standing.

The Concertación sought to manage labor relations through broad agreements negotiated at the national level. Tripartite negotiations among the government, the principal union confederation, the CUT,[8] and representatives of business, the CPC,[9] resulted in recognition of the CUT on the part of business, and recognition of the respect for private property by the CUT. The main benefit for labor that came out of these accords was an increase in the minimum wage in 1990. But these negotiations have been less successful than the government and organized labor had hoped. The Concertación's strategy of elite negotiations and social demobilization have made for a stable transition period, yet with few concessions won from the Right and big business.

That organized labor made such limited gains since the transition also reflects the weakness of labor as a movement. Unions have only recently begun to rebuild at the base. Between 1989 and 1991, thousands of new unions were formed. Yet in 1993, the number of workers who were members of active unions actually dropped by 5.5%.[10] At the same time that new unions were being established, others were going into "recess," no longer active. Many of the new unions, fruit of the high hopes and enthusiasm of the transition period, found that collective negotiations were not very successful. The bulk of firm-level unions, the only type of union that employers must negotiate with, have only 25-50 members, and correspondingly little power. In 1993, only 13.1% of the Chilean labor force was unionized, up from 9.8% in 1988, but down from 14.5% in 1991.[11] While the Aylwin administration saw major strikes, especially by state and state enterprise workers such as teachers, health workers and copper miners, on the whole, Chile under Aylwin was far more remarkable for its stability than its conflict.

In other changes and reforms, the Aylwin administration raised health and education budgets. The government set up a new social services fund, the Solidarity Fund for Social Investment, FOSIS. Under the slogan "Investing in People," FOSIS has developed a wide range of programs, including rural housing improvement, job training and micro-enterprise development. Most FOSIS programs are implemented through contracts with city governments and non-governmental organizations. Such programs were urgently needed to begin reconstructing Chile's atomized social fabric, and make up for the void in social programs left by the neo-liberals.

The Concertación addressed the severe housing shortage resulting from Pinochet's free market housing policy. The government dramatically increased housing subsidy programs. Some 400,000 poor and middle class families bought homes with government assistance in the first four years — a lot of houses for a country of 13.4 million people.

The Aylwin administration moved away from Pinochet's free market approach to public transportation problems. Through government negotiation with industry, a new set of regulations were put in place, reorganizing bus routes, enforcing bus stops, restricting the numbers of buses permitted in congested areas through competitive bidding, and phasing in catalytic converters. Fewer, fuller buses now move faster down the Alameda, Santiago's main boulevard. The government also increased the restrictions on personal car use, especially during the winter when Santiago's smog is at its worst. Such broad restrictions and regulations, desperately needed to combat Santiago's dangerous air quality, were only possible after the new government came into power, when public good could be placed above the "right" to drive a car at all times (at least for those who own them).[12]

In a step toward greater regulation of the environment the

Concertación also moved forward with a new environmental framework law, which came into effect only days before the end of Aylwin's term in March 1994. The new framework establishes processes for environmental impact review and for setting pollution standards.

Economy and Equity

In contrast to the dire predictions of the outgoing Pinochet regime, macroeconomic stability and economic growth were sustained during the Aylwin administration. The Concertación inherited a growing economy, and that growth continued, averaging 6.3% annually from 1990-93.[13] This compares to an average 3.5% per year for the period 1973-89, the years of the dictatorship, and 6.4% for the 1985-89 period, the years of economic recovery from the debt crisis.

During the Aylwin administration, the inflation rate dropped from 27.3% in 1990 to 12% in 1993.[14] National savings and annual investment rates increased.[15] Chile's overall debt situation improved, with external debt as a percentage of exports and as a percentage of GNP falling.[16]

Export volumes continued to grow, reaching an average annual rate of 9.3% from 1990-3, though export markets proved unstable, and with growth in exports dropping to 2% in 1993.[17] But growth in volumes did not translate directly into growth in export incomes, with export income falling 10% in 1993.[18] In the fruit trade, prices and volumes of exports to the US and Europe have been down in apples, grapes, kiwis and other major crops, though nectarine and berry exports have increased. The European Union's decision in 1993 to raise countervailing duties against Chilean apples caused huge losses. While the Chilean government and exporters have coped with declines in exports to the US and Europe by opening new markets in Asia, the Middle East and Latin America, the Chilean economy remains extremely vulnerable to price and market fluctuations of the natural resource exports on which the economy now depends.

Official unemployment fell to a 20-year low of 4.5% in 1992, from 27% in 1982 and 5.7% in 1990.[19] While official statistics underestimate the numbers of unemployed and under-employed, they still show a substantial reduction. At the same time, workers saw their week get longer, with the average increasing from 48.5 hours per week in 1990 to 50.5 hours in 1992.[20]

In innumerable speeches, the Concertación and president Aylwin affirmed their commitment to reducing poverty and gradually paying the "social debt." Indeed, during the Aylwin administration (1990-94) poverty rates declined, and the Frei administration began with a high-profile national campaign to eliminate poverty by the year 2000.[21]

During the first four years since General Pinochet left the presidency, the numbers of people officially defined as living in poverty fell from some five million to some four million, while over one million people were lifted over the indigence line,[22] according to the United Nations. There are now fewer poor people, and many of those who remain poor are less poor than they were before the transition.

The decline in poverty is the result of both government and market effects.[23] The increase in the minimum wage negotiated by the Aylwin government in 1990 accounts for much of the improvement, while the decrease in unemployment, and government social spending targeted at the poor were also important factors. The fall in the inflation rate improved the economic situation of wage-earners whose wages were indexed to past inflation.[24] Without government actions such as the increase in the minimum wage, and increases in social spending, the progress in reducing poverty during the Aylwin administration could never have been made.

Nevertheless, poverty rates remain much worse than before the neo-liberals took over national economic policy. Comparing the early 1990s with 1970 (before the redistribution that took place during the Allende years), we see a dramatic increase in the percentages of households living below the poverty and indigence lines. United Nations statistics show that while 17% of Chilean households were below the poverty line in 1970, 38% lived in poverty in 1986, and 35% in 1990.[25] The figure is 33.5% for 1992[26]. While incomes have been improving over the last several years, they have not made up for the magnitude of the reversal that neo-liberal restructuring wrought over the past 20 years.

Yet while strides have been made in poverty reduction, after ten straight years of economic growth, the neo-liberal model does not seem to be producing a more equal distribution of wealth. A 1993 study by Chilean economist Alvaro Díaz shows that the Chilean economy has continued to reproduce inequality. "[I]n spite of the increase in the real incomes of workers and of the poorest 40% of the population, there has been no significant change in the distribution of national and personal income. The share of national income attributable to wages in fact fell between 1990-92; and the richest 10% of all Chileans continues to receive around 45% of the total."[27]

It is not unemployment, but precarious employment and low wages which are the principal causes of poverty in Chile. Labor's weak bargaining power means wages have continually fallen short of productivity gains, and continued economic growth alone will not significantly reduce inequality. While the Center and the Left promoted "growth with equity" as an economic strategy during the 1960s and early 1970s, today growth and stability is the Concertación's mantra, and "growth with equity" has been demoted to the realm of principles and ideals.

Conclusion

Many of the improvements in Chile during the Aylwin administration were made through government interventions in the market, not by keeping to neo-liberal dogma. It was not just the magic of the market, but government actions such as raising the minimum wage and pensions, and other social policies, that contributed to poverty reduction under Aylwin. Given the institutions and structure of the economy, even these measures have had little effect on Chile's very unequal pattern of income distribution.

It remains to be seen to what degree Chile's economy will continue to rely on "flexible" cheap labor, or whether future Labor Code reforms, a re-organization of the labor movement and state policies facilitating worker training and technology transfer and development will fuel a second stage of more equitable development.

Moves toward more progressive and equitable economic and labor policies have been difficult in Chile's slow transition toward democracy. On the one hand, there is the challenge of developing alternatives that are feasible and more equitable. Emerging debates in Chile over industrial policy show that there is growing support for a stronger government role in guiding the economy, and fear that without such intervention, Chile will not move beyond low value added natural resource exports. On the other hand, the economic and political restructuring that took place during the dictatorship make change very difficult. The reduction of the state's role in economic planning and production under the neo-liberals also hinders the state's ability to guide the economy in a strategic way.

As his term came to an end in March 1994, President Aylwin became more openly critical of the neo-liberal economic model. In a controversial interview in the religious news magazine *Mensaje*, Aylwin expressed his concerns about how long this relative prosperity and security could last:

> Economic growth. Well, we have advanced and we have reasons to be satisfied, but how long is it going to last? Chile is a country that depends so much on the exterior. The recession in Europe means one billion US dollars less in exports this year, in a country whose total exports are 10 billion dollars. That's 10% of the total! This is equivalent to twice the income we receive from the tax reform, since that law produces 500 million dollars per year [in tax revenue]. This is explained by the fall in the price of copper, of fish meal, wood chips and fruit. What does this mean in terms of our capacity for social development, housing, health, education?[28]

Later, at a celebration of International Women's Day, Aylwin remarked, "There is no point in it [free market-based development] if the majority of human beings see it only on TV."[29]

Notes

Chapter 1

1. First sentence is from a speech by President George Bush to the Chilean Congress in Valparaiso, Chile, December 6, 1990. The other two sentences are from his speech at a state dinner in Santiago that evening.
2. Quoted by David L. Marcus, *Miami Herald International Edition*, May 10, 1992.
3. However appropriately or inappropriately, the appelation neo-liberal refers to 18th century British "liberal" economists such as Adam Smith. In the United States, "neo-conservative" is frequently used interachangeably with "neo-liberal." In this book we employ the term "free-market" and "neo-liberal" interchangeably. See Chapter 4.
4. *El Mercurio*, Chile's leading newspaper, in August 1988 went so far as to proclaim in a banner headline: "Chile Has Left Latin America," arguing that Chile should no longer be classified as a Latin American nation but as one of the booming Pacific Rim nations. This was the theme also in a *Wall Street Journal* feature article, "Free Market Model: Chile's Economy Roars As Exports Take Off in Post-Pinochet Era — 'Latin America's Tiger' Now Goes After the Next Step: Free Trade With the U.S. — Leaving Third World Behind," *The Wall Street Journal*, January 25, 1993. For an analysis and critique of the Asian economic "tigers," see Walden Bello and Stephanie Rosenfeld, *Dragons in Distress* (San Francisco: Food First Books, 1990).
5. Shirley Christian, *New York Times*, "Free Market Lessons of Chile's 'Chicago Boys,'" October 8, 1990.
6. Patricia Politzer, *Fear in Chile*, (New York, Pantheon Books, 1989).
7. Ricardo Infante and Emilio Klein, "Chile: Transformaciones del Mercado Laboral y sus Efectos Sociales: 1965-1990," PREALC, Programa Mundial del Empleo, OIT, Octubre 1992, Documento de Trabajo, Cuadro 12, p. 33.
8. See Larissa Lomnitz and Ana Melnick, *Chile's Middle Class: A*

Struggle for Survival in the Face of Neoliberalism. Boulder, Colorado: Lynne Rienner Publishers, 1991.

Chapter 2

1. An excellent general history of Chile is Brian Loveman, *Chile: the Legacy of Hispanic Capitalism* (New York: Oxford University Press, 2nd edition, 1988). Arnold Bauer, *Chilean Rural Society* (Cambridge: Cambridge University Press, 1975) is a fine study of the countryside.
2. Arturo Valenzuela, "Chile: Origins, Consolidation, and Breakdown of a Democratic Regime," in Larry Diamond, Juan J. Linz, and Seymour Martin Lipset, eds., *Democracy in Developing Countries; vol. 4, Latin America* (Boulder, Colorado: Lynne Rienner, 1989), p. 174.
3. José Pablo Arellano, *Políticas sociales y de desarrollo*, (Santiago: CIEPLAN, 1985), pp. 36-39.
4. Arturo Valenzuela, *The Breakdown of Democratic Regimes: Chile* (Baltimore: Johns Hopkins University Press, 1978), 118. In the aftermath of the Watergate scandals, Senate investigations of U.S. government covert activites produced *Covert Action in Chile, 1963-73, Staff Report of the Select Committee to Study Governmental Operations with Respect to Intelligence Activities* (Washington, D.C.: GPO, Dec. 18, 1975).
5. Seymour Hersh, *The Price of Power* (New York: Summit Books, 1983), p. 259.
6. Ronald Fischer, "Efectos de una apertura sobre la distribución del ingreso," *Colección Estudios Cieplan* N. 33, Diciembre de 1991, pp. 95-121.
7. A fine account of the conflict between Allende's directed program of socialist transformation and the "revolution from below" is Peter Winn's *Weavers of Revolution:The Yarur Workers and Chile's Road to Socialism.* (New York: Oxford University Press, 1986).
8. Interview with Daniel Gonzalo Martner, Santiago, January, 1990.
9. The U. S. government viewed Allende's election in terms of the East-West conflict as well as the threat nationalist movements posed to multinational capital. As Seymour Hersh suggests in his study of Kissinger's role in foreign policy,

> "The fear was not only that Allende would be voted into office, but that — after his six-year term — the political process would work and he would be voted out of office in the next election." The left's commitment to democracy was the wrong message to send to potential voters in Europe and Latin America, where left-leaning parties were increasingly popular. In the weeks following Allende's electoral victory, the highest levels of the

Nixon administration made contacts and payments to
right-wing vigilante and military groups in Chile in the
hopes that assassination or a military coup would pre-
vent Allende from taking office. After Allende's election
was confirmed by the Chilean Congress in October,
U.S. policy focused on intervening indirectly to accelerate divisions and undermine the economy — or as
Nixon declared to CIA director Richard Helms, to
"make the economy scream" — and thereby hasten the
end of the Popular Unity experiment."
Hersh, *The Price*, pp. 274-285.

10. U.S. Agency for International Development figures taken from
Gonzalo Martner, *El Gobierno de Salvador Allende, 1970-1973*,
(Santiago, Ediciones LAR, 1988), pp. 232, 240. In addition, the CIA
secretly funnelled millions of dollars to a wide variety of groups
opposing Allende, ranging from the right-wing newspaper *El
Mercurio* to the organizers of the devastating truckers' strike of July
1973. The hostility of the U.S. government, while not directly
instrumental in the overthrow of Allende, gave legitimacy and the
assurance of international tolerance to a wide variety of groups in
Chile that plotted Allende's overthrow.

Chapter 3

1. For a detailed history of the agreement between the University of
Chicago and the Catholic University of Chile, and of the "Chicago
Boys," the reader is referred to Juan Gabriel Valdes, *La Escuela de
Chicago: Operación Chile* (Buenos Aires: Zeta, 1989, especially chapters 3, 4, 5 and 6; see also (the adulatory but informed) Arturo
Fontaine, *Los Economistas y El Presidente Pinochet* (Santiago: Zig Zag,
2nd ed., 1988), chapter 2.
2. Philip J. O'Brien, "The New Leviathan: The Chicago School and the
Chilean Regime, 1973-1980," *IDS Sussex Bulletin* 13 (1981): 38.
3. Pamela Constable and Arturo Valenzuela, *A Nation of Enemies* (New
York: Norton, 1991), p. 167.
4. Harberger, who married one of his students at the end of his first
tour of duty in Chile as a visiting professor and regularly visited Chile
to select new candidates for studies in Chicago, came to be called the
Chicago Boys' "spiritual father."
5. For one list of the "Chicago Boys," see Manuel Délano and Hugo
Traslaviña, *La herencia de los Chicago boys* (Santiago: Ornitorrinco,
1989), pp. 32 ff. A few Chileans who received their doctorates from the
University of Chicago, such as Ricardo Ffrench-Davis, became prominent intellectual critics of the military government's economic policies.

6. Constable and Valenzuela, op. cit., drawing on Arturo Fontaine Aldunate, *Los economistas y el presidente Pinochet* (Santiago: Zig-Zag, 1988), p. 20.
7. The details of this account vary from source to source (cf. Aldunate, Délano and Traslaviña, Constable) but the thrust is the same in all versions. Constable and Valenzuela (*op. cit.*, chapter 7, footnote 3), comment that it is "likely that some aid was provided by the CIA," quite possibly channeled through corporations in Europe, Latin America and the United States. They cite a 1975 report by the U.S. Senate Select Committee to Study Governmental Operations with Respect to Intelligence Activities (established in the wake of the Watergate scandals) which found that the CIA helped finance "an opposition research organization" during the Popular Unity. See *Covert Action in Chile, 1963-73* (Washington, D.C.: Government Printing Office, December 18, 1975), p. 30.
8. Fontaine, *Los economistas...*, p. 54. See his chapter "Tomando posiciones" for many more such details of these early heated clashes.
9. Constable and Valenzuela, op. cit., p. 169.
10. Cited in and translation from Brian Loveman, *Chile, The Legacy of Hispanic Capitalism*, 2nd edition, (Oxford, New York, 1988), pp. 312-316.
11. *Fortune*, November 2, 1981, p. 140.
12. *Fortune*, November 2, 1981, p. 138; see also *Business Week*, January 12, 1976, p. 71.
13. *"El consejo del profesor,"* *Ercilla*, April 2, 1975, pp. 19-22.
14. Ibid.
15. This was also the time of a coup within the coup: Decree Law 966 gave Pinochet sweeping powers of "executive prerogative" to name all top government officials, a power previously shared by all four junta members. Shortly after his appointment, de Castro declared that the economic stagnation and poverty in Chile were "the result of years of demagogy and erroneous economic policies, the consequence of an exaggerated statism. . .[and] exaggerated protectionism that guaranteed monopoly profits. . .[and] the result of policies made to benefit special interest groups to the detriment of the majority of the population."
16. Fontaine, *op. cit.*, p. 94.
17. Details are taken from Fontaine's vivid account, *op. cit.*, pp. 93f.
18. *Business Week*, January 12, 1976, pp. 71-72. In many aspects, the "shock plan" anticipated the so-called structural adjustment plans imposed by the International Monetary Fund and the World Bank on many governments overwhelmed with foreign debts in the 1980s.
19. Figures from Banco Central de Chile, *Indicadores economicos y sociales, 1960-1988*, (Santiago, 1989) and Alejandro Foxley, in J. Samuel and Arturo Valenzuela, *Military Rule in Chile*, (Baltimore:

Johns Hopkins University Press, 1986).
20. Banco Central de Chile, *Indicadores economicos y sociales.*
21. Cite and translation from Loveman, *Chile*, p. 343.
22. Ricardo Ffrench-Davis, "Debt and Growth in Chile: Trends and Prospects," in David Felix, editor, *Debt and Transfiguration?*, (Armonk, N.Y.: M. E. Sharpe, 1990), p. 145.

Chapter 4

1. For a particularly accessible and influential presentation of the core doctrines, see Milton Friedman and Rose Friedman, *Free to Choose* (New York: Harcourt Brace Jovanovich, 1980).
2. This current of thought in the United States often has been journalistically and popularly dubbed "neo-conservative." See Joseph Ramos, *Neo-Conservative Economics in the Southern Cone of Latin America, 1973-1983* (Baltimore: The Johns Hopkins University Press, 1986).
3. Juan Gabriel Valdes, *La Escuela de Chicago: Operación Chile* (Buenos Aires: Grupo Editorial Zeta, 1989), pp. 99-102.
4. Milton Friedman, *Capitalism and Freedom.* (Chicago: University of Chicago Press, 1962), pp. 14f.
5. That professional associations are also seen as obstacles to the free functioning of markets is consistent with Milton Friedman's doctoral dissertation in economics (for Columbia University) which strongly criticized the American Medical Association for placing obstacles in the way of a free market in health services in the United States.
6. The "principle of subsidiarity of the state" is emphasized in the *Declaration of Principles of the Government of Chile* issued by the junta on March 11, 1974.
7. Pilar Vergara, *Auge y caida del neoliberalismo en Chile* (Santiago: FLACSO, 1985), p. 81.
8. Vergara, *Auge y caida*, pp. 94-95, has an especially insightful discussion of the neo-liberal view of social equality.
9. See Pilar Vergara, *Politicas hacia la extrema pobreza en Chile.*, pp. 38-40.
10. Vergara, *Auge y caida*, p. 96. Vergara's footnotes marshal illustrative quotes from the Chilean Chicago Boys and members of the junta.
11. Harry G. Johnson, "The Keynesian Revolution and the Monetarist Counter-Revolution," *American Economic Review* 61 (May 1971): pp. 7-11 provides a useful contrasting of the two competing economic philosophies.
12. Vergara, *Auge y caida*, p. 78.
13. Milton Friedman, *Dollars and Deficits* (Englewood Cliffs, N.J.: Prentice-Hall, 1968), p. 18.
14. Friedman, who was widely publicly attacked for his collaboration with the Pinochet regime, eventually attempted to distance himself

from Pinochet's notoriously repressive rule. For a critique of this attempt, see Elton Rayack, *Not So Free to Choose* (Westport: Praeger, 1987), esp. 59-62.

15. Manuel Délano and Hugo Traslaviña, *La herencia de los Chicago boys*, (Santiago: Ornitorrinco, 1989), p. 19.
16. *Que Pasa*, May 31, 1979, 31. Cited in Constable and Valenzuela, op. cit., p. 188.
17. Roberto Zahler, *"El neoliberalism en una version autoritaria,"* CPU *Estudios Sociales*, no. 31, 1982, p. 21.
18. Constable and Valenzuela, op. cit., p. 188. The de Castro quote is from *El Mercurio*, February 15, 1976, cited in Vergara, *Auge y caida*, pp. 98-99.
19. Interview by Nina Serafino, November 12, 1979, quoted in Constable and Valenzuela, op. cit., p. 171.
20. Constable and Valenzuela, op. cit., p. 171.
21. *El Mercurio*, July 25, 1982.
22. Center for International Policy, "Aid Memo" (Washington, D.C., May 30, 1986).
23. *Washington Post*, August 3, 1979, p. 16.
24. P. Vergara, *Auge y caida*, p. 90.
25. P. Vergara, *Auge y caida*, p. 99.
26. P. Vergara, *Auge y caida*, p. 100.

Chapter 5

1. Quoted in "Privatization and the Private Sector: Keys to Third World Development," *AID Highlights*, vol. 3, no. 2, Summer 1986, p. 1.
2. *Memoria Corfo*, 1987.
3. Mario Marcel, "Privatizacion y Finanzas Publicas," *Coleccion Estudios Cieplan*, 26, 1989, p. 28.
4. Marcel, "Privatizacion," p. 29.
5. This policy assumed the continued existence of CODELCO as a public enterprise, but at the same time severely limited CODELCO's scope. The considerable CODELCO revenues committed to the military could not be diverted either to further invest in the mines' productivity or to badly needed social services. By contrast, private foreign investment in copper mining increased dramatically in the 1980s, so that by the early 1990s over half of copper output was again in private hands. Bleeding CODELCO dry was a *de facto* privatization of the copper industry.
6. Sergio Bitar, *Chile para todos*, (Santiago: Planeta, 1988), p. 77.
7. Figures are based on published *Memorias* (1986-1989) and confidential CORFO reports as well as anonymous interviews within CORFO, 1990.

8. Marcel, "Privatization," p. 41; Gustavo Marin, "Privatizaciones en Chile: de la Normalizacion del 'Area Rara' a la Ley del Estado Empresario." Documento de Trabajo #24, (Santiago: Pries-Cono Sur, 1989), p. 19.
9. Interview, anonymous CORFO official, Santiago, December 1990. During the Pinochet regime, CORFO officials were not permitted to use the word "losses" in their annual reports in relation to privatizations, referring instead to "negative results." See CORFO, *Memorias*, 1985-1989.
10. Marcel, "Privatization," p. 41.
11. Cristian Larroulet, "Impact of Privatization: The Chilean Case 1985-1989," paper presented at the Insitute of the Americas of San Diego, California, November 1992, p. 35.
12. Marcel, "Privatization," p. 41.
13. Gustavo Marin, "Trayectoria de las privatizaciones en Chile durante el regimen dictatorial, 1973-1989." Documento de Trabajo, (Santiago: PRIES-Cono Sur, 1990), p. 25
14. Marin, "Trayectoria," p. 32.
15. Marin, "Trayectoria," p. 40.
16. Interview with Raul Saez, Santiago, January 1991.
17. Interview with Raul Saez, Santiago, January 1991.
18. Bitar, *Chile para todos*, p. 74.

Chapter 6

1. For an excellent account of the "debt crisis" see Susan George, *A Fate Worse than Debt* (New York: Grove Press, 1988), especially chapters 8 and 9.
2. Ricardo Ffrench-Davis and Jose de Gregorio,"Origines y efectos del endeudamiento externo," *CIEPLAN Notas Tecnicas* 99, (1987) pp. 3-5.
3. Ricardo Ffrench-Davis, "Debt and Growth in Chile: Trends and Prospects" in David Felix, editor, *Debt and Transfiguration?*, (Armonk, N.Y.: M. E. Sharpe, 1990), p. 147.
4. Ffrench-Davis, "Debt and Growth," p. 147.
5. James Livingston, "Chile and debt-equity conversion" in Robert Wesson, editor, *Coping with the Latin American Debt*, (New York: Praeger, 1988), p. 142
6. As the Argentine writer Jacobo Timerman explains the accord, "Pinochet does not inquire of the newspaper owners, the Edwards family, what they have done with the $100 million, and *El Mercurio* does not ask Pinochet what he has done with the seven hundred who have disappeared in Chile after being arrested by the military." Jacobo Timerman, *Chile: Death in the South*, (New York: Knopf, 1987)
7. Ffrench-Davis, "Debt and Growth," p. 145.

8. World Bank, *World Debt Tables* (Washington, D.C.: World Bank, 1992-1993), v. 1, p. 74.
9. Ffrench-Davis, "Debt and Growth," p. 152.

Chapter 7

1. Jose Piñera, *La Revolución Laboral en Chile*, (Santiago: Zig-Zag, 1990), p. 38.
2. Jaime Ruiz-Tagle, *El sindicalismo chileno después del plan laboral.* (Santiago: PET, 1985), p. 181.
3. Manuel Barrera and J. Samuel Valenzuela, "The Development of Labor Movement Opposition," in J. Samuel Valenzuela and Arturo Valenzuela, *Military Rule in Chile*, (Baltimore: Johns Hopkins University Press, 1986), p. 234.
4. Interview with Manuel Bustos in Patricia Politzer, *Fear in Chile*, (New York: Pantheon, 1989), pp. 174-199.
5. Figures from ILO report cited in Delano and Traslaviña, *La Herencia*, p. 76.
6. Of 2,279 recognized victims of human rights violations, 571 were *obreros. Informe Rettig, Informe de la Comisión Nacional de Verdad y Reconciliación*, (Santiago, 1991), Tomo II, p. 887.
7. Barrera and Valenzuela, "The Development of Labor Opposition," p. 236.
8. Statements quoted in Barrera and Valenzuela, "The Development of Labor Opposition," p. 246, 248.
9. Jaime Gatica Barros, *Deindustrialization in Chile* (Boulder: Westview, 1989) pp. 64, 152.
10. Peter Winn and Maria Angelica Ibañez, "Textile Entrepreneurs and Workers in Pinochet's Chile, 1973-1989." (New York: Institute of Latin American and Iberian Studies — Columbia University, 1989), p. 4.
11. Winn and Ibañez, "Textile Entrepreneurs," p. 5
12. Winn and Ibañez argue that the trauma of bankruptcy and unemployment was instrumental in the reorganization of the textile sector. Winn and Ibañez, "Textile Entrepreneurs," p. 2.
13. Piñera, *La Revolucion Laboral,* p. 101.
14. Eugenio Tironi, *Los Silencios de la Revolución*, (Santiago: Puerta Abierta, 1988) p. 73.
15. Barrera and Valenzuela, "The Development of Labor Opposition," p. 255.
16. Bustos in Patricia Politzer, *Fear in Chile*, p. 188.
17. Ruiz-Tagle, *El Sindicalismo Chileno,* p. 181.
18. Eugenio Tironi, *Los Silencios*, p. 72.
19. Piñera euphemistically refers to the military junta as the "legislative branch." Piñera, *La Revolución Laboral,* p. 63.

20. Alan Angell, "Unions and Workers in Chile During the 1980s" in Paul Drake and Ivan Jaksic, eds., *The Struggle for Democracy in Chile, 1982-1990,* (Lincoln: University of Nebraska, 1991), p. 193 fn.
21. Joaquin Lavin and Luis Larrain, *Chile, Sociedad Emergente,* (Santiago: Zig-Zag, 1989), p. 24.
22. Lavin and Larrain, *Chile, Sociedad Emergente,* p. 25.
23. Wage and economic growth from Banco Central, cited in Jaime Ruiz-Tagle, "Crisis de la Experiencia Neoliberal en Chile," (Santiago: PET, 1989) and (no author), "Evolución Económica y Situación de los Trabajadores en la Transición a la Democracia," (Santiago: PET, 1990).
24. Ruiz-Tagle,"Crisis de la Experiencia Neoliberal," p. 16; Tironi, *Los Silencios,* p. 74; PET, "Evolucion Económica," p. 34.
25. René Cortázar, "Que hacer con los salarios minimos?" *Notas Tecnicas,* no. 107 (December 1987), cited in Angell, "Unions and Workers," p. 190.
26. Piñera, *La Revolución Laboral,* p. 63
27. Figures based on Ruiz-Tagle, "Crisis de la Experiencia Neoliberal," p. 17.
28. PET, "Evolucion Económica," p. 25. PET figures include those in PEM/POCH and those who had occasional work as unemployed.
29. Bradford Barham, et. al, "Nontraditional Agricultural Exports in Latin America," *Latin American Research Review,* 27:2, 1992, p. 65.
30. PET, "Evolucion Económica," p. 27.
31. Soledad Ugarte, "Salud Laboral: Riesgos y Beneficios," *Vida Médica,* 1988, 132-134.
32. Ugarte, "Salud Laboral", p. 133-134.
33. Ugarte gives the example of a bank clerk who developed tendonitis of the flexores cubitales, was reinstated, then fired. Ugarte, "Salud Laboral", p. 134.
34. Mariana Schkolnik, and Berta Teitelbolm, "Segunda Encuesta de Empleo en el Gran Santiago," (Santiago: PET, 1989), p. 79.
35. Banco Central, *Indicadores Economicos y Sociales,* 1989, p. 445.
36. Instituto Nacional de Estatidistica, *Encuesta Suplementaria de Ingresos,* (Santiago, 1989) and Ronald Fischer, "Efectos de una apertura sobre la distribución del ingreso," *Colección Estudios Cieplan N.* 33, Diciembre de 1991, pp. 95-121.
37. Figures for the percentage of Chileans living in poverty are in relative agreement: two United Nations organizations put the figure at 44 percent (ECLA) and 49 percent (PREALC) for 1987, and the Catholic church-based Programa de Economía del Trabajo estimated 49 percent in 1988.
38. Barrera and Valenzuela, "Development," p. 258.
39. Winn and Ibañez,"Textile Entrepreneurs," p. 17.
40. Jaime Ruiz-Tagle, *El Sindicalismo Chileno,* p. 104.

41. Throughout the world, a return to a version of the free-market policies in vogue in the nineteenth century could potentially result in similar patterns of open conflict.
42. *Chile Information Project* newsletter, Santiago, June 15, 1992.

Chapter 8

1. Joaquín Lavín and Luis Larraín, *Chile, sociedad emergente*, (Santiago: Zig-Zag, 1989), p. 31.
2. Lavín and Larraín, *Chile, sociedad emergente*, p. 41.
3. Joseph Scarpaci, ed., *Health Services Privatization in Industrial Societies*, "Dismantling Public Health Services in Authoritarian Chile," (New Brunswick, NJ: Rutgers University Press, 1989), p. 238.
4. Joseph Scarpaci, "Restructuring Health Care Financing in Chile," *Social Sciences and Medicine*, vol. 21, no. 4, pp. 417 f. See also Joseph Scarpaci, *Primary Medical Care in Chile* (Pittsburgh: University of Pittsburgh Press, 1988).
5. Joseph Scarpaci, "Restructuring Health Care Financing in Chile," *Social Science and Medicine*, vol. 21, no. 4, p. 417, citing G. Arroba, "La financiación de la seguridad social en los paises en desarrollo. Estudios Seguridad Social, 19, pp. 5-31, 1979 and M. I. Roemer, Medical Care in Latin America (Washington, D.C.: Pan American Health Union, 1964).
6. Zita Elsa Barrueto, "Evaluating the Effects of Economic Recession on Child Welfare in Chile," Ph.D. dissertation, University of California, Berkeley, 1990, p. 42.
7. Barrueto, p. 42
8. There is some debate about whether the first was established in Puerto Rico during the U.S. administration of Franklin Roosevelt.
9. Barrueto, p. 42.
10. Mariano Raquena B. *"Marco historico del sistema de cuidado de la salud chileno,"* unpub. ms., pp 3 f., and Barrueto, pp. 42 f.
11. "Testimonios de Medicos Exonerados Durante el Regimen Militar," *Vida Medica*, April 1990.
12. Ibid.
13. Ibid. Several doctors and other health workers we interviewed were themselves targets of official terror.
14. A. Goic. "La salud en Chile: el problem de fondo," *Mensaje* 282, p. 560, 1979.
15. D. Chanfreau, "Professional ideology and the health care system in Chile," *International Journal of Health Services*, vol. 9, pp. 86-105, 1979.
16. Alejandro Foxley and Dagmar Raczynksi, "Vulnerable Groups in Recessionary Situations: The Case of Children and the Young in Chile," *World Development*, vol. 12, no. 3, pp. 223-246, 1984.

17. F. Schuerch and P. Retamal, 1989, cited by Dr. Rafael Sepulveda in *Vida Medica*, 41, September–October 1989.

18. E. Lira and E. Weinstein, "Desempleo y Daño Psicologica" FASIC, Chile 1980. See also "La Salud Pública en Chile 1985," *Vida Médica*, 1986.

19. Joseph Scarpaci, *Primary Medical Care in Chile* (Pittsburgh: University of Pittsburgh Press, 1988) focuses on this distinction.

20. Ministry of Health, "Diagnóstico," January 28, 1991, using data from CASEN 1987.

21. Jaime Lavados, *"Revolucion en salud?" Vida Médica*, 1988.

22. Jaime Sepúlveda, *"El desafio de la salud en el gobierno democratico,"* unpub. ms. (December 1990), p. 17, citing government data.

23. Interview (January 17, 1991) with Dr. Raul Donckaster, Medical Association.

24. Sepúlveda, *op. cit.*, p. 16, citing FONASA publications.

25. Sepúlveda, *op. cit.*, pp. 19 ff.

26. Ministerio de Salud. *Indicadores Financieros Sector Salud Público* 1974–1988.

27. Pilar Vergara, *Politicas hacia la extrema pobreza en Chile, 1973–1988* (Santiago: FLACSO), 1990, p. 250.

28. *The South Pacific Mail,* December 1990. Somewhat more was spent in the wake of the 1988 earthquake which badly damaged several facilities and happened during the politically sensitive period for the regime leading up to the plebiscite on Pinochet's future.

29. Requena, *"Marco Histórico,"* p. 3.

30. Eugenio Tironi, *Los Silencios de la revolucion* (Santiago: La Puerta Abierta, 1988), p. 37.

31. See Vergara, *op. cit.*, p. 254 and Cuadro A-1.

32. *The South Pacific Mail,* December 1990, p. 234.

33. Requena. *"Marco Historico"* chart 4, drawn from World Health Organization data.

34. Requena, *"Marco Historico"* p. 10 using data from FONASA.

35. José Pablo Arellano, *La salud en los años 80, análisis desde la economía* (Santiago: CIEPLAN, 1987).

36. Scarpaci, in *Health Services Privatization,* p. 229.

37. Arellano, *op. cit.*, p. 20.

38. Joseph Scarpaci, personal correspondence, September 15, 1991.

39. All data from the Ministry of Health, "Estructura Porcentual del Estado de Resultados de las Isapre Abiertas" (1991).

40. Lavín and Larraín, p. 44.

41. J. Lavín, *Chile: A Quiet Revolution* (Santiago: Zig-Zag, 1988), pp. 150 f.

42. *The South Pacific Mail,* December 1990, p. 233.

43. Requena, *"Marco Historico,"* p. 12, citing data from the Banco Central and the Ministerio de Salud.

44. Calculations are from Joseph Scarpaci, personal correspondence,

September 15, 1991, referring to his chapter in *Health Services Privatization*.

45. Cited in J. Scarpaci, *Health Services Privatization*, p. 235.
46. See Jorge Jiménez and Margarita Gili, "Municipalización de la Atención Primaria en Salud," *Estudios Sociales* No. 62 (1989), p. 125 for a complete tabulation of the three waves of municipalization.
47. Scarpaci, *Health Services Privatization*, 236.
48. Jiménez and Gili, *op. cit.*, 132.
49. Interviews at Consultorio Yazigi, Lo Prado, December 13, 1990.
50. "Culpan de aumento de TBC a municipalización," *La Epoca*, October 27, 1990.
51. Jiménez and Gili, *op. cit.*, pp. 138 f.
52. Jorge Jiménez, "La salud pública en Chile 1985," *Vida Médica*, vol. 36, no. 1, 1985.
53. Vergara, *op. cit.*, p. 276.
54. For a chronological detailing on these targeting measures, see Tarscicio Castañeda, *Innovative Social Policies for Reducing Poverty: Chile in the 1980s* (Washington, D.C.: World Bank), 1989, p. 67. Since 1980 the CAS index system based on a socioeconomic survey has been used to determine the benficiary populations of the social programs administered by the municipalities or the central government.
55. Clara S. Haignere, "The Application of the Free-Market Economic Model in Chile and the Effects on the Populaton's Health Status," *International Journal of Health Services*, vol. 13, no. 3, 1983, pp. 398 f.
56. Ibid.pp. 397 f. Castañeda puts the figure at $600 in 1987 but even at that level admits that "the cost is high." Castañeda p. 71.
57. Clara S. Haignere, "The Application of the Free-Market Economic Model in Chile and the Effects on the Populaton's Health Status," *International Journal of Health Services*, vol. 13, no. 3, 1983, 403.
58. See, for example, Dagmar Raczynski and César Oyarzo, "Por qué caé la tasa de mortalidad infantil en Chile?" *Colecccion Estudios CIEPLAN*, December 1981, 45-84 in which many studies are cited. Also Barrueto, *op. cit.* In our own research we interviewed on this issue health policy experts Dr. G. Solimano and Dr. Roberto Belmar among others.
59. Ibid.
60. Ministry of Health statistics.
61. Interview, Luz Ramirez, December 19, 1991.
62. Barrueto, pp 92-100.
63. Barrueto, p. 128
64. Barrueto, pp. 106 - 113.
65. Greater Santiago's population in 1985 was estimated to be 4.6 million, 42 percent of the entire nation's population.
66. Robert Edelman and Myron M. Levine, "Summary of an International Workshop on Typhoid Fever," *Reviews of Infectious*

Diseases. vol. 8, no. 3, May-June 1986, p. 344.

67. Colegio Medico, *Algunas consideraciones sobre la salud en Chile*, pp. 15-29, 1983 cited in Joseph Scarpaci, "Restructuring Health Care Financing in Chile."
68. Scarpaci, "Restructuring Health Care Financing in Chile," p. 427, citing an interview in 1984.
69. See, for instance, J. Scarpaci, *Health Services Privatization*, p. 233 f. or J. Scarpaci "Restructuring health care..," p. 427.
70. Clara S. Haignere, "The Application of the Free-Market Economic Model in Chile and the Effects on the Populaton's Health Status," *International Journal of Health Services*, vol. 13, no. 3, 1983, p. 393.
71. Programa de Economía del Trabajo (PET), *"El desigual acceso a la salud,"* 1989, p. 1
72. Ibid. Also see Eugenio Tironi and Eugenia Weinstein, "Frustración, agresividad y violencia en grupos marginales de Santiago: informe de una encuesta," Sur, Documento de Trabajo, 1988.
73. Poll by Bestland Company published in *El Mercurio,* cited in Mariano Requena, *"Marco Historico ..."* .

Chapter 9

1. Programa Interdisciplinario de Investigaciones en Educación (PIIE), *Ruptura y construccion de consensos en la educación Chilena* (Santiago: PIIE), 1989, p. 16.
2. Lavín and Larraín, *Chile: sociedad emergente,* (Santiago: Zig-Zag), 1989, p. 96.
3. See, for instance, Lavín and Larraín, pp. 97 f.
4. Approximate figures for the school year ending 1990. See Beatriz Fried and Mario Abuhadba, "Reforms in higher education: the case of Chile in the 1980s," in *Higher Education,* vol. 21, 1991, p. 137.
5. PIIE, *Ruptura,* p. 12 and p. 77.
6. PIIE, ibid, p. 77.
7. See E. Tironi, *Silencios,* p. 89.
8. UNESCO, *Anuario estadistico de America Latina y el Caribe,* Paris, 1975.
9. Rafael Echeverría, *Evolucion de la matricula en Chile,* 1935-1981, *PIIE Estudios,* 1982.
10. PIIE, *Ruptura,* pp. 77f.
11. Corporación de Promoción Universitaria, *Informe sobre la educacion superior en Chile 1988* (Santiago: CPU), 1988, cuadro No. A-3, p. 9. University students were a major force in a number of nationally important political parties and movements.
12. Rafael Echeverría, *Evolución de la matricula en Chile,* 1935-1981, *PIIE Estudios,* 1982.

13. Corporación de Promoción Universitaria, La educación superior privada en Chile. Antecedentes y perspectivas. (Santiago: CPU), 1988, p. 76.
14. Interview with Ivan Nuñez, Ministry of Education, December 13, 1990.
15. El Mercurio, May 19, 1968.
16. Manuel Figueroa-Unda, "Violence and Education: The Legacy of Repression in the Educational Systems of Latin America: A Case Study on Chile," unpub. ms. California State University-Fresno, March 1991, p. 28, citing a former faculty member of the School of Education, Catholic University of Valparaiso, June 15, 1978.
17. Manuel Figueroa, p. 34.
18. Le Maitre, M.J. and Lavados, I. "Antecedentes, Restricciones y Oportunidades de la Educacion Superior en Chile" in Le Maitre, M.J. and Lavados, I., eds., La educacion superior en Chile: riesgos y oportunidades en los '80. (Santiago: CPU), 1986, p. 83.
19. Banned authors included Freud, Nietzsche, and Nobel Prize winner Pablo Neruda. See interview with teacher in Politizer, Fear in Chile.
20. What in the United States is often referred to as a "voucher system."
21. Clarisa Hardy, La ciudad escindida, (Santiago: PET), 1989, p. 148.
22. As one report by a respected Jesuit-affiliated institute on education commented, "In this way, the existence of different qualities [of schools] in accordance with the socio-economic level of their students — better for those who have more, inferior for those who have less — is legitimized." Espinola, V. cf. Hardy, p. 148, footnote 5.
23. By 1989 higher education received only 22 percent of total national government expenditures on education; cf. Fried and Abuhadba, p. 142, Table 2.
24. Hardy, p. 153.
25. In the initial drafting of the decree, all universities including the new ones were to be eligible to receive the per-student payments for the top students, but the final version of the decree excluded new private universities from this "indirect government funding" (in contrast to the eligibility of most private primary and secondary schools for per-student government payments). Tarsicio Castañeda, Innovative Social Policies for Reducing Poverty: Chile in the 1980s (Washington, D.C.: World Bank), ms. p. 41.
26. Corporacion de Promocion Universitaria, Informe sobre la educacion superior en Chile 1988, p. 23 Cuadro No. B-4.
27. Corporación de Promoción Universitaria, Informe sobre la educación superior en Chile 1988, p. 22.
28. Ministerio de Educacion, "Analisis de Remuneraciones del Personal del Sector Subvencionado," internal unpub. paper, March 1990, table number 8.
29. Tironi, Silencios, p. 91.

30. Tironi, *Silencios*, p. 90. and IBRD p. 19.
31. Ivan Nuñez, "*Diagnóstico del sistema escolar*," PIIE unpub. ms., 1989.
32. Informe Final 1990, PIIE, Carmen Luz Latorre et al, draft, p.50.
33. Interview. December 3, 1990. with administrative staff person of Liceo Dario E. Salas.
34. Interview December 13, 1990 with Ivan Nuñez, advisor to the minister of education.
35. In the upper middle-class municipality of Nuñoa in metropolitan Santiago the test scores of the municipal and the subsidized private schools in Spanish and mathematics averaged almost the same and were well above the national average, although they were about 14 points below the private tuition-charging schools in the municipality. Seemingly what counts is not whether a school is publicly run or privately run (with a government subsidy) but the level of financial resources mobilized and the socioeconomic status of the students' families.
36. Hardy, p. 154.
37. In 1987 the government decreed on a permanent basis adjustment in the per-student payments in accord with the adjustment in the wages and salaries of public sector employees, in accordance with the estimated costs per grade level.
38. Interview with Ivan Nuñez. December 13, 1990.
39. Interview with principal of Lord Cochrane School, Santiago, December 13, 1990.
40. Informe Final 1990, PIIE, Carmen Luz Latorre et al, draft, p. 68.
41. Ibid., pp. 63 f.
42. Hardy, p. 152. citing studies by Rojas et al, PET.
43. Some involved in education have suggested to us that the actual situation is worse. They allege that in order to get more payments from the government some schools boost the attendance figures and that, even though there are government inspectors, the Pinochet government itself had an interest in keeping up school attendance figures.
44. Hardy, pp 154 f.
45. Ivan Nuñez, in *Chile 2000*, p. 99.
46. Corporación de Promoción Universitaria, *Informe sobre la educacion superior en Chile 1988*, p. 10 Cuadro No. A-4.
47. Corporación de Promoción Universitaria, *Informe sobre la educacion superior en Chile 1988*, p. 10 Cuadro No. A-4. This does not take into consideration the 10,609 students enrolled in the public professional institutes and the 19,047 in private professional institutes. Nonetheless, there is an obvious considerable decline in the percentage of university-age youths enrolled in universities and professional institutes.
48. Including, for instance, a sharp reduction in meals for grade-school pupils. In 1972, 68 percent of grade-school pupils received a light

meal; in 1988, only 22 percent. Over the same period, the percentage receiving lunch fell from 32 percent to 22 percent.

49. Hardy, p. 153.
50. Hardy, Table 47, p. 254.
51. By December 1991 the number had jumped to 43.
52. Corporacion de Promocion Universitaria, *La educaçion superior privada en Chile* (Santiago: CPU), 1989 (?), p. 189.
53. By law, they must offer three of the twelve undergraduate degree programs that the public universities are required to offer.
54. Corporacion de Promocion Universitaria, *La educacion superior privada en Chile* (Santiago: CPU), 1989 (?), p. 199.
55. Interview with Luis Torres, rector, Universidad Arcis, December 17, 1990.
56. Corporacion de Promocion Universitaria, *La educacion superior privada en Chile*, p. 180 notes that one university, Diego Portales, in recent years has started to be a little academically selective.
57. Interview with Luis Torres. Each new private university goes through a legally mandated period of five years of review of each undergraduate degree program by professors from the traditional universities. But certification is a "business," we were told, especially for a poor provincial university. The university in Iquique, for instance, has reportedly been under so much pressure to finance itself that it has tested students even in fields it does not offer.
58. Castañeda. p. 38.
59. The same Bank report goes on to suggest that there is no call for concern since higher education is just the "lengthening of the growing-up period before work and even [the] coping with the high rates of youth unemployment."
60. Pilar Vergara and Teresa Rodriguez, "*Libre Mercado y Educación Técnica Postsecundaria: La Experiencia de los Centros de Formación Técnica*, FLACSO, March 1986.
61. Ibid. See Part II for the findings.
62. Ibid, p. 78.
63. Ibid.
64. Ibid, p. 131. Students from such families, as Vergara and Rodriguez note, have more employment opportunities in any case.
65. Ibid., p. 126.
66. Officially, the private universities (unlike the private professional institutes and technical formation centers) are legally required to be "non-profit." In fact, they make a good return given how small the capital investments are and seek to accumulate capital. (Most operate on a rollover basis, that is, by securing a bank loan secured by the total tuition that the enrolled students are committed to pay.) Often the top officials are well-paid. And, we were told, directors often own or are otherwise connected to profitable businesses that hold univer-

sity contracts.
67. Pilar Vergara and Teresa Rodriguez, FLACSO no. 285, March 1986, p. 93.
68. Pilar Vergara and Teresa Rodriguez, FLACSO no. 285, March 1986, p. 83.
69. Vergara and Rodriguez, ibid.
70. Vergara and Rodriguez, pp. 83-84.
71. Interview with Manuel Délano, December 16, 1990.
72. Vergara and Rodriguez, pp. 101-102.
73. Vergara and Rodriguez, pp. 91-92.
74. Vergara and Rodriguez, p. 130.
75. Corporación de Promoción Universitaria, *Informe sobre la educación superior en Chile 1988*, p. 16.
76. Rodriguez and Tironi, *"El otro Santiago,"* *Proposiciones*, Number 13, pp. 15 f.
77. The latest study we know on this point goes up to only 1981, the time of the changes that arguably have worsened the situation. Guillermo Briones, *Las universidades chilenas en el modelo de economia neo-liberal.* (Santiago; PIIE), 1981.
78. ODEPLAN, *Informe Social* 1984-1985, p. 21.

Chapter 10

1. Cited in Jorge Scherman Filer, *Techo y Abrigo*, (Santiago: PET, 1990), p. 24.
2. Scherman Filer, *Techo*, p. 25.
3. Edwin Haramoto, "Politicas de Vivienda Social: Experiencia Chilena de las tres Ultimas Decadas," in Joan MacDonald, editor, *Vivienda Social*, (Santiago, 1983), pp. 92-93.
4. See for example Joan MacDonald, "25 años de Vivienda Social. La Perspectiva del Habitante" in MacDonald, *Vivienda Social.*
5. Fernando Kusnetzoff, "Urban and Housing Policies under Chile's Military Dictatorship 1973-1985," *Latin American Perspectives*, 14, 33, Spring (1987), pp. 157-86.
6. Manuel Castells, *The City and the Grassroots*, (Berkeley: University of California Press, 1983), p. 200.
7. Haramoto, "Politicas," p. 101.
8. Banco Central de Chile, *Indicadores Economicos y Sociales* (1989), p. 113.
9. Clarissa Hardy, *La Ciudad Escindida*, (Santiago: PET, 1990) p. 60.
10. Pablo Trivelli Oyarzun, "Intra-urban Socio-Economic Settlement Patterns, Public Intervention, and the Determination of the Spatial Structure of the Urban Land Market in Greater Santiago, Chile," Ph.D. Thesis, (Cornell,1987), p. 137.

11. For a comparison of Santiago with other Latin American cities, see Alejandro Portes, "Latin American Urbanization during the Years of the Crisis," *Latin American Research Review*, 1989, #3.
12. Eduardo Morales et al, *Erradicados en el Regimen Militar*, (Santiago: FLACSO, 1990), p.4.
13. Trivelli, "Intra-urban patterns," p. 148.
14. Trivelli, "Intra-urban patterns," p. 140.
15. E. Morales, et al. FLACSO, 170; and E. Tironi, *Los Silencios de la Revolucion*, (Santiago: Puerta Abierta, 1988), p. 27.
16. E. Morales, "Erradicados," p. 170.
17. E. Morales, "Erradicados," chapter 4.
18. *Santiago, Dos Ciudades*, Centro de Estudios del Desarrollo (Santiago, 1990), 47.
19. E. Morales, "Erradicados," pp. 57-58.
20. Tironi, *Silencios*, p. 27.
21. E. Morales, "Erradicados," p. 26.
22. Tironi, *Silencios*, p. 26.
23. Figure based on MINVU estimates in Haramoto, "Politicas," p. 110.
24. La Coordinadora Metropolitan de Pobladores, "Los Allegados; un problema nacional," 1990.
25. "Encuesta Sur," published in *Revista Proposiciones* #13, p. 17.
26. Scherman Filer, *Techo*, p. 33.
27. Arellano, *Politicas sociales*, p, 230.
28. Kusnetzoff, "Urban Housing Policies," p. 166.
29. Scherman Filer, *Techo*, p. 30.
30. Arellano, *Politicas sociales*, 235-240.
31. Pilar Vergara, *Politicas hacia la Extrema Pobreza*, (Santiago: FLACSO, 1990), ch. 4.
32. Tarsicio Castañeda, *Para Combatir la Pobreza*, (Santiago: Centro de Estudios Publicos, 1990), p. 180.
33. Vergara, *Politicas*, p. 233.
34. Scherman Filer, *Techo*, p. 33.
35. Arellano, *Politicas sociales*, p. 258.
36. Castañeda, *Combatir*, p. 217.
37. Arellano, *Politicas sociales*, p. 252.
38. Trevelli, "Intra-urban patterns," p. 162.
39. Vergara, *Politicas*, p. 230.
40. Arellano, *Politicas sociales*, p. 263.
41. Vergara, *Politicas*, p. 219.
42. It is worth noting that the centerpiece of the housing policy of the government of Patricio Aylwin, called "progressive housing," is to even further reduce the size of the original housing unit while providing a later subsidy for expansion.
43. Interview in *Dominical*, October 2, 1988, p. 12.
44. Arellano, *Politicas sociales* p. 269.

45. Interview with Veronica Silva, Social Services department of the municipality of La Florida, December 1990.
46. Vergara, *Politica*, p. 243.
47. Vergara, *Politica*, p. 227.
48. See claims in Castañeda, *Para Combatir*,p. 213; and rebuttal in Scherman Filer, *Techo*, pp. 16-17.
49. *Minuta Politica de Vivienda y Desarrollo Urbano*, Gabinete de Subsecretario, Ministerio de Vivienda, internal document, (1990); Scherman Filer, *Techo*, p. 14.
50. The surcharge amounted to the difference between the amount of the loan and its value on the domestic loan market.
51. Scherman Filer, *Techo*, p. 54.
52. *Dominical*, October 2, 1988.
53. Scherman Filer, *Techo*, pp. 49, 62.
54. Interview with Carlos Aguilar Chuecos, FEDHACH, Santiago, December 1989.
55. Hardy, *La Ciudad Escindida*, pp. 141-143; FEDHACH survey cited in Hardy, p. 144.
56. Default of private bank loans was 14 percent, while default among what is left of the old savings and loan associations loans reached 17 percent. Scherman Filer, *Techo*, 57.
57. Interview with Carlos Aguilar Chuecos, FEDHACH, Santiago, December 1989.
58. Ana Maria Barrenechea, "Financiamiento Habitacional," unpublished manuscript.
59. Jaime Estevez, "Una Solucion justa a la deuda habitacional," FEDHACH, 1987, p. 13.
60. Scherman Filer, *Techo*, p. 59.
61. This group broke off from FEDHACH after the plebiscite of 1988 and still uses the name FEDHACH.
62. *Dominical*, October 2, 1988, p. 11
63. *Dominical*, October 2, 1988, p. 11.
64. For statistics on voting patterns for greater Santiago, see Hardy, *La Ciudad Escindida*, p. 211.

Chapter 11

1. United Nations Economic Commission for Latin America (ECLA), Transport and Communications Division, "Urban Bus Deregulation in Chile," July 1990, p.1.
2. Ibid. Of the 5,435 buses, 710 were full-sized, 90-passenger, buses belonging to the publicly owned company; 3,167 were privately owned buses known as "micros" each with a capacity, counting standees, for approximately 78 passengers; and 1,558 were privately

owned taxibuses, each with a capacity for 40 passengers (also including standees, although, up to that year, they were officially authorized to carry only seated passengers).

3. Ibid.

4. Ian Thomson, interview, December 11, 1990.

5. ECLA, "Urban Bus...," p. 2.

6. Ian Thomson, interview, January 8, 1992.

7. ECLA, "Urban Bus...," p. 2.

8. Interview with bus owner Dec. 13, 1990. He estimated that on an investment of 4.6 million pesos the net return was 400,000 pesos a month and that profits used to be much higher.

9. Ironically, the thousand or so buses on the Alameda run directly above a fast, electric metro built under Frei, Allende and completed early in the Pinochet regime. The metro remains a public company, but under the doctrine that public firms must make themselves self-financing it has had to put fares up high enough to cover costs and therefore it is under-utilized.

10. ECLA, *Diagnostico del sector transporte colective en Santiago de Chile: los efectos de la desreglamentacion*, June 1990, p. 63.

11. Ibid., p. 70.

12. Expressed in U.S. dollars. ECLA, *El diagnostico*, p. 72.

13. ECLA, *El Diagnostico*, pp 41f.

14. Interview with bus owner, Dec. 13, 1990.

15. Medical Association, 1988.

16. James F. Smith, *Los Angeles Times*, July 22, 1989, p. 33.

17. The free-market policies furthered the disproportionate growth of Santiago and many other urban areas in Chile. The reversal of previous agrarian reform policies undercut the development of year-round rural livelihoods and thereby accelerated the outflow to the cities. Even many employed in the booming fruit and vegetable export industry found only seasonal work and live in Santiago and other urban areas, forced to seek catch-as-catch-can jobs.

18. "*El problema del medio ambiente en Chile: violacion de un derecho humano*," José Aylwin and Ana Scozia, Comision chilena de derechos humanos, August 1989, p. 20. In our interview with Gabriel Sanhueza, member of the Pollution Commission, he put the figure of the responsibility of diesel buses at 70 percent.

19. *Programa de descontaminación ambiental del área metroplitana de Santiago*. Special Commission for Decontamination of the Metropolitan Region, Santiago, April 1990, p. 9.

20. The *New York Times*, "Studies Say Soot Kills Up To 60,000 in U.S. Each Year," July 19, 1993.

21. James F. Smith, op. cit.

22. Ibid.

23. See, for instance, Dra. Haydeé López Cassou, "Nuevos Agentes

Patogenos: Los gases tóxicos," *Vida Médica*, 1985, pp. 38f.

24. "Urban Bus ...," p.3.
25. Nathaniel C. Nash, *The New York Times*, July 6, 1992.
26. Ibid.
27. Ibid.

Chapter 12

1. Carmelo Mesa Lago, *El Desarrollo de la Seguridad Social en America Latina*, (New York: United Nations, 1985), p. 99.
2. Jose Pablo Arellano, *Politicas Sociales y Desarrollo, Chile 1924-1984*, (Santiago: CIEPLAN, 1988), p. 83.
3. Jose Pablo Arellano points out that in the case of public employees, the cost to the government was really an accounting problem; since the government didn't pay its share as an employer, it ended up paying for public workers from fiscal funds. Arellano, *Politicas Sociales*, p. 98; A United Nations report shows that in 1980, 53 percent of the state contribution to Social Security went to public employees, while another 44 percent went to health and maternity programs, Mesa Lago, *El Desarrollo*, 116.
4. Interview with Hugo Sanfuentes, Secretaria de Seguridad Social, January 1991.
5. Arellano, *Politicas Sociales*, p. 90.
6. Arellano, *Politicas Sociales*, p. 139.
7. Total withholdings from a Chilean worker's paycheck usually include: retirement 10 percent, disability 3.5 percent and the 7 percent for health through FONASA or ISAPRES.
8. Arellano, *Politicas Sociales*, pp. 148, 151.
9. PREALC, *El Desafio de la Seguridad Social: el caso Chileno*, Documento de trabajo #340,(Santiago: PREALC, 1990), p. 8.
10. PET, *Pagina Economica* #34, June 1985.
11. PREALC, *El Desafio*, p. 16.
12. PREALC, *El Desafio*, pp. 8, 34.
13. Study cited in Arellano, *Politicas Sociales*, p. 106.
14. Armando Barrientos, "Pension Reform and Economic Development in Chile," *Development Policy Review*, vol. 11, 1993, pp. 99-100.
15. PREALC, *El Desafio*, p. 9.
16. Gillion and Bonilla, "Analysis," p. 178.
17. Centro de Estudios Publicos (CEP), *Puntos de Referencia* #32 (no date).
18. Jaime Ruiz-Tagle, *La Seguridad Social en Chile: Realidad Actual y Propuestas Alternativeas*, (Santiago: PET, 1988) p. 24.
19. Arellano, *Politicas Sociales*, p. 170.
20. Ruiz-Tagle, *La Seguridad Social*, chart, p.16.

21. Mesa Lago, *El Desarrollo,* p. 123.
22. Interview with Pedro Corona in *El Diario,* December 12, 1990.
23. Pedro Corona, interview.
24. *El Mercurio,* November 15, 1980, cited in Arellano, p. 171.
25. PREALC, *El Desafío,* p. 3.
26. Tarsicio Casteñeda, *Innovative Social Policies for Reducing Poverty: Chile in the 1980s,* unpublished manuscript, (Washington, D.C.: World Bank), p. 185.
27. One study based on 1987 wage levels estimates that only 22 percent of the work force in 1987 made a salary sufficient to allow them to retire with more than minimum benefits. Ruiz-Tagle, *La Seguridad Social,* p. 24; Tarsicio Casteñeda, *Para Combatir la Pobreza,* (Santiago: Centro de Estudios Publicos, 1990), p. 251.
28. Gillion and Bonilla, "Analysis," pp. 186-187.
29. Banco Central de Chile, *Indicadores Economicos y Sociales, 1960-1988,* p. 406. This pattern, by which the debt related to the transition costs of social security crowds out social spending is confirmed by Colin Gillion and Alejandro Bonilla, "Analysis of a national private pension scheme: The case of Chile," *International Labour Review,* Vol. 131, no. 2, pp. 191-192.
30. PREALC, *El Desafío,* p. 32.
31. Casteñeda, *Innovative Social Policies,* p. 2.
32. Interview with Aurelio Becerra, Santiago, December 1990.

Chapter 13

1. In 1991 dollars. Nonetheless all of Chile's fruit exports add up to only 3 percent of the fruit in international trade (far and away dominated by bananas from tropical areas). Moreover, even with the reality of the "fruit boom," Chile remained first and foremost an exporter of copper and other minerals which accounted at the end of the decade for two-thirds of the value of Chile's exports. Fresh fruit exports, as astonishing and well-known as is their "boom," account for a little under 10 percent of total Chilean exports.
2. U.S. Embassy (Santiago, Chile), *Chilean Agriculture: Integrating into World Markets,* mimeo, May 1990, p. 1.
3. Sergio Gomez, "La Uva Chilena en el Mercado de los Estados Unidos," unpub. ms., Santiago, November 1991, p. 12.
4. Lovell S. Jarvis, "Changing Private and Public Sector Roles in Technological Development: Lessons from the Chilean Fruit Sector," mimeo, Department of Agricultural Economics, University of California, Davis, August 1992, p. 4.
5. S. Gomez, pp. 8 f, citing data from the Asociación de Exportadores de Frutas y la Fundación Chile.

6. Walter L. Goldfrank, "Chilean Fruits of Counter-revolution," *Hemisphere*, Fall 1988, p. 11.
7. Lovell S. Jarvis, "Chilean Fruit Development Since 1973: Manipulating the Cornucopia to What End?" mimeo, University of California, Davis, April 1991, p. 2.
8. Lovell S. Jarvis, "Changing Private and Public Sector Roles in Technological Development: Lessons from the Chilean Fruit Sector," August 20, 1992, p. 5.
9. For a detailed study refer to United Nations Economic Commission for Latin America (ECLA), *The Distribution Chain and the Competitiveness of Latin American Exports.* (Santiago: ECLA), 1989.
10. In fact, the figures suggest that about 30 percent of the population consume fresh fruit in the winter months. Gomez, p. 10.
11. Goldfrank, p. 11.
12. Clavier presents evidence that this has in fact been the experience with table grapes. G. P. Clavier, "An Analysis of the Effects of Inter-Seasonal Trade: The Case of U.S. Imports of Chilean Table Grapes," Paper presented at the XVI (1991) International Congress of the Latin American Studies Association, Washington, D.C.
13. Sergio Gomez, "La Uva Chilena en el Mercado de los Estados Unidos," p. 11.
14. At the other end of the pole, more than 116,000 small farms (*"minifundios"*) had to make do with a mere 7 percent of the total agricultural land.
15. Lovell S. Jarvis, *Chilean Agriculture Under Military Rule: From Reform to Reaction, 1973-1980*, Research Series no. 59 (Berkeley: University of California, Institute of International Studies, 1985), p. 10.
16. Cristobal Kay, "Agrarian Change after Allende's Chile," in Hojman, David E. (ed.) *Chile after 1973: Elements for the Analysis of Military Rule*, p. 102, and Lovell S. Jarvis, *Chilean Agriculture Under Military Rule: From Reform to Reaction, 1973-1980*, pp. 10 and 26 f.
17. U.S. Embassy, op. cit., p. 8.
18. David E. Hojman, *Neo-Liberal Agriculture in Rural Chile* (New York: St. Martin's Press, 1990), p. 5.
19. Sergio Gomez and Jorge Echenique, *La agricultura Chilena* (Santiago: FLACSO, 1988), pp. 165 f.
20. Lovell S. Jarvis, "The Unraveling of Chile's Agrarian Reform, 1973-1986 in William C. Thiesenhusen (ed.) *Searching for Agrarian Reform in Latin America* (Boston: Unwin Hyman, 1989), pp. 244 f.
21. Gomez and Echenique, op. cit., p. 95.
22. Jarvis, 1st version, p. 14.
23. U.S. Embassy, Chilean Agriculture: Integrating into World Markets, May 1990, p. 9.
24. Jarvis, "The Role of Markets and Public Intervention in Chilean Fruit Development since the 1960s: Lessons for Technological

Policy," October 1991, p. 14.

25. For a discussion of the role of the "reserve army of labor" in contemporary Chilean agriculture, see Harry P. Diaz, "Proletarianisation and Marginality: the Modernisation of Chilean Agriculture," in ed. David E. Hojman, *Neo-Liberal Agriculture in Rural Chile* (New York: St. Martin's Press 1990), pp. 127-144.

26. Tironi, *Silencios*, p. 76.

27. U.S. Embassy, op cit., p. 18.

28. See, for instance, Gomez and Echeverría. Their book's subtitle (in English) is "The Two Faces of Modernization."

29. Study cited (without further reference) in Sarah Bradshaw, "Women in Chilean Rural Society," in David E. Hojman (ed.), *Neo-Liberal Agriculture in Rural Chile*. New York: St. Martin's Press, 1990, p. 114.

30. Gomez and Echenique, p. 64.

31. Gonzalo Falabella, unpub. ms., 1990, "La Casa del Temporero."

32. See Harry P. Diaz, "Proletarianisation and Marginality: the Modernisation of Chilean Agriculture," in David E. Hojman, *Neo-Liberal Agriculture in Rural Chile*. New York: St. Martin Press, 1990, and passim.

33. See Daniel Rodriguez and Sylvia Venegas, *De Praderas a Parronales*. (Santiago: GEA, 1989), pp. 167f.

34. See Gomez and Echinique, *La agricultura chilena*, p. 64.

35. Interviews with Maria Elena Cruz, GIA, December 18, 1989 and December 19, 1990.

36. Sarah Bradshaw, op. cit., p. 124.

37. Ibid.

38. U.S. Embassy, op. cit., p. 16.

39. GIA concluded that in the 1989-1990 season some workers in the packing plants made up to $14 a day but only by packing some 300 crates and working very long hours to do so. Cited in Maria Elena Cruz, "*Condiciones de vida de los trabajadores ligados a la agroexportacion*," Santiago: GIA, November 1990.

40. Gonzalo Falabella, "Trabajo temporal y desorganizacion social," *Proposiciones 18* (Santiago: Sur, 1990). Profits do not take into consideration any interest charges for borrowed capital.

41. GIA study cited in Maria Elena Cruz, "*Condiciones de Vida de Los Trabajadores Ligados a la Agroexportacion*," Santiago: GIA, November 1990.

42. Cruz cites Rodriguez and Venegas 1990.

43. Cruz, p. 102.

44. Gonzalo Falabella, *El sistema de trabajo temporal*, Santiago: Sur, 1989, pp. 11f.

45. Campana and Cruz, 1988, cited in Cruz, p. 104.

46. Hernan Sandoval, "*Contaminación Ambiental*," in *Cuadernos Med-Soc.*, XXX, 1, 1989, p. 8.

47. Tironi, *Los Silencios de la Revolución*, p. 78.
48. Figures are from Gonzalo Falabella, "Reestructuracion y respuesta sindical," mimeo presented at the XVII Congress of the Latin American Studies Association (LASA), September 1992, p. 1.
49. Maarten M. J. Derksen, "Santa Sabina: Surviving in a Rural Shanty Town," in D. Hojman (ed.), *Neo-Liberal Agriculture in Rural Chile*, p. 184.
50. Personal communication, Stephanie Rosenfeld, July 1993.
51. Jarvis, "The Role of Markets....," p. 2.
52. The excellent research and analysis on the technological development of the Chilean fruit industry by Lovell S. Jarvis (University of California at Davis) who came to the research with years of experience in agrarian issues in Chile has been fundamental for this section of the chapter. Also illuminating on these issues are Chileans Sergio Gomez and Jorge Echnique. Anyone further interested in the points we can only touch upon here are strongly encouraged to turn to the work of these researchers and analysts.
53. Jarvis, "Changing Private and Public Sector Roles," p. 25.
54. Certain pests and diseases are not economically significant in California but cause considerable losses for Chilean growers; the research on how to control them therefore is not being carried out in California and so cannot be transferred.
55. Jarvis, "Changing Private and Public Sector Roles," p. 19.
56. Jarvis, "Changing Private and Public Sector Roles," p. 18.
57. Jarvis, "The Role of Markets and Public Intervention in Chilean Fruit....," p. 19.
58. Jarvis, "The Role of Markets and Public Intervention in Chilean Fruit," p. 3.
59. Jarvis, "The Role of Markets and Public Intervention in Chilean Fruit," p. 14.
60. Patricio Silva, "State Subsidiarity in the Chilean Countryside," in D. Hojman (ed.), *Neo-Liberal Agriculture in Rural Chile*, p. 28
61. Jarvis, "The Role of Markets and Public Intervention," p. 18.
62. Sergio Gomez, *"La uva Chilena en el mercado de los Estados Unidos,"* mimeo, esp. pp. 15f.
63. Case study in the Valley of Aconcagua cited by Sergio Gomez, op. cit., p. 16.

Chapter 14

1. Joaquin Lavín, *Chile, A Quiet Revolution*, (Santiago: Zig Zag, 1988), p. 60; *Estadisticas Forestales* (Santiago: CORFO, 1989).
2. Claudio Donoso, cited in Cruz and Rivera, *La realidad Forestal Chileno*, (Santiago: GIA, 1983), p. 9.

3. Contreras, *Mas alla del Bosque,* (Santiago: Amerinda, 1989), p. 50.
4. Contreras, *Mas alla,* p. 87.
5. Contreras, *Mas alla,* p. 32.
6. Interview with Jose Leyton, Santiago, December 1990.
7. The military government reluctantly fulfilled pacts initiated under the previous government, the program ending in 1978. Jose Leyton, *El fomento Forestal y su impacto sobre el desarrollo rural en Chile,* (Santiago: CEPAL, 1985), p. 114.
8. Contreras, *Mas alla,* p. 40.
9. Harry Polo, "Forestry Labour, Neo-liberals and the Authoritarion State: Chile, 1973-1981." Ph.D. dissertation, York University 1983, pp. 113-116.
10. Maria Elena Cruz and Rigoberto Rivera, *La realidad Forestal Chilena,* (Santiago: Gia 1983), p. 17.
11. *Estadisticas Forestales* 1989, p. 64.
12. Direct planting by CONAF includes fulfillment of pacts and minimum employment programs 1983-85. CONAF, *Informe Estadistico* #27, "Plantaciones, 1988"; also Contreras, *Mas alla,* p. 57; CONAF, internal document, "Bonificaciones", marzo 1990.
13. For a study comparing costs of direct and subsidized plantings, see Cruz y Rivera, *La realidad forestal,* p. 21.
14. Cruz y Rivera, *La realidad forestal,* p. 21; CONAF *Informe Estadistico* #27, p. 18.
15. Quote cited in Harry Polo, "Forestry Labour," p. 116.
16. Contreras, *Mas alla,* p. 184; Jose Leyton, *El Fomento Forestal,* p. 67; Antonio Lara et al, "Consideraciones para un politica forestal,"(Santiago: CODEFF, 1989), p. 4.
17. Leyton, *El Fomento Forestal,* p. 92.
18. Contreras, *Mas alla,* p. 189; Leyton estimates forestry employment from 1965-73 at 100,000. *El Fomento,* pp. 122-123.
19. The number of forestry workers organized in unions rose to 20% in the final year of the Pinochet government. Contreras, *Mas alla,* pp. 189, 209.
20. Harry Polo, "Forestry Labour," p. 162.
21. Arzobispado de Concepcion, *La Otra Cara...,* (Concepcion: Vicaria de Pastoral Obrera, 1984) p. 41.
22. Equipo Capacitacion Forestal Concepcion, "Primer Taller Forestal: Una Perspectiva de los trabajadores," in *Boletin Estudios Agrarias,* Santiago: Grupo de Estudios Agro-Regionales, 22 Mayo 1988, p. 13.
23. Harry Polo, p. 160; in the first half of 1990, over fifteen forestry workers died of accidents on the job, *La Epoca,* August 30, 1990; Vicaria de Concepcion, *La otra cara...,* p. 2.
24. Quote cited in Leyton, *El Fomento,* p. 129.
25. Interview, Claudio Donoso, in Valdivia, December 1990.
26. Claudio Donoso, *La Epoca,* 27 junio 1988.

27. Claudio Donoso, *La Epoca*, 27 junio 1988.
28. CODEFF, "Crecimiento Forestal Chileno y Medioambiente," 1988.
29. Statement by CORMA, cited in *La Epoca*, Nov. 12, 1990.
30. *La Epoca*, 18 marzo 1990.
31. *The Ecologist*, August 13, 1990.
32. Andres Gomez-Lobo, "Desarrollo Sustentable del Sector Pesquero Chileno en los anos 80," (Santiago: Cieplan, no date), p. 2.

Chapter 15

1. *Chile Economic Report*, #224, (Santiago: CORFO, April 1990); Omar Cerda, "Analisis del Sector Pesquero," *La Caleta*, Nov. 1988, p. 1.
2. CORFO, *El Sector Pesquero*, (Santiago: CORFO, 1987); Omar Cerda, "Analisis," p. 15.
3. Alejandro Zuleta, "Sustentabilidad del recurso e impacto en el desarrollo regional" in CIPMA, *Sector Pesquero*, (Santiago: CIPMA, 1990), p. 63.
4. Omar Cerda, "Analisis," p. 15.
5. We use the term fishmeal here to refer to both the production of oil and meal, both processed from the same pelagic fish. Fish oil generally makes up around 15 percent of total production weight. Solange Duhart, Jacqueline Weinstein, *Pesca Industrial: Sector Estrategico y de alto Riesgo*, (Santiago: PET, 1988), v. II, p. 39.
6. Zuleta, "Sustentabilidad," p. 69; Duhart and Weinstein, *Pesca Industrial,* p. 35.
7. Eschewing quotas, the government did finally freeze entry of new ships into the fishmeal industry.
8. Zuleta, "Sustentabilidad," p. 71; Andres Gomez-Lobo, "Desarrollo Sustentable del Sector Pesquero Chileno en los anos 80," *Cieplan.* no date. pp. 18, 19, 21.
9. CORFO, *El Sector Pesquero Chileno*, 1987.
10. Factory trawlers pay a registration fee of $1000 plus $60 per ton of ship weight. Max Aguero and Vilma Correa, "Analisis de rentabilidad relativa y perspectivas de los barcos factorias en Chile," p. 90, in *Estudios en Pesquerias Chilenas*, ed. Teofilo Melo, (Santiago, 1985); Juan Carlos Cardenas, *Pesqueria Chilena y Desarrollo Sostenible*, p. 14, (Santiago: CODEFF, 1985).
11. In the United States, factory trawlers are prohibited everywhere but off the coast of Alaska. Juan Carlos Cardenas, *Pesqueria Chilena*, p. 13.
12. Carlos Vignolo, "Sobreinversion y congestion en la pesquera demersal Austral" in *Chile Pesquero*, Sept-Dic. 1989, p. 36.
13. Vignolo, "Sobreinversion," p. 39.
14. Juan Carlos Cardenas, *Pesqueria Chilena*, p. 105.
15. Hector Vera B., *El Boom Pesquero* (Santiago, 1989), p. 18.

16. Juan Carlos Cardenas, *Pesqueria Chilena*, p. 12; and interview with Juan Carlos Cardenas, Santiago, December 1990.
17. Vignolo, "Sobreinversion," p. 37.
18. Vignolo, "Sobreinversion," p. 39.
19. Andres Gomez-Lobo, "Desarrollo Sustentable," p. 25.
20. IFOP, *Sistemas Informaciones Pesqueras*, 1991.
21. Cardenas, *Pesqueria Chilena*, p. 11.
22. Interview with Dr. Phillippe Cavalie, Lago Ranco, January 1991. See also Shirley Christian, *The New York Times*, October 15, 1990.
23. *La Tercera*, 25 marzo 1990; Interview with Dr. Phillippe Cavalie, January 1991.
24. Cardenas, *Pesqueria Chilena*, p. 12.
25. Vera, *El Boom*, p. 29.
26. Juan Carlos Cardenas, *Pesqueria Chilena*, p. 8.
27. Vera, *El Boom*, p. 42.

Epilogue

1. "Continuity and Change" became a slogan of the Concertación government under president Aylwin.
2. This formula is spelled out clearly in *Un Gobierno para los Nuevos Tiempos: Bases programáticas del segundo gobiern"la Concertación*, (Santiago: 1993), p. 5.
3. The "designated" senators represent institutions, such as the armed forces, rather than an electoral district. Their terms expire in 1997, when president Frei will name two senators, the Supreme Court designates three, and the National Security Council designates four.
4. The National Security Council is composed of the President, the President of the Senate, the Controller General, the president of the Supreme Court, and the Commanders in Chief of the Armed Forces and the police.
5. There are sectors who are more critical of Chile's neo-liberal model of development both inside the Concertación, such as some tendencies of the Socialist Party, and outside, such as the Communist Party and the movements associated with outsider 1993 presidential candidate and environmentalist Manfred Max-Neef. They have had little impact on economic policy, and do not have a comprehensive alternative proposal. The weakness of these sectors reflects the historic defeat of Left under Pinochet, among other factors.
6. Oscar Muñoz Goma, Carmen Celedon, "Chile en Transición: Estrategia económica y política," *Colección Estudios CIEPLAN* No. 37, June 1993, p. 102.
7. José Piñera, *La Revolución laboral en Chile*, (Santiago: Zig-Zag, 1990), p. 28.

8. Central Unitaria de Trabajadores
9. Confederación de Producción y Comercio
10. Dirección del Trabajo, 1994.
11. Dirección del Trabajo, 1994.
12. Due to the terrible pollution, even the dictatorship began to experiment with transportation restrictions, but significant reforms were phased in during 1992-3, after the transition to civilian rule.
13. Patricio Meller, Sergio Lehmann, Rodrigo Cifuentes, "Los Gobiernos de Aylwin y Pinochet: Comparación de indicadores nómicos y sociales," *Apuntes CIEPLAN* No. 118, September 1993.
14. *Apuntes CIEPLAN, No.* 118.
15. National savings averaged 21.4% during the Aylwin administration 1990-93, compared with 15.3% from 1974-89, and 15.9% from 1985-89, the period during the dictatorship of economic recovery from the debt crisis. Annual investment as a percent of GNP averaged 24.8% from 1990-93, compared with 18.7% from 1974-89, and 19.8% from 1985-89 *Apuntes* CIEPLAN, No. 118.
16. *Economic and Social Progress in Latin America* (1993), Interamerican Development Bank.
17. *Apuntes* CIEPLAN, No. 118.
18. "Patricio Aylwin se confiesa con *Mensaje*," *Mensaje*, No. 426, (Santiago: Jan-Feb 1994), p. 33.
19. Alvaro Díaz, "Restructuring and the New Working Classes in Chile: Trends in Waged Employment, Informality and Poverty"3-1990," *UNRISD Discussion Paper* 47, p. 22.
20. Alvaro Díaz, "Restructuring...," p. 22.
21. Un Gobierno para los Nuevos Tiempos..., p. 6.
22. For urban areas, "indigents" are defined as people who, if they spend 100% of their income on food, still would not be able to afford a basic diet. Those who earn twice the indigence level of income are no longer considered to be living poverty.
23. See Alvaro Díaz, "Restructuring...," for an excellent discussion of poverty and the restructuring of the labor market.
24. The minimum wage is now indexed to anticipated inflation, not past inflation.
25. CEPAL, Latin American Poverty Profiles for the Early 1990s....p 15.
26. Alvaro Díaz, "Restructuring...," p. 22.
27. Alvaro Díaz, "Restructuring...," p. 22.
28. "Patricio Aylwin se confiesa...," p. 33, translation by the author.
29. CHIP, *La Nacion, El Mercurio*, March 9, 1994.

Selected Bibliography

A. Goic. "*La salud en Chile: el problem de fondo.*" *Mensaje* 282, 1979.

Aguero, Max and Vilma Correa. "Analisis de rentabilidad relativa y perspectivas de los barcos factorias en Chile," in *Estudios en Pesquerias Chilenas*, ed. Teofilo Melo, Santiago, 1985.

Angell, Alan. "Unions and Workers in Chile during the 1980's" in Paul Drake and Ivan Jaksic, eds., *The Struggle for Democracy in Chile, 1982-1990*. Lincoln: University of Nebraska, 1991.

Arellano, Jose Pablo. *Politicas Sociales y Desarrollo, Chile 1924-1984*. Santiago: CIEPLAN, 1988.

Arellano, Jose Pablo. "La salud en los años 80: analisis desde la economia," monograph no. 100, CIEPLAN, August, 1987.

Arzobispado de Concepcion. *La Otra Cara...*, Concepcion: Vicaria de Pastoral Obrera, 1984.

Aylwin, José and Ana Scozia. "*El problema del medio ambiente en Chile: violacion de un derecho humano,*" Comision chilena de derechos humanos, August 1989.

Banco Central de Chile. *Indicadores economicos y sociales, 1960-1988*, Santiago, 1989.

Barham, Bradford, Mary Clark, Elizabeth Katz, and Rachel Schurman. "Nontraditional Agricultural Exports in Latin America," *Latin American Research Review* 27:2 (1992), 43-82.

Barrenechea, Ana Maria. "Financiamiento Habitacional," unpublished manuscript, Santiago, no date.

Barrera, Manuel and J. Samuel Valenzuela. "The Development of Labor Movement Opposition," in J. Samuel Valenzuela and Arturo Valenzuela. *Military Rule in Chile*. Baltimore: Johns Hopkins University Press, 1986.

Barrientos, Armando. "Pension Reform and Economic Development in Chile," *Development Policy Review*, vol 11, 1993.

Barrueto, Zita Elsa. "Evaluating the Effects of Economic Recession on Child Welfare in Chile," Ph.D. dissertation, University of California, Berkeley, 1990.

Bauer, Arnold. *Chilean Rural Society*. Cambridge: Cambridge University Press, 1975.

Bello, Walden and Stephanie Rosenfeld. *Dragons in Distress*. San

Francisco: Food First Books, 1990.

Bengoa, Jose. *El Campesinado Chileno despues de la reforma agraria.* Santiago: Ediciones SUR, 1983.

Bitar, Sergio. *Chile para todos.* Santiago: Planeta, 1988.

Bradshaw, Sarah. "Women in Chilean Rural Society," in David E. Hojman, ed., *Neo-Liberal Agriculture in Rural Chile.* New York: St. Martin's Press, 1990.

Briones, Guillermo. *Las universidades chilenas en el modelo de economia neo-liberal.* Santiago; PIIE, 1981.

Briones, Guillermo et al.. *Desigualdad Educativa en Chile.* Santiago: PIIE, no year given.

Cardenas, Juan Carlos. *Pesqueria Chilena y Desarrollo Sostenible.* Santiago: CODEFF, 1985.

Castañeda, Tarsicio. *Para Combatir la Pobreza.* Santiago: Centro de Estudios Publicos, 1990.

Castañeda, Tarsicio. *Innovative Social Policies for Reducing Poverty: Chile in the 1980s.* unpublished manuscript, Washington, D.C.: World Bank.

Castells, Manuel. *The City and the Grassroots.* Berkeley: University of California Press, 1983.

Center for International Policy. "Aid Memo." Washington, D.C., May 30, 1986.

Centro de Estudios del Desarrollo. *Santiago, Dos Ciudades.* Santiago, 1990.

Centro de Estudios Publicos (CEP). *Puntos de Referencia* #32 (no date).

Cerda, Omar. "Analisis del Sector Pesquero," *La Caleta,* Nov. 1988.

Cereceda, Luz E. and Max Cifuentes. *Qué comen los pobres?* Santiago: Instituto de Sociologia de la Pontificia Universidad Católica de Chile, 1987.

Chanfreau, D. "Professional ideology and the health care system in Chile," *International Journal of Health Services,* vol. 9, pp. 86-105, 1979.

Chavkin, Samuel. *Storm Over Chile.* Chicago: Lawrence Hill Books, 1989 (rev. ed.).

Chile Economic Report, #224, Santiago: CORFO, April 1990.

Chile Information Project newsletter, Santiago, June 15, 1992.

Clavier, G. P. "An Analysis of the Effects of Inter-Seasonal Trade: The Case of U.S. Imports of Chilean Table Grapes," Paper presented at the XVI (1991), International Congress of the Latin American Studies Association, Washington, D.C.

CODEFF, "Crecimiento Forestal Chileno y Medioambiente," Santiago, 1988.

Comisión Nacional de Verdad y Reconciliación. *Informe Rettig: Informe de la Comision Nacional de Verdad y Reconciliación.* Santiago: Ornitorrinco, 1991.

CONAF, "Plantaciones, 1988," *Informe Estadistico* #27.

CONAF, "Bonificaciones," internal document, Marzo 1990.

Constable, Pamela and Arturo Valenzuela. *A Nation of Enemies.* New York:

Norton, 1991.

CORFO, *El Sector Pesquero Chileno*, Santiago: CORFO, 1987.

CORFO, *Memorias*, 1985-1989.

CORFO. *Estadisticas Forestales.* Santiago: CORFO, 1989.

Corporación de Promoción Universitaría, *Informe sobre la educacion superior en Chile 1988* Santiago: CPU, 1988.

Corporación de Promoción Universitaría. *La educación superior privada en Chile. Antecedentes y perspectivas.* Santiago: CPU, 1988.

Cortázar, Rene and Patricio Meller. *Los dos Chiles y las estadisticas oficiales: una version didactica.* Santiago: CIEPLAN, December 1987.

Cortázar, René. "Qué hacer con los salarios minimos?" *Notas Tecnicas,* no. 107 (December 1987).

Cruz, Maria Elena. *La experiencia neoliberal en la agricultura Chilena: sus exitos y su pobreza,* mono., Santiago: GIA, 1988.

Cruz, Maria Elena. *De inquilinos a temporeros, de la hacienda al poblado rural,* mono. Santiago: GIA, 1986.

Cruz, Maria Elena. *Condiciones de vida de los trabajadores ligados a la agroexportacion,* Santiago: GIA, November 1990.

Cruz, Maria Elena and Rigoberto Rivera. *La realidad Forestal Chileno.* Santiago: GIA, 1983.

Délano, Manuel and Hugo Traslaviña. *La herencia de los Chicago Boys.* Santiago: Ornitorrinco, 1989.

Derksen, Maarten M. J. "Santa Sabina: Surviving in a Rural Shanty Town," in D. Hojman ed., *Neo-Liberal Agriculture in Rural Chile.*

Diaz, Harry P. "Proletarianisation and Marginality: the Modernisation of Chilean Agriculture," in ed. David E. Hojman, *Neo-Liberal Agriculture in Rural Chile.* New York: St. Martin's Press, 1990.

Duhart, Solange and Jacqueline Weinstein, *Pesca Industrial: Sector Estrategico y de alto Riesgo,* Santiago: PET, 1988.

Echeverría, Rafael. *Evolucion de la matricula en Chile, 1935-1981,* PIIE Estudios, 1982.

ECLA, *Diagnostico del sector transporte colective en Santiago de Chile: los efectos de la desreglamentacion,* June 1990.

Edelman, Robert and Myron M. Levine. "Summary of an International Workshop on Typhoid Fever," *Reviews of Infectious Diseases.* vol. 8, No. 3, May-June 1986.

Equipo Capacitacion Forestal Concepcion, "Primer Taller Forestal: Una Perspective de los trabajadores," in *Boletin Estudios Agrarias,* Santiago: Grupo de Estudios Agro-Regionales, 22 mayo 1988, pp. 7-16.

Errazuriz, Enrique, Rodolfo Fortunatti, Cristian Bustamante, *Hauchipato, de empresa publica a empresa privada, 1947-1988.* Santiago: Programa de Economia del Trabajo, 1989.

Errazuriz, Enrique, Rodolfo Fortunatti, Cristian Bustamante, *Industria azucarera nacional 1952-1989.* Santiago: Programa de Economia del Trabajo, 1989.

Estevez, Jaime. "Una Solucion justa a la deuda habitacional," Santiago: FEDHACH, 1987.

Falabella, Gonzalo. "Trabajo temporal y desorganizacion social," *Proposiciones 18*. Santiago: Sur, 1990.

Falabella, Gonzalo. *El sistema de trabajo temporal*, Santiago: SUR, 1989.

Falabella, Gonzalo. "Reestructuracion y respuesta sindical," paper presented at the XVII Congress of the Latin American Studies Association (LASA), September 1992.

Ffrench-Davis, Ricard. "Debt and Growth in Chile: Trends and Prospects" in David Felix, editor, *Debt and Transfiguration?* Armonk, N.Y.: M. E. Sharpe, 1990.

Ffrench-Davis, Ricardo and Jose de Gregorio. "Origines y efectos del endeudamiento externo," *CIEPLAN Notas Tecnicas* 99 (1987): pp. 3-5.

Figueroa-Unda, Manuel. "Violence and Education: The Legacy of Repression in the Educational Systems of Latin America: A Case Study on Chile," unpub. ms. California State University-Fresno, March 1991.

Fischer, Ronald. "Efectos de una apertura sobre la distribución del ingreso," *Colección Estudios Cieplan* N. 33 (December 1991), pp. 95-121.

Fontaine, Arturo. *Los Economistas y El Presidente Pinochet*. Santiago: Zig Zag, 2nd ed., 1988.

Foxley, Alejandro. *Experimentos neoliberales en America Latina*. Mexico: Fondo de Cultura Economica. 1988.

Foxley, Alejandro and Dagmar Raczynksi. "Vulnerable Groups in Recessionary Situations: The Case of Children and the Young in Chile," *World Development*, vol. 12, no.3, pp. 223-246, 1984.

Fried, Beatriz and Mario Abuhadba, "Reforms in higher education: the case of Chile in the 1980s," in *Higher Education*, vol. 21, 1991.

Friedman, Milton and Rose Friedman. *Free to Choose*. New York: Harcourt Brace Jovanovich, 1980.

Friedman, Milton. *Capitalism and Freedom*. Chicago: University of Chicago Press, 1962.

Friedman, Milton. *Dollars and Deficits*. Englewood Cliffs, N.J.: Prentice-Hall, 1968.

Gatica Barros, Jaime. *Deindustrialization in Chile*. Boulder: Westview, 1989.

George, Susan. *A Fate Worse than Debt*. New York: Grove Press, 1988.

Gillion, Colin and Alejandro Bonilla, "Analysis of a national private pension scheme: The case of Chile," *International Labour Review*, Vol 131, no. 2.

Goldfrank, Walter L. "Chilean Fruits of Counter-revolution," *Hemisphere*, Fall 1988.

Gomez, Sergio. "La Uva Chilena en el Mercado de los Estados Unidos," unpub. ms., Santiago, November 1991.

Gomez, Sergio and Jorge Echenique. *La agricultura Chilena*. Santiago: FLACSO, 1988.

Gomez-Lobo, Andres. "Desarrollo Sustentable del Sector Pesquero Chileno en los anos 80," Santiago: Cieplan, no date.

Haignere, Clara S. "The Application of the Free-Market Economic Model in Chile and the Effects on thePopulaton's Health Status," *International Journal of Health Services*, vol. 13, no. 3, 1983.

Haramoto, Edwin. "Politicas de Vivienda Social: Experiencia Chilena de las tres Ultimas Decadas," in Joan MacDonald, editor, *Vivienda Social*, Santiago, 1983.

Hardy, Clarissa. *La Ciudad Escindida*. Santiago: PET, 1990.

Hersh, Seymour. *The Price of Power*. New York: Summit Books, 1983.

Hojman, David E. *Chile: The Political Economy of Development and Democracy in the 1990s*. Pittsburgh: University of Pittsburgh Press, 1993.

Hojman, David E. (ed.). *Chile after 1973: Elements for the Analysis of Military Rule*.

Hojman, David E. *Neo-Liberal Agriculture in Rural Chile*. New York: St. Martin's Press, 1990.

IFOP, *Sistemas Informaciones Pesqueras*, 1991.

Instituto Nacional de Estatidistica, *Encuesta Suplementaria de Ingresos*, Santiago, 1989.

Jarvis, Lovell S. "Changing Private and Public Sector Roles in Technological Development: Lessons from the Chilean Fruit Sector," mimeo, Department of Agricultural Economics, University of California, Davis, August 1992.

Jarvis, Lovell S. "Chilean Fruit Development Since 1973: Manipulating the Cornucopia to What End?" mimeo, University of California, Davis, April, 1991.

Jarvis, Lovell S. "Changing Private and Public Sector Roles in Technological Development: Lessons from the Chilean Fruit Sector," August 20, 1992.

Jarvis, Lovell S. *Chilean Agriculture Under Military Rule: From Reform to Reaction, 1973-1980*. Research Series no. 59, Berkeley: University of California, Institute of International Studies, 1985.

Jarvis, Lovell S. "The Unraveling of Chile's Agrarian Reform, 1973-1986" in William C. Thiesenhusen (ed.). *Searching for Agrarian Reform in Latin America*. Boston: Unwin Hyman, 1989.

Jarvis, Lovell S. "The Role of Markets and Public Intervention in Chilean Fruit Development since the 1960s: Lessons for Technological Policy," October 1991.

Jiménez, Jorge and Margarita Gili. "Municipalización de la Atención Primaría en Salud," *Estudios Sociales*, no. 62, 1989.

Johnson, Harry G. "The Keynesian Revolution and the Monetarist Counter-Revolution," *American Economic Review* no. 61, May 1971, pp. 7-11.

Kay, Cristobal. "Agrarian Change after Allende's Chile," in Hojman, David E. (ed.). *Chile after 1973: Elements for the Analysis of Military Rule*.

Kusnetzoff, Fernando. "Urban and Housing Policies under Chile's Military Dictatorship 1973-1985," *Latin American Perspectives*, 14, 33, (Spring 1987): pp. 157-86.

La Coordinadora Metropolitan de Pobladores. "Los Allegados; un problema nacional," 1990.

Lara, Antonio et al. "Consideraciones para un politica forestal," Santiago: CODEFF, 1989.

Larroulet, Cristian. "Impact of Privatization: The Chilean Case 1985-1989," paper presented at the Insitute of the Americas of San Diego, California, November 1992.

Latorre, Carmen Luz et al. *Informe Final 1990*, PIIE, draft.

Lavados, Jaime. "Revolucion en salud?" *Vida Médica*, 1988.

Lavín, Joaquin and Luis Larraín. *Chile, Sociedad Emergente*. Santiago: Zig-Zag, 1989.

Lavín, Joaquin. *Chile, A Quiet Revolution*. Santiago: Zig-zag, 1988.

Le Maitre, M.J. and Lavados, I. "Antecedentes, Restricciones y Oportunidades de la Educacion Superior en Chile" in Le Maitre, M.J. and Lavados, I., eds., *La educación superior en Chile: riesgos y oportunidades en los '80*. Santiago: CPU, 1986.

Leyton, Jose. *El fomento Forestal y su impacto sobre el desarrollo rural en Chile*. Santiago: CEPAL, 1985.

Lira, E. and E. Weinstein, "Desempleo y Daño Psicologica" FASIC, Chile 1980. See also "La Salud Pública en Chile 1985," *Vida Médica*, 1986.

Livingston, James. "Chile and debt-equity conversion" in Robert Wesson, ed., *Coping with the Latin American Debt*, New York: Praeger, 1988.

Lomnitz, Larissa and Ana Melnick. *Chile's Middle Class: A Struggle for Survival in the Face of Neoliberalism*. Boulder, Colorado: Lynne Rienner Publishers, 1991.

López Cassou, Haydeé. "Nuevos Agentes Patogenos: Los gases tóxicos," *Vida Médica*, 1985.

Loveman, Brian. *Chile, The Legacy of Hispanic Capitalism*. 2nd edition, Oxford, New York, 1988.

MacDonald, Joan, ed. *Vivienda Social*, Santiago, 1983.

MacDonald, Joan. "25 anos de Vivienda Social. La Perspectiva del Habitante," in MacDonald, *Vivienda Social*.

Marcel, Mario. "Privatización y Finanzas Públicas," *Colección Estudios Cieplan*, 26, 1989.

Marin, Gustavo. "Privatizaciones en Chile: de la Normalizacion del 'Area Rara' a la Ley del Estado Empresario." Documento de Trabajo #24, Santiago: Pries-Cono Sur, 1989.

Marin, Gustavo. "Trayectoria de las privatizaciones en Chile durante el regimen dictatorial, 1973-1989." Documento de Trabajo, Santiago: PRIES-Cono Sur, 1990.

Martner, Gonzalo. *El Gobierno de Salvador Allende, 1970-1973*, Santiago: Ediciones LAR, 1988.

Martner, Gonzalo D. *El Hambre en Chile.* Geneva: UNRISD, 1989.

Mesa Lago, Carmelo. *Desarrollo de la Seguridad Social en America Latina.* NewYork: United Nations, 1985.

Ministerio de Educación, "Analisis de Remuneraciones del Personal del Sector Subvencionado," internal unpub. paper, March 1990.

Ministerio de Salud, Chile. "Diagnóstico," January 28, 1991.

Ministerio de Salud, Chile. *Indicadores Financieros Sector Salud Público,* 1974-1988.

Ministerio de Vivienda. *Minuta Politica de Vivienda y Desarrollo Urbano,* Gabinete de Subsecretario, internal document, 1990.

Morales, Eduardo, et al. *Erradicados en el Regimen Militar.* Santiago: FLACSO, 1990.

Nuñez, Ivan. *Diagnostico del sistema escolar,* PIIE unpub. ms., 1989.

O'Brien, Philip J. "The New Leviathan: The Chicago School and the Chilean Regime, 1973-1980," *IDS Sussex Bulletin* 13 (1981).

ODEPLAN, *Informe Social* 1984-1985.

Ortega, Eugenio and Ernesto Tironi, *Pobreza en Chile.* Santiago: CED, 1988.

PET, *Pagina Economica* #34, June 1985.

Piñera, Jose. *La Revolución Laboral en Chile.* Santiago: Zig-Zag, 1990.

Politzer, Patricia. *Fear in Chile.* NewYork: Pantheon, 1989.

Polo, Harry. "Forestry Labour, Neo-liberals and the Authoritarion State: Chile, 1973-1981." Ph.D. dissertation, York University 1983.

Portes, Alejandro. "Latin American Urbanization during the Years of the Crisis," *Latin American Research Review,* 1989, #3.

PREALC. *El Desafio de la Seguridad Social: el caso Chileno.* Documento de trabajo #340, Santiago: PREALC, 1990.

Programa de Economia del Trabajo (PET). "El desigual acceso a la salud," Santiago: PET, 1989.

Programa del Economía del Empleo. "Evolución Económica y Situación de los Trabajadores en la Transición a la Democracia," Santiago: PET, 1990.

Programa Interdisciplinario de Investigaciones en Educacion (PIIE). *Ruptura y construccion de consensos en la educación Chilena,* Santiago: PIIE, 1989.

Raczynski, Dagmar and Claudia Serrano. *Vivir la porbreza.* Santiago: CIEPLAN, 1985.

Raczynski, Dagmar and César Oyarzo. "Por qué cae la tasa de mortalidad infantil en Chile?" *Coleccccion Estudios CIEPLAN,* December 1981.

Ramos, Joseph. *Neo-Conservative Economics in the Southern Cone of Latin America, 1973-1983.* Baltimore: The Johns Hopkins University Press, 1986.

Raquena B., Mariano. "*Marco historico del sistema de cuidado de la salud chileno,*" unpub. ms.

Rayack, Elton. *Not So Free to Choose.* Westport: Praeger, 1987.

Rodriguez, Daniel and Sylvia Venegas. *De Praderas a Parronales*. Santiago: GEA, 1989.

Rozas, Patricio and Gustavo Marin. *Concentracion y transnacionalizacion del sistema financiero chileno*. Santiago: PRIES, 1987.

Ruiz-Tagle, Jaime. *El sindicalismo chileno después del plan laboral*. Santiago: PET, 1985. 181.

Ruiz-Tagle, Jaime. "Crisis de la Experiencia Neoliberal en Chile," Santiago: PET, 1989.

Ruiz-Tagle, Jaime. *La Seguridad Social en Chile: Realidad Actual y Propuestas Alternativeas*. Santiago: PET, 1988.

Sandoval, Hernan. "Contaminacion Ambiental," in *Cuadernos Med-Soc.*, vol. XXX, no. 1, 1989.

Scarpaci, Joseph, ed. *Health Services Privatization in Industrial Societies*, "Dismantling Public Health Services in Authoritarian Chile," New Brunswick, NJ: Rutgers University Press, 1989.

Scarpaci, Joseph. "Restructuring Health Care Financing in Chile," *Social Sciences and Medicine*, vol. 21, no 4.

Scarpaci, Joseph. *Primary Medical Care in Chile*. Pittsburgh: University of Pittsburgh Press, 1988.

Scarpaci, Joseph. "Restructuring Health Care Financing in Chile," *Social Science and Medicine*, vol. 21, no. 4.

Scherman Filer, Jorge. *Techo y Abrigo*. Santiago: PET, 1990.

Schkolnik, Mariana and Berta Teitelbolm, "Segunda Encuesta de empleo en el Gran Santiago," Santiago: PET, 1989.

Sepúlveda, Rafael. *Vida Medica*, 41, September-October 1989.

Sepúlveda, Jaime. "*El desafio de la salud en el gobierno democratico*," unpub. ms. December 1990.

Silva, Patricio. "State Subsidiarity in the Chilean Countryside," in D. Hojman ed., *Neo-Liberal Agriculture in Rural Chile*.

Special Commission for Decontamination of the Metropolitan Region. *Programa de descontaminación ambiental del área metroplitana de Santiago*. Santiago, April 1990.

"Testimonios de Medicos Exonerados Durante el Regimen Militar," *Vida Medica*, April 1990.

Thiesenhusen, William C. (ed.). *Searching for Agrarian Reform in Latin America*. Boston: Unwin Hyman, 1989

Timerman, Jacobo. *Chile: Death in the South*, New York: Knopf, 1987.

Tironi, Eugenio. *Los Silencios de la Revolución*. Santiago: Puerta Abierta, 1988.

Tironi, Eugenio and Eugenia Weinstein. "Frustración, agresividad y violencia en grupos marginales de Santiago: informe de una encuesta," Sur, Documento de Trabajo, 1988.

Trivelli Oyarzun, Pablo. "Intra-urban Socio-Economic Settlement Patterns, Public Intervention, and the Determination of the Spatial Structure of the Urban Land Market in Greater Santiago, Chile,"

Ph.D. Thesis, Cornell, 1987.

U.S. Embassy (Santiago). "Chilean Agriculture: Integrating into World Markets." May 1990.

U.S. Senate. *Covert Action in Chile, 1963-73, Staff Report of the Select Committee to Study Governmental Operations with Respect to Intelligence Activities.* Washington, D.C.: GPO, Dec. 18, 1975.

Ugarte, Soledad. "Salud Laboral: Riesgos y Beneficios," *Vida Medica,* 1988.

UNESCO, *Anuario estadistico de America Latina y el Caribe,* Paris, 1975.

United Nations Economic Commission for Latin America (ECLA), Transport and Communications Division. "Urban Bus Deregulation in Chile," July 1990.

United Nations Economic Commission for Latin America (ECLA). *The Distribution Chain and the Competitiveness of Latin American Exports.* Santiago: ECLA, 1989.

USAID. *AID Highlights,* vol. 3, no. 2, Summer 1986, p. 1.

Valdes, Juan Gabriel. *La Escuela de Chicago: Operación Chile.* Buenos Aires: Zeta, 1989.

Valdes, Teresa. *Venid, benditas de mi Padre. Los Pobladoras, sus rutinas y sus seuños,* Santiago: FLACSO, 1988.

Valdes, Juan Gabriel. *La escuela de Chicago: operacion Chile* Buenos Aires: Grupo Editorial Zeta, 1989.

Valenzuela, J.S. and A. Valenzuela. eds. *Military Rule in Chile.* Baltimore: Johns Hopkins.

Valenzuela, Arturo. "Chile: Origins, Consolidation, and Breakdown of a Democratic Regime," in Larry Diamond, Juan J. Linz, and Seymour Martin Lipset, eds., *Democracy in Developing Countries; vol. 4, Latin America.* Boulder, Colorado: Lynne Rienner, 1989.

Valenzuela, Arturo. *The Breakdown of Democratic Regimes: Chile.* Baltimore: Johns Hopkins University Press, 1978.

Vera B., Hector. *El Boom Pesquero.* Santiago, 1989.

Vergara, Pilar. *Politicas hacia la Extrema Pobreza.* Santiago: FLACSO, 1990.

Vergara, Pilar. "Changes in the Economic Functions of the Chilean State under the Military," pp. 85-117 in J.S. Valenzuela and A. Valenzuela (eds.), *Military Rule in Chile.* Baltimore: Johns Hopkins.

Vergara, Pilar and Teresa Rodriguez. *Libre Mercado y Educación Técnica Postsecundaria: La Experiencia de los Centros de Formación Técnica.* FLACSO, March 1986.

Vergara, Pilar. *Politicas hacia la extrema pobreza en chile, 1973-1988.* Santiago: FLACSO , 1990.

Vergara, Pilar. *Auge y caida del neoliberalismo en Chile .* Santiago: FLACSO, 1985.

Vignolo, Carlos. "Sobreinversion y congestion en la pesquera demersal Austral," in *Chile Pesquero,* Sept-Dic. 1989.

Viteri, María Antonieta. "Asunto de vida o muerte," *Que Pasa,* June 28, 1990.

Winkler, Donald R. *Higher Education in Latin America: Issues of Efficiency and Equity.* Washington, D.C.: World Bank, 1990.

Winn, Peter. *Weavers of Revolution: The Yarur Workers and Chile's Road to Socialism.* New York: Oxford University Press, 1986.

Winn, Peter and Maria Angelica Ibañez, "Textile Entrepreneurs and Workers in Pinochet's Chile, 1973-1989." New York: Institute of Latin American and Iberian Studies — Columbia University, 1989.

Zahler, Roberto. "El neoliberalism en una version autoritaria," *CPU Estudios Sociales,* no. 31, 1982.

Zuleta, Alejandro. "Sustentabilidad del recurso e inmpacto en el desarrollo regional," in CIPMA, *Sector Pesquero,* Santiago: CIPMA, 1990.

INDEX

149, 151, 154, 207, 209, 271
pacts, 204-207
Private universities, 126, 129-130,
134, 136, 141-142
Professional institutes, 125, 129-
130, 143-144, 147
Public health, 8, 94, 98-101, 105,
108-110, 113, 120-121, 240, 246

R

Reagan, Ronald, 39
Repression, 21, 25, 52, 56, 68, 70-
72, 96-98, 151-152, 156, 209,
260
Rodriguez, Teresa, 144, 288, 316
Rottenberg, Simon, 23

S

Sáez, Raul, 29
Safety, 86-87, 97, 209-211
Salmon cultivation, 226-227
Sanitation, 122, 246
Santiago municipalities
Reorganization of, 154
Public services, 153-154
Schools, 125-130, 132-140, 143,
147, 247
primary, 126, 128-129, 133,
136-139, 148
secondary, 128-129, 133, 135-
139, 148
Schultz, Theodore, 23
Social security, 14, 31, 57, 167-
179, 181, 196, 249
Social services, 4, 6, 31, 154, 247,
255
Subsidiary role of the State, 41,
116, 122, 128, 157, 186, 232

T

Tariffs, 14, 30, 34, 72-74
Tomic, Radomiro, 17
Transportation, 155, 231-234,
235, 240, 248-249
Typhoid fever, 120-123, 246

U

Unemployment, 28, 43, 67, 71-
72, 74-76, 79, 84-85, 97, 266-
267
Unions, 49, 56, 69-72, 75-80,
198, 235, 253, 263

V

Vergara, Pilar, 42, 115, 144

W

Wages, 82-85, 101, 162-163, 177,
196, 262, 266-267
Wheat, 11, 26

About the Authors

Joseph Collins, Ph.D., co-founded in 1975 the Institute for Food and Development Policy in California, after several years at the Institute for Policy Studies in Washington, D.C. and the Transnational Institute in Amsterdam. His previous books include *Food First: Beyond the Myth of Scarcity*, *Aid As Obstacle*, *No Free Lunch*, *Nicaragua: What Difference Could a Revolution Make?*, *World Hunger: Twelve Myths* and *The Philippines: Fire on the Rim*. A John Simon Guggenheim Fellow, he is a frequent conference and university lecturer and a consultant on development issues to United Nations and non-governmental organizations. His experiences in Chile date back over thirty years.

John Lear, Ph.D., is a graduate of Harvard University and the University of California-Berkeley. He is an historian specializing in Latin America and labor issues and is completing a book on workers in Mexico City during the revolution. Following a year as a Visiting Research Fellow at the Center for U.S.-Mexican Studies at the University of California-San Diego, he joined the faculty at the University of Puget Sound.

Walden Bello, Ph.D., is a senior analyst at Food First and the author of *Dark Victory: The U.S., Structural Adjustment, and Global Poverty* and **Stephanie Rosenfeld** is a research associate at Food First and is the co-author of *Dragons in Distress: Asia's Miracle Economies in Crisis* with Walden Bello.

Institute Publications

Books

Alternatives to the Peace Corps: A Directory of Third World and US Volunteer Opportunities by Becky Buell and Annette Olson. Now in its sixth edition, this guide provides essential information on voluntary service organizations, technical service programs, work brigades, study tours, as well as alternative travel in the Third World and offers options to the Peace Corps as the principle route for people wishing to gain international experience. $6.95

Brave New Third World? Strategies for Survival in the Global Economy by Walden Bello. Can Third World countries finish the next decade as vibrant societies? Or will they be even more firmly in the grip of underdevelopment? The outcome, Bello argues, depends on their ability to adopt a program of democratic development which would place them on equal footing in the global economy. $6.00

Circle of Poison: Pesticides and People in a Hungry World by David Weir and Mark Shapiro. In the best investigation style, this popular expose documents the global scandal of corporate and government exportation of pesticides and reveals the threat this poses to consumers and workers throughout the world. $7.95

Dark Victory: The U.S., Structural Adjustment, and Global Poverty by Walden Bello, with Shea Cunningham and Bill Rau. Offers an understanding of why poverty has deepened in many countries, and analyzes the impact of Reagan-Bush economic policies which resulted in a decline of living standards in much of the Third World, but also in the U.S. The challenge for progressives in the 1990's is to articulate a new agenda based on the reality that the people of the South and North share the tragedy of being victims of the same process that serves the interest of a global minority. $12.95

Diet for a Small Planet by Frances Moore Lappé. This revised, 20th anniversary edition of Lappé's best-seller draws on more than a decade of research to explain how political and economic systems keep people hungry. Charts, tables, resource guides, and recipes. *20th Anniversary Ed. (large format)* $14.00 *10th Anniversary Ed.* $6.99

Don't Be Afraid, Gringo: A Honduran Woman Speaks from the Heart translated and edited by Medea Benjamin with photos by Susan Meiselas. Elvia Alvarado, a courageous peasant organizer, tells about the struggle to regain land taken from the poor in Honduras and how she has been harassed, imprisoned, and tortured for her efforts. $10.00

Dragons in Distress: Asia's Miracle Economies in Crisis by Walden Bello and Stephanie Rosenfeld. Economists often refer to South Korea, Taiwan, and Singapore as "miracle economies," and technocrats regard them as models for the rest of the Third World. The authors challenge these established notions and show how, after three decades of rapid growth, these economies are entering a period of crisis. The authors offer policy recommendations for structural change that would break the NIC's unhealthy dependence on Japan and the U.S. and examine both the positive and negative lessons of the NIC experience for the Third World. $12.95

Education for Action: Graduate Studies with a Focus on Social Change by Andrea Freedman and Nooshi Borhan. A guide to progressive graduate programs and educators in agriculture, anthropology, development studies, economics, ethnic studies, history, law, management, peace studies, political science, public health, sociology, urban planning and women's studies. $6.95

Food First: Beyond the Myth of Scarcity by Frances Moore Lappé and Joseph Collins. This landmark study draws on a worldwide network of research to demystify such complex and vital issues as: rapid population growth, the green revolution, U.S. foreign aid, the World Bank, and agribusiness. $5.95

Kerala: Radical Reform as Development in an Indian State by R.W. Franke and B.H. Chasin. Analyzes both the achievements and the limitations of the Kerala experience. In the last eighty years, the Indian state of Kerala has undergone an experiment in the use of radical reform as a development strategy that has brought it some of the Third World's highest levels of health, education, and social justice. 1994 revised edition $9.95

Needless Hunger: Voices from a Bangladesh Village by James Boyce and Betsy Hartmann. The Global analysis of Food First is vividly captured here in a single village. The root causes of hunger emerge through the stories of both village landowners and peasants who live at the margin of survival. Now in its sixth printing! $6.95

No Free Lunch: Food and Revolution in Cuba Today by Medea Benjamin, Joseph Collins and Michael Scott. Based on sources not readily available to Western researchers, this examination of Cuba's food and farming system confirms that Cuba is the only Latin American country to have eradicated hunger. $9.95

People and Power in the Pacific: The Struggle for the Post-Cold War Order by Walden Bello. Examines the extent to which events in the Asia-Pacific reflect the so-called new world order; the future role of the U.S. and the emergence of Japan as a key economic power on the world stage. $12.00

The Philippines: Fire on the Rim by Joseph Collins. Looks at the realities following the People Power revolution in the Philippines. A choir of voices from peasants, plantation managers, clergy, farmers, prostitutes who serve U.S. military bases, mercenaries, revolutionaries and others, speak out. *Hardcover* $9.50, *Paper* $5.00.

Taking Population Seriously by Frances Moore Lappé and Rachel Schurman. The authors conclude that high fertility is a response to anti-democratic power structures that leave people with little choice but to have many children. The authors do not see the solution as more repressive population control, but instead argue for education and improved standard of living. $7.95

Trading Freedom: How Free Trade Affects Our Lives, Work, and Environment edited by John Cavanagh, John Gershman, Karen Baker and Gretchen Helmke. Contributors from Mexico, Canada and the U.S. analyze the North American Free Trade Agreement. Drawing on the experiences of communities in Canada, the U.S., and Mexico, this comprehensive collection provides a hard-hitting critique of the current proposals for a continental free trade zone through an intensive examination of its impact on the environment, workers, consumers, and women. $5.00

World Hunger: Twelve Myths by Frances Moore Lappé and Joseph Collins. A revealing and often shocking book that shatters common beliefs about the causes of hunger and the present approaches to a solution. Each chapter is a concise, self-contained essay, written in popular style, but with thorough documentation. $10.95

Curricula

Exploding the Hunger Myths: A High School Curriculum by Sonja Williams. With an emphasis on hunger, twenty-five activities provide a variety of positive discovery experiences — role playing, simulation, interviewing, writing, drawing — to help students understand the real underlying causes of hunger and how problems they thought were inevitable can be changed. 200 pages, 8.5x11 with charts, reproducible illustrated hand-outs, resource guide and glossary. $15.00

Food First Curriculum by Laurie Rubin. Six delightfully illustrated units span a range of compelling topics including the path of food from farm to table, why people in other parts of the world do things differently, and how young people can help make changes in their communities. 146 pages, three-hole punched, 8.5x11 with worksheets and teacher's resources. $12.00

Food First Comic by Leonard Rifas. An inquisitive teenager sets out to discover the roots of hunger. Her quest is illustrated with wit and imagination by Rifas, who has based his comic on *World Hunger: Twelve Myths*. $1.00

Write for information on bulk discounts.

All publications orders must be prepaid and CA residents must add 8.5% sales tax.

Please include shipping charges of 15% ($2 minimum) for each order. Add 20% for UPS within the U.S.; add 45% ($5 minimum) for air mail delivery outside the U.S.

Food First Books
Institute for Food and Development Policy
398 60th Street, Oakland, CA 94618
(800) 888-3314

About the Institute

The Institute for Food and Development Policy, publisher of this book, is a nonprofit research and education for action center. The Institute works to identify the root causes of hunger and poverty in the United States and around the world, and to educate the public as well as policymakers about these problems.

The world has never produced so much food as it does today — more than enough to feed every child, woman, and man. Yet hunger is on the rise, with more than one billion people around the world going without enough to eat.

Institute research has demonstrated that the hunger and poverty in which millions seem condemned to live is not inevitable. Our Food First publications reveal how scarcity and overpopulation, long believed to be the causes of hunger, are instead symptoms — symptoms of an ever-increasing concentration of control over food-producing resources in the hands of a few, depriving so many people of the power to feed themselves.

In 55 countries and 20 languages, Food First materials and investigations are freeing people from the grip of despair, laying the groundwork — in ideas and action — for a more democratically controlled food system that will meet the needs of all.

An Invitation to Join Us

Private contributions and membership dues form the financial base of the Institute for Food and Development Policy. Because the Institute is not tied to any government, corporation, or university, it can speak with a strong independent voice, free of ideological formulas. The success of the Institute's programs depends not only on its dedicated volunteers and staff, but on financial activists as well. All our efforts toward ending hunger are made possible by membership dues or gifts from individuals, small foundations, and religious organizations. We accept no government or corporate funding.

Each new and continuing member strengthens our effort to change a hungry world. We'd like to invite you to join in this effort. As a member of the Institute you will receive a 25 percent discount on all Food First books. You will also receive our quarterly publication, Food First News and Views, and our timely Action Alerts. The alerts provide information and suggestions for action on current food and hunger crises in the United States and around the world.

All contributions to the Institute are tax deductible.

To join us in putting food first, just clip and return the attached coupon to:

Institute for Food and Development Policy,
398 60th Street, Oakland, CA 94618
(510) 654-4400

Name _____

Address _____

City/State/Zip _____

Daytime Phone ( ) _____

□ I want to join Food First and receive a 25% discount on this and all subsequent orders. Enclosed is my tax-deductible contribution of:

□ $100   □ $50   □ $30

PAGE	ITEM DESCRIPTION	QTY	UNIT COST	TOTAL
	T-shirts □ XL □ L □ M □ S		$12.00	

Member discount -25% $ _____

CA Residents 8.5% $ _____

SUBTOTAL $ _____

Postage/15%–UPS/20% ($2 min.) $ _____

Membership(s) $ _____

Contribution $ _____

TOTAL ENCLOSED $ _____

Payment Method: □ Check   □ Money Order   □ Mastercard   □ Visa

For gift mailings, please see other side of this coupon.

Name on Card _____

Card Number _____ Exp. Date _____

Signature _____

Please send a Gift Membership to:

Name _____

Address _____

City/State/Zip _____

From _____

Please send a Gift Book to:

Name _____

Address _____

City/State/Zip _____

From _____

Please send a Resource Catalog to:

Name _____

Address _____

City/State/Zip _____

Name _____

Address _____

City/State/Zip _____